Good Practice in Working with Violence

Good Practice Series

Edited by Jacki Pritchard

This series explores topics of current concern to professionals working in social work, health care and the probation service. Contributors are drawn from a wide range of settings, both in the voluntary and statutory sectors.

Good Practice in Child Protection
A Manual for Professionals
Edited by Hilary Owen
and Jacki Pritchard
ISBN 1 85302 205 5
Good Practice 1

Good Practice in Supervision
Statutory and Voluntary Organisations
Edited by Jacki Pritchard
ISBN 1 85302 279 9
Good Practice 2

Good Practice in Risk Assessment and Risk Management 1
Edited by Hazel Kemshall
and Jacki Pritchard
ISBN 1 85302 338 8
Good Practice 3

Good Practice in Working with People Who Have Been Abused
Edited by Zetta Bear
ISBN 1 85302 424 4
Good Practice 4

Good Practice in Risk Assessment and Risk Management 2
Key Themes for Protection, Rights and Responsibilities
Edited by Hazel Kemshall
and Jacki Pritchard
ISBN 1 85302 441 4
Good Practice 5

of related interest

Elder Abuse Work
Best Practice in Britain and Canada
Edited by Jacki Pritchard
ISBN 1 85302 704 9

Working with Victims of Crime
Policies, Politics and Practice
Brian Williams
ISBN 1 85302 450 3

Violence in Children and Adolescents
Edited by Ved Varma
ISBN 1 85302 344 2

Assessing Men Who Sexually Abuse
A Practice Guide
David Briggs, Paddy Doyle,
Tess Gooch and Roger Kennington
ISBN 1 85302 435 X

Working with Sex Offenders
Alec Spencer
ISBN 1 85302 767 7

Managing Child Sexual Abuse Cases
Brian Corby
ISBN 1 85302 593 3

Forensic Psychotherapy
Crime, Psychodynamics and the Offender Patient
Edited by Christopher Cordess
and Murray Cox
ISBN 1 85302 240 3 hb
ISBN 1 85302 634 4 pb

A Practical Guide to Forensic Psychotherapy
Edited by Estela Welldon
and Cleo Van Velsen
ISBN 1 85302 389 2

Play Therapy with Abused Children
Ann Cattanach
ISBN 1 85302 193 8

Good Practice in Working with Violence

Edited by

Hazel Kemshall and Jacki Pritchard

Good Practice Series 6

Jessica Kingsley Publishers
London and Philadelphia

First published in the United Kingdom in 1999 by

Jessica Kingsley Publishers Ltd
116 Pentonville Road
London N1 9JB, England
and
325 Chestnut Street
Philadelphia, PA 19106, USA

www.jkp.com

Library of Congress Cataloging in Publication Data
A CIP catalog record for this book is available from the Library of Congress

British Library Cataloguing in Publication Data
Good practice with violence
1.Violent crimes - Great Britain 2.Criminals - Great Britain
I.Kemshall, Hazel II.Pritchard, Jacki
364.3'0941
ISBN 1 85302 641 7

Printed and bound in Great Britain by
Athenaeum Press, Gateshead, Tyne and Wear

Contents

Out of this nettle, danger,
we pluck this flower, safety
King Henry IV, Part I

Introduction

Hazel Kemshall and Jacki Pritchard

Why, at a time of greater personal safety than ever before, are we more fearful of personal violence? (Mirrlees-Black, Mayhew and Percy 1996). This is nowhere better exemplified than in the BBC's *Crimewatch* programme, which, whilst portraying crimes of violence against the person, attempts to reassure us with the catchphrase 'Don't have nightmares'. The paradox of such a programme is that whilst attempting to reassure us about personal safety, it also contributes to public perceptions of violence and danger (Gunter 1987). Safety and violence seem to be a pre-occupation of the current time.

Violence has always been with us in one form or another, ranging from the ritualised state execution of being hanged, drawn and quartered so graphically described by Foucault (1977), to murders to achieve political ends (e.g. the killing of the Princes by Richard III), domestic violence (portrayed so vividly by Anne Brontë in *The Tenant of Wildfell Hall*), ritualised killing of women (Jack the Ripper and the Yorkshire Ripper) and the killing of children (the Moors Murders).

Media coverage of notorious cases, such as the murder of Jamie Bulger and the massacre at Dunblane, has heightened public awareness of violence throughout the 1990s. The extent of media influence on public perception of violence and dangers has long been the subject of public and academic debate (Gerbner 1970, 1972; Gunter 1987; Reiner 1988; Sparks 1992; Young 1987). However, there can be little doubt that certain cases have the power to pass into folklore and public consciousness, and have the power to frame public understanding of violent crime. However, most violent crime is *not* of this extreme nature but often occurs within families, trusted personal relationships and familiar situations. So what is violence and how is it addressed in this book?

The Oxford and Collins English Dictionaries define violence as:

- the unlawful use of force
- the exercise or an instance of physical force, usually effecting or intended to effect injuries, destruction
- powerful, untamed or devastating force.

These quotes illustrate that violence can be understood as a continuum ranging from acts which result in minor physical discomfort to those which result in death. The Butler Committee (1975) also recognised psychological trauma as an important component of violence. This has most recently come to public awareness through acts of stalking. The latter has resulted in a legal response through the introduction of the Protection from Harassment Act 1997, which has created an 'aggravated indictable offence involving the fear of violence' (Lawson-Cruttenden 1997).

In addition to legal definition, understandings of violence are bound up with public values and attitudes. This is most often expressed in terms of levels of acceptability and tolerance of certain violent acts over others. A simple contrast between responses to corporate recklessness and negligence resulting in injury and death (e.g., P&O Herald of Free Enterprise) and public and legal reaction to Fred and Rosemary West illustrates differing levels of reaction to acts which have the same outcome.

Outcomes are not always clearly defined as death or serious injury. The Robert Maxwell Pension Fund fraud illustrates how it is possible not to commit a violent crime but to cause significant psychological trauma nevertheless. In this instance it was a crime which had many victims and had a significant impact but fell outside the legal definition of a violent crime. This illustrates that violence is as much about perception and definition over time as it is about being an objective reality. In recent times we have seen the 'discovery' of domestic violence, stalking and bullying.

The recording of actual violent crimes and the prevalence of violence are not necessarily the same. Under-reporting has long hindered the accurate identification of the incidence of violence. In addition the processing and mechanisms for reporting also present barriers to identifying the prevalence of violent crime. These problems can be compounded by agency procedures (e.g., referrals not being recorded properly because the database does not cater for the correct input of information) and the reaction of agency personnel (e.g., refusal to deal with an incident because it happened so long ago). Specialisms within social care agencies can result in artificial categorisation of service users and their problems. This can result in certain service users falling outside the net or between responses (e.g., managers arguing about which team should deal with a case where the victim of violence has both a learning disability and a mental health problem).

Whilst the public perception of violence *might* be exaggerated, this does not make such perceptions less real (Sparks 1992). Exposure to information on violence can contribute to an amplified perception of its prevalence. An individual's calculation of the risk of harm is influenced by such exposure (e.g., the siting of a nuclear power station or likelihood of falling to crime [Slovic, Fischoff and Lichtenstein 1980]). If this exposure is involuntary (e.g., location of sex offenders in one's own road), the fear of the harm is heightened,

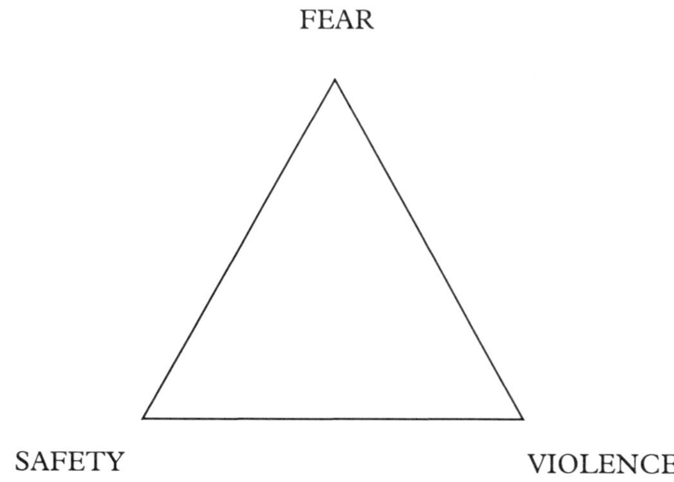

Figure 1

leading to what some commentators have labelled 'dread' (Slovic 1987). Such harms are not only feared but resented. This results in a potent cocktail of high fear and low acceptability. This is most often expressed in demands for safety and, in this context, avoidance of violent harms. This is the context in which managers and practitioners have to work with violence.

This book is primarily concerned with identifying best practice in work with perpetrators of violence and addresses the following themes:

- the assessment of violent persons and the extent to which violent behaviours can be predicted
- the production of reliable assessment methods for use in the field
- the moral and ethical issues presented by such assessments
- the extent to which violent behaviours can be successfully managed in the community and institutions, and the most effective intervention techniques for work with perpetrators of violence
- multi-agency responses to violent offenders to monitor and control behaviours
- issues of public protection.

The desire for public protection has increasingly focused attention on the identification and assessment of those most likely to commit acts of violence. The quest for accurate violence prediction has longed taxed both practitioners and academics (Walker 1996). Agencies in developing policies and procedures related to violence need to be proactive rather than reactive. This may mean emphasising the knowledge and skills required for work with violence as much as the formulation and implementation of policies and procedures. Staff need to be equipped to carry out this challenging work. This will require giving attention to raising awareness of violence, training, knowledge and skill development, and adequate supervision and support – including appropriate counselling for workers who are themselves victims of violence.

This book came out of the editors' desire to promote good practice in this area of work. Also, we felt that although there are many texts on violence, few address the issue of working *with* violence. A limited number of subject areas were chosen for their topicality. We recognise that it is an arbitrary collection and some areas of equal merit have been omitted. Some of these will be addressed in Volume 2, which will be concerned with the victims of violence. The areas included in this volume are:

- violent offending
- family violence
- violence to children
- violence in residential settings
- management issues
- training issues.

It is generally agreed that one never stops learning and that practice should be about continuing development. Our present assumptions and stereotypes of violence may need critical review (e.g., women are rarely violent or that dangerous carers are predominantly male). This book is a prompt to current thinking and to stimulate debate. Books of this nature can only give a snapshot of a complex issue and the concern here has been with the perpetrator of violence. Volume 2 will address the issues of working with victims of violence. Very often, managers and practitioners are concerned with the protection issues and the prevention of violence before it occurs. Relatively little attention is given to long-term support and therapeutic intervention for those who have been victimised. The needs of victims should be re-prioritised and Volume 2 will address the pressing issue of working with victims.

REFERENCES

Brontë, Anne (first published 1848) *The Tenant of Wildfell Hall.* Harmondsworth: Penguin.

Butler Committee, Home Office and Department of Health and Social Security (1975) *Committee on Mentally Abnormal Offenders.* Cmnd. 6244. London: HMSO.

Foucault, M. (1977) *Discipline and Punishment.* London: Allen Lane.

Gerbner, G. (1970) 'Cultural Indicators: the case of violence in television drama.' *Annals of the American Academy of Political Science,* 38, 69–81.

Gerbner, G. (1972) 'Violence in television drama: trends and symbolic functions.' In G. Comstock and E. Rubenstein (eds) *Television and Social Behaviour* Vol 1. Rockville, MD: US Department of Health, Education and Welfare.

Gunter, B. (1987) *Television and the Fear of Crime.* London: John Libby/I.B.A.

Lawson-Cruttenden, T. (1997) 'Harassment and Domestic Violence.' *Journal of Family Law,* 429–431.

Mirrlees-Black, C., Mayhew, P. and Percy, A. (1996) *The 1996 British Crime Survey, England and Wales*. London: Home Office Statistical Bulletin.

Protection from Harassment Act (1997) London: HMSO.

Reiner, R. (1988) 'British criminology and the state.' In P. Rock (ed) *A History of British Criminology*. Oxford: Clarendon Press.

Slovic, P. (1987) 'Perception of risk,' *Science*, 236, 280–285.

Slovic, P., Fischoff, B. and Lichtenstein, S. (1980) 'Facts and fears: understanding perceived risk.' In R.C. Schwing and W.A. Albers (eds) *Societal Risk Assessment: How Safe is Safe Enough?* New York: Plenum Press.

Sparks, R. (1992) *Television and the Drama of Crime*. Buckingham: Open University Press.

Walker, N. (ed) (1996) *Dangerous People*. London: Blackstone Press.

Young, J. (1987) 'The tasks facing a realist criminology.' *Contemporary Crises*, 11, 337–356.

CHAPTER 1

Sentencing Violent Offenders

Judge D.R. Bentley QC

There is widespread ignorance about how the sentencing system works. The year-in-year increase in violent crime is blamed by the tabloid press upon 'soft' sentencing, and yet the courts are today sending more people to prison and for longer terms than ever before.[1]

A point frequently overlooked is that judges and magistrates are not, as their critics seem to assume, free to impose whatever sentence they see fit. The punishment imposed for an offence may not exceed the maximum penalty prescribed by law. It is idle to criticise a judge for not sending an offender to prison for ten years for an offence carrying a maximum penalty of six months. Nor is this the only constraint. By section 1 of the Criminal Justice Act 1991, a court may not sentence an offender to custody unless of the opinion that his offence is so serious that only a custodial sentence can be justified or, in the case of a sexual or violent offence, that only a custodial sentence would be adequate to protect the public from serious harm from him. The same Act limits severely the power of courts to sentence offenders under 18 to custody. The Crime Sentences Act 1997, on the other hand, obliges judges to sentence to life imprisonment those convicted on a second occasion of 'serious' offences. Magistrates' courts are subject to an additional fetter: by

1 The prison population has risen by over 50 per cent since the end of 1992 from 40,606 to 62,948 in October 1997 (Penal Affairs Consortium, The Prison System – Some Current Trends (October 1997) London: Penal Affairs Consortium).

statute the maximum prison sentence which they may impose is normally six months.[2]

As well as being fettered by statutory constraints, sentencers are also obliged to have regard to decisions of the Court of Appeal laying down guideline (or tariff) sentences for particular offences. Such decisions are reported in the *Criminal Appeal (Sentencing) Reports* and summarised in journals such as *Sentencing News, Current Law* and the *Criminal Law Review.* There are also practitioners' books, of which the most authoritative are *Current Sentencing Practice* and *The Crown Court Index* (copies of both are supplied to all full-time Crown Court judges).[3] In magistrates' courts an important source of ready reference is the Magistrates' Association's *Sentencing Guidelines* (issued by the Association with the blessing of the Lord Chancellor and the Lord Chief Justice).[4]

To ensure that sentencers understand and keep up to date on current sentencing practice, they are required to undergo periodic training organised by the Judicial Studies Board. Before they are permitted to sit, Crown Court judges are required to attend a training course and to spend at least a week sitting as pupil to an experienced judge. Every three years they must attend a refresher course, a significant part of which will be devoted to sentencing. Magistrates undergo training conducted by their clerk under the overall supervision of the Judicial Studies Board.

One of the principal objectives which training seeks to achieve is consistency in sentencing. Ideally, the identity of the sentencer ought not to affect sentence, but, inevitably, it does. It is possible to construct a table showing which magistrates' courts make the most extensive use of imprisonment as a punishment and which the least. The variations thrown up by such research are striking. What is true of magistrates is true of judges. Some judges have reputations for severity, others for leniency. There is, in some quarters, a belief that women judges are more harsh sentencers of their own sex than their

2 Magistrates' Courts Act 1980, ss. 31 and 32.

3 D. Thomas (1982–1997) *Current Sentencing Practice.* London: Sweet and Maxwell; P. Morrish, I. McLean and D. Selwood (1998) *Crown Court Index* 19th edition. London: F.T. Law and Tax.

4 The Magistrates' Association (1997) *Sentencing Guidelines.* London: The Magistrates Association.

male brethren ('Sisters of Little Mercy'). The factors responsible for such variation no doubt include differences in temperament and social background, perception of the seriousness of certain offences and the efficacy of particular sentencing disposals. The problem is not new. In the nineteenth century those convicted in the higher criminal courts had no right of appeal against sentence, but by the 1890s the High Court bench had become so concerned about inconsistency in sentencing that it recommended that a Court of Criminal Appeal be established with power to give authoritative guidance to sentencers.[5] In 1907 such a court was finally established with power to hear appeals against sentence from those convicted in the higher criminal courts. The ability of the court to alter sentences, together with its pronouncements on the sentencing process, serve as an important corrective to harsh sentencing. The problem of over-lenient sentencing went ignored until 1988, when the Attorney-General was given the power to refer to the Court of Appeal a sentence passed in the Crown Court which appeared to be 'unduly lenient'.[6] It is from the decisions of the court upon sentence appeals that much of the present law on sentencing derives.

VIOLENT ADULTS

In sentencing violent offenders, courts are concerned to achieve four objectives: retribution, deterrence (both of the individual offender and of others who may be minded to commit like offences), protection of the public and reform of the offender. Imprisonment is, in the case of those who have never previously experienced custody, capable, in theory at least, of achieving all four objectives. Individualised sentences, such as probation, which attempt to help the offender address his offending and change his behaviour may achieve his reformation, and thereby protect the public from him in the future, but are unlikely either to deter others or to satisfy the demands of retribution.

All offences of violence are imprisonable – murder carrying a mandatory sentence of life imprisonment. Life imprisonment is also

5 Report of the Council of Judges PP 1894 (127) LXXXI, 173.
6 Criminal Justice Act 1988, ss. 35 and 36.

the maximum sentence for attempted murder, conspiracy to murder, soliciting murder, manslaughter, infanticide and wounding/causing grievous bodily harm with intent contrary to section 18 of the Offences against the Person Act 1861. For unlawful wounding, inflicting grievous bodily harm contrary to section 20 of the 1861 Act and assault occasioning actual bodily harm, the maximum sentence is five years, whilst violent disorder, affray and common assault carry maximum sentences of four years, three years and six months respectively.[7] Grave violence is almost invariably punished with imprisonment – the need to deter and to punish being considered paramount – but, in the case of less serious offences, courts are more ready to consider a non-custodial

7 Definitions of offences:

- Murder: unlawful killing with malice aforethought – that is with the intention of killing or causing grievous bodily harm ('really serious harm').
- Manslaughter (by violence) comprises two categories: 'voluntary manslaughter' (a killing which would have been murder had the killer not been provoked or suffering from diminished responsibility) and involuntary manslaughter (killing caused by an unlawful act done with the intention of causing physical harm to the victim but not intended to kill or to cause grievous bodily harm).
- Infanticide: the killing of a child under twelve months of age by a mother whose mind was disturbed due to her not having recovered fully from the effects of giving birth to the child.
- Wounding/causing grievous bodily harm with intent contrary to section 18 of the Offences against the Person Act 1861: unlawfully causing a wound (a cut involving the full thickness of the skin) or grievous bodily harm (really serious harm) to another with the intention of causing grievous bodily harm.
- Wounding/causing grievous bodily harm contrary to section 20 of the Offences against the Person Act 1861: unlawfully causing a wound or grievous bodily harm to another, the offender not having the intention of causing grievous bodily harm to his victim.
- Assault occasioning actual bodily harm contrary to section 47 of the Offences against the Person Act 1861: an assault (a deliberate and unlawful use of force on another) causing the victim some bodily injury which need be neither permanent nor serious.
- Common assault: an assault which causes no injury to the victim.
- Violent disorder: three or more persons present together using or threatening unlawful violence such as would cause a person of reasonable firmness present at the scene to fear for his own safety – that is to fear being caught up in violence.
- Affray: the use of or threats of violence towards another such as would cause a person of reasonable firmness present at the scene to fear for his own safety.

disposal, such as community service, probation, a combination order (probation and community service combined) or a fine. Following the introduction of the suspended prison sentence in 1967, violent offenders were often dealt with in this way, particularly if of good character and considered unlikely to reoffend. Where the suspended sentence imposed was longer than six months, it could be combined with supervision (a form of probation). In 1991 the power of courts to pass such sentences was severely curtailed. It was enacted that a suspended sentence might only be passed in 'exceptional circumstances'.[8] Where a prison sentence is suspended, the term imposed may not exceed two years and the maximum period for which it can be suspended is also two years.

A sentencing court will usually have the assistance of a pre-sentence report (a report prepared by a probation officer following an interview with the accused with a view to assisting a court to determine the most suitable method of dealing with him) and, if the offender is mentally ill, psychiatric reports. References and testimonials from employers, friends and others are sometimes placed before the court. Where the accused is in ill-health, a medical report will often be produced.

The first question which the sentencer must ask himself when dealing with a violent offender is whether the offence is so serious that only a custodial sentence can be justified or would be adequate to protect the public from the risk of serious harm from the offender. However, the mere fact that he concludes that the offence falls within this category does not mean that he must impose a prison sentence; there may be mitigating factors present which are sufficiently compelling to enable him to step back from a prison sentence and adopt a non-custodial disposal. Where an offence involves the use of very grave violence, it will usually be difficult, if not impossible, to do other than send the offender to prison. The sentencer's only concern in such a case will be to decide how long the prison sentence shall be. In determining sentence length he will have regard to the maximum sentence available, the dangerousness

8 Powers of Criminal Courts Act 1973, s 22(2)(b).

of the offender (as demonstrated by his record and reports about him), the tariff for such an offence (indicated by Court of Appeal sentencing guidelines) and the presence or absence of mitigating factors. The graver the offence, the less weight will be given to mitigating factors. Sentencers are also enjoined to have regard to the statutory provisions as to early release of prisoners.[9] They must bear in mind that the maximum sentence is to be reserved for the worst offences of that kind. If the sentencer concludes that the offence is not so serious that only a custodial sentence is justified, or concludes that – despite the fact that the offence passes the custodial threshold – a non-custodial disposal is appropriate, he will determine the penalty having regard to the seriousness of the offence and the circumstances of the offender. Before sentencing to community service or a combination order, he must have evidence from the probation service that the offender has been assessed as suitable to do community service and that there is work available for him to do.

Where an offender falls to be sentenced for two or more offences (not forming part of the same incident), consecutive sentences may be imposed, but, in this event, care must be taken to ensure not merely that the individual sentences imposed are not excessive but also that the total sentence is not excessive (known as 'the totality principle').

The use of life imprisonment

An adult convicted of murder must be sentenced to life imprisonment. There are other offences of violence, including attempted murder, conspiracy to murder, soliciting murder, manslaughter, infanticide and wounding/causing grievous bodily harm with intent, for which life imprisonment is the maximum penalty. Prior to the coming into force of the Crime Sentences Act 1997, the passing of a life sentence for such offences was dis-

9 Practice Statement (Crime Sentencing) [1992] 1 WLR 948. The early release provisions (which are set out in Part II of the Criminal Justice Act 1991) are as follows: an offender sentenced to a term of imprisonment or detention of under 4 years will be released after serving half of his sentence; if sentenced to a term of 4 years or more he will not be released until he has served 2/3 of his sentence (unless the Parole Board recommends his earlier release). A released prisoner who, before his sentence has expired, commits a further offence may be ordered back to prison to serve the unexpired part of the sentence.

cretionary and exceptional. The sentence was, in practice, 'reserved for offenders who for one reason or another [could] not be dealt with under the provisions of the Mental Health Act [1983], yet who are in a mental state which makes them dangerous to the life or limb of members of the public'.[10] Where this criterion of dangerousness was satisfied, a life sentence might have been considered appropriate even where the instant offence was not of the first seriousness. Under the 1997 Act, where an offender over 18 who has previously been convicted of a 'serious offence'[11] is convicted of a violent offence punishable by life imprisonment committed after 1 October 1997, the passing of a life sentence is no longer discretionary; the sentencing judge must impose a life sentence unless satisfied that there are exceptional circumstances which justify him in not doing so. The power to impose discretionary life sentences in other cases remains unaffected and the discretion will continue to be exercised in the same way as before the Act.

The Home Secretary has power to release a life prisoner on licence.[12] A judge sentencing for murder may recommend 'a minimum period which should elapse before the offender is released on licence'.[13] He is not, however, bound to do so. Similarly, a judge passing a life sentence for an offence other than murder may specify how long the offender ought to serve before his case is referred to the Parole Board for consideration of release on licence.[14] The object of these provisions is to enable the trial judge to indicate how long the offender ought to serve in prison to satisfy the demands of punishment and deterrence, leaving the question of his ultimate release to be determined in the light of his perceived dangerousness at the time. At the expiry of the period specified by the trial judge, the Home Secretary must refer the case of a prisoner serving life for an offence other than murder to the Parole Board and, if they

10 Per Lawton CJ in Wilkinson (1983) 5 Cr App Rep (S), 105 at p.108.

11 As defined in s. 2 (5) to (7) of the Act; attempted murder, manslaughter, and offences under s. 18 of the Offences against the Person Act 1861 are amongst those included in the definition.

12 A life prisoner released on licence is liable to be recalled to custody if his licence is revoked, which it may be at any time if the Parole Board so recommends or the Home Secretary considers revocation to be in the public interest.

13 Murder (Abolition of Death Penalty) Act 1965, s. 1 (2).

14 Criminal Justice Act 1991, s. 34.

recommend release, he must release him. Not so with murder. There the Home Secretary is not bound by the trial judge's recommendation and, although he cannot release except upon the recommendation of the Parole Board and after consultation with the Lord Chief Justice and the trial judge, he is not bound to order release even where the Board recommend it. The effect is to make murder the only offence for which the length of time served in prison is determined by a politician. Whether this state of affairs can survive the imminent incorporation into English Law of the European Convention on Human Rights remains to be seen, but some doubt it.

Determinate prison sentences

Where the maximum sentence available for a violent offence is life imprisonment but the criteria for imposing a life sentence are not satisfied, the court, if it concludes that a custodial sentence is appropriate, will, in fixing the length of that sentence, have regard to the sentencing tariff for the offence and to any aggravating and mitigating circumstances.

Aggravating features so far as violent offences are concerned include the infliction of grave injury, the use of a weapon, premeditation, racial motivation, absence of provocation, the fact that the offender has previous convictions for offences of violence, the fact that he was on bail at the time of the offence and the fact that the offence is of a kind which is very prevalent and gives rise to considerable public concern (as, for example, so-called 'road rage' attacks).

Matters which will normally be regarded as mitigating such an offence include the fact that it was committed as a result of provocation or at a time when the offender was in a state of emotional distress. That he was in drink or under the influence of drugs (voluntarily consumed or taken) is no mitigation. Previous good character will tell in an offender's favour, as will a good work record, and an offender with a criminal record who has since his last conviction made real efforts to keep away from crime will receive credit for this. Meritorious conduct unconnected with the offence – for example, saving a child from drowning, helping prison staff during a riot or fire – may also earn some discount in sentence. Help given to the police which has led to the detection and prosecution of serious crime may lead to an offender receiving a much reduced sentence, as may serious (especially terminal) illness. Young offenders and those age 60 or over normally receive some discount on account of age. The fact that conviction or imprisonment will lead to an offender losing his job, or his home or, if a soldier, to his discharge from the army, is a matter which a court is entitled to take into account in deciding whether to sentence him to custody and, if so, for how long. Hardship which imprisonment will cause to the offender's family or dependants will normally be disregarded, save where it is extreme (e.g., if it will lead to a young child being deprived of all parental care). An early plea of guilty will always earn an offender a reduction in sentence. Such pleas save the public the expense of a trial, save court time and spare victims and witnesses anxiety and distress. Where there has been substantial delay between the accused's arrest and his ultimate prosecution which cannot be laid at his door, so that he has had to live with the matter hanging over him for many months, the court will normally reflect this by making some reduction in his sentence.

The tariff

ATTEMPTED MURDER

Sentences for attempted murder are rarely less than seven years. Where the victim is left gravely injured, the tariff appears to be ten years plus. The highest sentences are reserved for those who attempt to kill diplomats or political rivals (30 to 35 years), terrorists who plant bombs (30 years) and those who attempt to kill in order to escape arrest or to silence a witness to crime (12 to 15 years).

MANSLAUGHTER

Cases of manslaughter vary infinitely and not all involve the use of violence (as in killings by neglect or gross negligence).[15] The sentencing tariff reflects this. An offender who kills whilst suffering from diminished responsibility will often be dealt with by way of a hospital order (as to which see below). Killings under provocation

15 Murder (Abolition of Death Penalty) Act 1965, s. 1(2).

normally attract sentences of at least seven years, rising to ten where the offender had armed himself with a weapon in advance. For manslaughter in the course of a fight, the tariff appears to be two to seven years. Sentences at the lower end of the bracket are reserved for cases where death is caused by a single blow which, through bad luck, proves fatal (because, for example, the victim falls backwards and strikes his head on a kerb sustaining a fatal fracture, or where the victim has an abnormally thin skull). Where the victim was struck repeated blows or a weapon was used, the sentence is likely to be in the region of seven years. Manslaughter committed in an attempt to avoid or escape arrest will attract a sentence of at least ten years.

INFANTICIDE

This rare offence is invariably dealt with by way of probation or the making of a hospital order.

WOUNDING/CAUSING GRIEVOUS BODILY HARM WITH INTENT (CONTRARY TO SECTION 18 OF THE OFFENCES AGAINST THE PERSON ACT 1861) AND UNLAWFUL WOUNDING/UNLAWFULLY INFLICTING GRIEVOUS BODILY HARM (CONTRARY TO SECTION 20 OF THE ABOVE ACT)

These two offences are conveniently considered together. The section 20 offence, which carries a lesser maximum sentence, is an alternative to that under section 18. The common ingredient is in the nature of the injury inflicted on the victim: grievous bodily harm (really serious harm) or a wound (a cut involving the full thickness of the skin). The difference between them is that for a person to be convicted of an offence under section 18 it must be proved not only that he caused a wound or grievous bodily harm to his victim by the deliberate use of unlawful violence but also that at the time he did so his intention was not merely to hurt or injure his victim but to cause him really serious harm. If such intent is lacking, he is guilty only of an offence under section 20. A section 18 offence can only be tried in the Crown Court but a section 20 offence can be tried either in the Crown Court or summarily (i.e. by a magistrates' court) if both magistrates and accused agree; if, having tried and convicted an offender for a section 20 offence, magistrates consider their powers of sentence inadequate, they may commit him for sentence to the Crown Court, which will be able to sentence up to the five year statutory maximum.

The kinds of conduct which most commonly result in charges of, and convictions for, section 18 and section 20 offences are 'glassings' and attacks with weapons such as knives, guns, baseball bats and feet (although this does not pretend to be comprehensive list). Pushing a glass or bottle into a victim's face is a form of violence common in night clubs and public houses. The attacker (who will usually be male) will commonly be under the influence of drink. Sometimes, the glass or bottle is deliberately broken before being used; in other cases it breaks on impact. Typical injuries are facial scarring, although sometimes the victim loses an eye. Such attacks are commonly charged as section 18 offences. To secure a conviction for such an offence the Crown must satisfy a jury that the accused's intention when he struck out with the glass was to cause grievous bodily harm to his victim. This is relatively easy to prove where the glass was deliberately broken beforehand. An accused charged with a section 18 offence may offer to plead guilty to section 20 wounding; such a plea may be accepted where the prosecution case on intent (or generally) is weak. Also, it is always open to a jury to convict an offender charged with a section 18 offence of the lesser offence, which it may well do it if feels that such a verdict meets the justice of the case. An offender convicted of, or pleading guilty to, a 'glassing' offence must expect an immediate custodial sentence, even though of hitherto good character. In 1979 the Court of Appeal stated that three years' imprisonment must be regarded as the minimum for a section 18 'glassing'.[16] Recent Appeal Court decisions suggest that the tariff has gone up since then and is now of the order of four to five years (on a plea of guilty).[17] The presence of aggravating factors, such as the striking of repeated blows with the glass, the infliction of grave injury or a previous conviction for a 'glassing' offence, will lead to a sentence substantially above the tariff. Provocation will tend to keep the sentence at the bottom end of the bracket. Even where the conviction in a 'glassing' case is not for a section 18 but for a section 20 offence, the offender will rarely

16 Harwood (1979) 1 Cr App Rep (S) 354.
17 Attorney General's Reference (No 14 of 1994) 16 Cr App Rep (S) 376.

escape custody. The tariff in such cases would appear to be in the range 18 months to two years.

Section 18 offences involving the use of weapons such as knives, guns, sticks, and kicking will attract broadly the same tariff sentence as 'glassings', with sentences of up to 12 to 15 years imposed where grave permanent injury is caused.

Section 20 offences involving relatively minor injury (such as a small wound) are often dealt with summarily but even here, as the *Magistrates' Association Guidelines* make clear, the presumption is in favour of custody, with the use of a weapon and kicking treated as aggravating factors. Attacks on bus conductors, taxi drivers and police officers normally result in sentences of immediate custody, as do 'road rage' attacks and football violence. Where the injury caused was at the bottom end of the scale and no weapon was used, a non-custodial disposal will generally be both appropriate and possible, especially where there are mitigating factors present, such as provocation, youth and previous good character. If the offender is seen as in need of help and guidance, probation or a combination order (probation and community service combined) is the most likely disposal. An offender whose offence is considered close to the custody threshold is likely to be ordered to do community service, particularly if he has previous convictions for violence or for public order offences. If the offence occurred on licensed premises or at a football match, the court may, in addition to any other penalty, ban him from specified licensed premises or from football matches for periods of up to two years and three months respectively. Since imprisonment deprives a person of his earning capacity, compensation orders are rarely made against violent offenders sentenced to immediate custody. However, where the offender escapes custody and has the means to pay, the court will consider making such an order. To assist courts fix the amount of compensation the Magistrates' Association has produced a suggested tariff, with figures ranging from £2500 for a simple fracture of the leg to £50 for a graze. The amount actually ordered should be a sum which the offender will be able to pay off within twelve months. First offenders not in need of assistance and considered unlikely to offend again are often dealt with by way of a fine or an order of conditional discharge coupled with a compensation order.

ASSAULT OCCASIONING ACTUAL BODILY HARM CONTRARY TO SECTION 47 OF THE 1861 ACT

This offence is triable in the Crown Court, or summarily if both magistrates and accused agree. A section 47 offence may involve the use of a weapon and, indeed, the causing of a wound. Those charged with a section 20 offence will not infrequently offer to plead guilty to an offence under section 47 because they perceive it to be a less serious crime, notwithstanding that both carry the same maximum penalty. The perception may be realistic since a non-custodial disposal is relatively common for this offence. Indeed, the *Magistrates' Association Guidelines* indicate that the presumption is that a community penalty (i.e. community service, probation or a combination order) is the appropriate disposal. In deciding whether to send to custody at all and, if not, what non-custodial disposal to adopt, a sentencing court will carry out the usual balancing exercise. A bad record for violence or evidence that the attack was racially motivated will usually tip the balance in favour of custody and, as with section 20 offences, custody will normally be meted out where the victim was a taxi driver, bus conductor or a police officer, or the violence was caused in a 'road rage' attack or at a football match. What has been said as to non-custodial sentencing for section 20 offences holds good here also.

COMMON ASSAULT, ASSAULTING A POLICE CONSTABLE IN THE EXECUTION OF HIS DUTY

Common assault, like the offence of assaulting a police constable in the execution of his duty, is only triable summarily and carries a maximum sentence of six months' imprisonment. As the *Magistrates' Association Guidelines* indicate, the presumption in the case of common assault is that a non-custodial disposal is appropriate; in the case of assault upon a constable it is that custody is called for.

PUBLIC ORDER OFFENCES

Those guilty of public disorder may end up being charged with one of three offences: (i) violent disorder (three or more persons present together using or threatening unlawful violence such as would cause a person of reasonable firmness present at the scene to fear for his own safety, that is to fear being caught up in violence); (ii) affray (the use of or threats of violence towards another such as would cause a person of reasonable firmness present at the scene to fear for his own safety); (iii) using threatening, abusive or insulting words or behaviour. Violent disorder and affray are triable in the Crown Court but may be tried summarily if the magistrates agree and the accused consents. Using threatening behaviour is triable summarily, carrying a maximum sentence of 6 months' imprisonment. Violent disorder and affray, even when dealt with summarily, are normally punished by custody. Where such offences involve prolonged use of violence, Crown Court sentences are usually in the region of 18 months and upwards. Affrays arising spontaneously in places such as restaurants and public houses usually attract, even in the case of an offender of good character, sentences of between 3 and 12 months' imprisonment. The *Magistrates' Association Guidelines* indicate that for offences of threatening behaviour there is a presumption in favour of disposal by way of community penalty. However, this presumption is relatively easily displaced if the offender has previous convictions for violence or the offence itself was of an aggravated character (e.g., committed at a football match or in the Accident and Emergency Department of a busy hospital).

MENTALLY DISORDERED OFFENDERS

Where there is evidence from two registered medical practitioners, one of whom is approved for the purpose of the Mental Health Act 1983, that an offender, convicted of an offence other than murder, is suffering from a treatable mental disorder (the definition includes psychopathic disorder), the court, if satisfied that a hospital order is the most suitable method of dealing with him and that a hospital place is available, may make an order committing him to that hospital for treatment. Unless the court, at the same time as making a hospital order, also makes a restriction order (that is, an order which prevents his being discharged without the approval of the Home Office), an offender committed under a such an order may be discharged by the hospital at any time and must be discharged after six months unless the hospital's authority to detain him is renewed. Magistrates are not empowered to make restriction orders and, where a magistrates' court is minded to make a hospital order but thinks a restriction order necessary, it must commit the case for sentence at the Crown Court. Where a mentally disordered offender is considered dangerous to the public, a hospital order will not normally be considered unless there is a place available for him in one of the four special hospitals (Broadmoor, Rampton, Ashworth and Park Lane) or in a secure hospital or unit and, where it is made, it will invariably be coupled with a restriction order without limit of time. Where a patient the subject of a restriction order is discharged, such discharge will usually be conditional in the first instance, enabling the hospital to recall him if he shows signs of deterioration. By no means all dangerous violent offenders suffering from mental disorder end up being made the subject of a hospital order. In some cases lack of a hospital place obliges a court to pass a prison sentence. In others the fact that his condition is untreatable (as is often the case with psychopaths) acts as a bar to a hospital order. A court which is considering making a hospital order may, if certain conditions are satisfied, make an interim order committing the offender to a named hospital for 28 days so that the suitability of such a disposal can be investigated.

Violent offenders suffering from mental disorder who do not require hospitalisation, but who do need medical treatment, may be made the subject of a 'psychiatric' probation order – that is, a probation order, a condition of which is that the offender receive medical treatment under the supervision of a named medical practitioner.

PERSISTENT OFFENDERS

The fact that an offender convicted of a violent offence has previous convictions for such offences is an aggravating factor and may lead to him receiving a more severe sentence. Persistent violent offenders who commit grave offences and are considered unstable and dangerous may well be dealt with by imposing a discretionary life sentence or a hospital order coupled with a restriction order without limit of time. Since 1 October 1997 they are also at risk of receiving a mandatory life sentence under the provisions of the Crime Sentences Act. A persistent violent offender who commits an offence which does not carry life imprisonment and who does not satisfy the conditions for the making of a hospital order may, if the court is satisfied that there is a substantial risk of his committing serious violent offences in the future, be given a 'longer than normal' sentence.[18] Such a sentence may not exceed the statutory maximum for the offence but will be longer than the normal tariff sentence. Courts dealing with violent offenders who are not considered a danger to the public, but whose offending is associated with drink, drug abuse, poor self-control or psychiatric problems, may, in an attempt to assist them, make a probation order with a condition attached to the order that they attend for a period of up to 60 days a course run by or under the auspices of the probation service.

YOUNG OFFENDERS

Violent young offenders are much less likely than their adult counterparts to receive a custodial sentence. Youth is a powerful mitigating factor and the law places substantial restrictions upon the power of courts to sentence those under 18 to custody. Murder is an exceptional case. An offender convicted of murder, if under 18, must be sentenced to be detained during Her Majesty's Pleasure; if between 18 and 21, to custody for life. Offenders between 15 and 21 convicted of offences of violence other than murder cannot be sentenced to imprisonment. They may, however, be sentenced to detention in a young offender institution. Where an offender is aged over 18, the maximum length of sentence which may be imposed is the same as in the case of an adult (if he attains 21 whilst still serving the sentence it is converted automatically into a sentence of imprisonment). Where he is aged 15, 16 or 17, the maximum sentence which may be passed upon him is 24 months or the maximum term for the offence, whichever is less. Offenders under 15 cannot be sentenced to youth custody at all, although in areas served by the newly opened Medway Secure Training Centre[19] it is now possible to make a secure training order for a term of between six months and two years in the case of an offender over 12 who has at least three previous convictions for imprisonable offences and who has failed to respond to supervision. The effect of the above is that, save in the case of murder, a violent offender, if between 10 (the

18 Criminal Justice Act 1991, s. 2(2)(b).
19 See *The Times*, 15 April 1998.

age of criminal responsibility) and 15, cannot normally be sent to custody at all, and, if aged between 15 and 17, cannot be sentenced to more than two years' detention. However, to this general rule there is an important exception. To ensure that the law is not powerless to visit retribution upon juveniles who commit grave offences, it is provided by s. 53 of the Children and Young Persons Act 1933 that an offender aged between 10 and 17 convicted of an offence punishable with 14 years' imprisonment or more in the case of an adult (so far as violent offences go, this means a section 18 offence or worse) can be ordered to be detained for a term not exceeding that for which an adult offender could be imprisoned. The court may, however, only impose such a sentence if it is satisfied that no other method of dealing with the offender is appropriate, and after carefully exploring all other methods of dealing with him. The Court of Appeal has indicated that a sentence under s. 53 should normally be for at least two-and-a-half years.

Where a court dealing with a young offender is prevented by statute from sentencing him to custody, or concludes that custody, although available, is not appropriate, it has a wide range of other sentencing disposals open to it. These range from attendance at an attendance centre, a supervision order (where the offender is under 18), an order for supervision with intermediate treatment (i.e. with a requirement that the offender participate for a period of up to 90 days in specified activities), a hospital order, a community service or combination order (where the offender is over 16), a fine, a compensation order, orders of conditional and absolute discharge. There is also power to bind over the parent or guardian of an offender under 18 to take proper care of, and exercise proper control over, him (if the binding over is breached the parent or guardian is liable to forfeit a specified sum of money).

CONCLUSION

Present sentencing practice can be summarised thus. The sentence for grave offences of violence is almost invariably custody or confinement in a secure psychiatric hospital. Only where an offence of violence is not of the first seriousness will a non-custodial disposal be considered. The introduction of the Crime and Disorder Act 1998 will make far-reaching changes to the sentencing regime for young offenders. The power of youth court magistrates to sentence under-eighteens to custody will be greatly extended and the sentence of detention in a young offender institution will be replaced by a new form of sentence – 'the custody and training order'. One result of the Act is likely to be more young offenders being sent away to custody for offences of violence in much the same way as the Crime Sentences Act, as it begins to bite, will cause a slow but steady growth in the number of life prisoners. The public will doubtless approve.

CHAPTER 2

Young Offenders Who Commit Grave Crimes

The Criminal Justice Response

Gwyneth Boswell

INTRODUCTION

Section 53 offenders are children and young people between the ages of 10 and 17 inclusive who commit grave crimes and are sentenced to be detained, some indeterminately, under Section 53 of the Children and Young Persons Act 1933. Their crimes invariably involve violence or intended violence. Because this offender population is relatively small in number across child care and prison systems (1172 on 30.9.97), it is quite rare for one who is serving a lengthy sentence to come the way of social work and criminal justice professionals. Yet, with a potential age range of 10–65 (in terms of the known population), some of these young offenders can experience very long custodial careers and become 'lost' in the system. Certainly, as adults, they are rarely recognised as Section 53 offenders, with potential implications for the meeting of treatment needs and the accurate assessment of risk. The surrounding legislation is complex and the young (and sometimes not so young) offenders themselves are often both frightened and frightening, frequently combining both victim and offender in one person. Both they and those at risk from them deserve an informed and skilled response from responsible professionals. In particular, communication, assessment and intervention skills with this high-risk group need to stem directly from a strong and value-aware professional knowledge base. In turn, this requires a sound grasp of the surrounding historical and legislative context, an awareness of prevailing custodial career practice and a critical understanding of key research findings and theoretical underpinnings. Through examination of these factors this chapter will seek to provide a framework for the professional response to this small, but singular, group of offenders.

THE HISTORICAL AND LEGISLATIVE CONTEXT

Undoubtedly the most notorious case to attract a Section 53 sentence in recent memory is that of two 11-year-old boys convicted in November 1993 of the murder of two-year-old James Bulger. This case received unprecedented media attention when it came to trial, the general feeling being that it was unique – though those old enough to remember the conviction of Mary Bell in 1968 for the manslaughter of two small children knew otherwise. Indeed, as a catalogue of over fifty case histories shows, children of both sexes, some under the age of 10 years, have killed both adults and other children since time immemorial (Wilson 1973).

The separate and distinctive status of children and young persons convicted of murder and other specified violent crimes first became enshrined in the Children and Young Persons Act 1933. Section 53 of that Act made special provision for juveniles convicted on indictment by the Crown Court of murder or other serious offences. Section 53[1] provided that a person under the age of 18 years, convicted of murder, be detained during Her Majesty's Pleasure in such place and under such conditions as the Secretary of State (the Home Secretary) may direct. This sentence is indeterminate, controversially often treated as a life sentence and has not been significantly varied or amended by any subsequent legislation. It is the only sentence which a court can dispense in respect of 10 to 17-year-olds convicted of murder.

Section 53[2] of the 1933 Act provided for longer terms of detention with no statutory minimum but up to the adult maximum (i.e. life) for those under the age of 17 (raised to 18 in 1991). This was for the specified offences of attempted murder, manslaughter and wounding with intent to do grievous bodily harm – subsequently extended by the Criminal Justice Act 1961 to 'any offence punishable in the case of an adult with imprisonment for 14 years or more'.

The 1993 Act was also, however, the first measure to combine the two principles of criminal justice and welfare for children. It was stated that: 'Every Court in dealing with a child or young person who is brought before it, either as being in need of care or protection or as an offender or otherwise, shall have regard to the welfare of the child or young person' (Children and Young Persons Act 1933: Section 44[1]). This welfare requirement has not been repealed or amended by any subsequent legislation.

A significant landmark in the development of Section 53[2] sentencing emerged in 1968 with the conviction of 11-year-old Mary Bell for the manslaughter of two small boys aged 3 and 4 respectively. Like the James Bulger case in 1993, this case was also described as unique (Sereny 1974). In 1968 the trial judge's inability to make the Hospital Order which was his preference (because no hospital felt it could offer the combination of treatment and containment required) led to Mary Bell's detention in a special secure unit of a local authority children's home. Similar establishments were the location for the detention of the two young killers of James Bulger, who will move to Young Offender Institutions when they are 16 and Adult Prisons when they are 21 years of age.

An important development for Section 53[1] and Section 53[2] life detainees, during the 1980s, was the introduction of the tariff date for those serving life sentences, a procedural measure which began to be implemented around 1984. This meant that, for the first time, those sentenced to life would receive from the trial judge a notional date by which they would have served society's requirement for punishment and deterrence and which would constitute the earliest date at which they could be released. In respect of adult murderers and Section 53[1] detainees, this date could be varied first by the Lord Chief Justice and second by the Home Secretary. In practice, this often meant that the tariff was increased – so that this measure has carried particularly far-reaching consequences for children and adolescents convicted of murder, such as those in the James Bulger case who were initially given an 8-year tariff which was ultimately extended to 15 years by the Home Secretary.

The Criminal Justice and Public Order Act 1994 doubled the Young Offender Institution (YOI) maximum sentence to two years and introduced the Secure Training Order for 12 to 14-year-olds, effectively raising the minimum length of a Section 53[2] sentence to in excess of 2 years. In addition, Section 53[2] could now be used for the first time ever for 10 to 13-year-olds (the only previous exceptions being those convicted of homicidal offences or jointly charged with an adult).

Overall, then, Section 53 legislation during the twentieth century has constituted an unfolding picture, which, more than any other section of youth justice, has served to highlight the welfare/justice dichotomy for young offenders and for those involved in their care and rehabilitation.

THE CUSTODIAL CAREER PATTERN

Many of those receiving a Section 53 sentence are remanded in custody or secure units prior to their trial. The killers of James Bulger, remanded in separate secure units for nine months and, reportedly, severely traumatised, were given no access to treatment lest it prejudice their evidence at the trial. In respect of one child, the consultant psychiatrist considered that his capacity to instruct his lawyers and testify in his defence had been impaired by the continuing, untreated symptoms of post-traumatic stress disorder (James Smith 1994). Further, a research study of 24 Section 53 offenders and their institutional staff (Boswell 1991) showed that it was not unusual for younger Section 53 respondents to have been detained on remand first in police cells, then in remand wings of Young Offender Institutions, or, in some cases, adult prisons, before being placed in a child care establishment. One under-sized 16-year-old recounted to the researcher horrific bullying experiences in his YOI establishment and wanted to stay in the interview room, where he felt safe, for as long as possible. This was not long after another teenager had committed suicide in the same institution after alleged experiences of bullying and sexual assault. In a later study of abuse and loss (Boswell 1995), several respondents recounted experiences of depression, self-harm, bullying by other inmates and attempts at suicide consistent with official reports (Liebling 1992; Howard League for Penal Reform 1993).

Not surprisingly, young people remanded in prisons or local authority secure units are likely to be vulnerable to receiving harsh sentences because they have already been assessed as high-risk enough to require secure containment. Additionally, in more serious cases, perhaps involving high profile media coverage, these periods of remand can be prolonged because of extended trial procedures and it is not impossible for such periods to exceed the sentence finally meted out. During this time there appears to be little preparation of remandees for what might follow (Boswell 1991).

A 10 to 15-year-old Section 53 offender serving an indeterminate or long determinate sentence will, following assessment, almost certainly be placed in a local authority secure unit or Youth Treatment Centre set up to provide long-term care for a minority of severely disturbed and anti-social children and adolescents. In each of these settings there will be a proportion of other children, usually with extreme behaviour problems, who are in local authority care primarily in the interests of their welfare and whom staff will be encouraging to work towards a realistic date for discharge from care. The fact that this group of young people lives with and works to the same regime as Section 53 offenders, frequently displaying worse behaviour problems, but is aiming for a discharge from care date rather than a release from custody date highlights immediately the position of each group on the welfare/justice continuum (Boswell 1996). This is not to suggest that the position is simple, however. Other writers who have researched the issue of long-term care/custody have observed the irony of a situation where a 'welfare' ethos is espoused but the professional discourse and structure of the regime mean that it is a 'punishment' ethos which is practised (Jones and Fowles 1984; Kelly 1992).

Equally, within the punishment ethos espoused by the criminal justice system for young delinquents lies a welfare ideology ('This is for your own good') which has been criticised as a smokescreen for social control (Rutherford 1986). More realistically, perhaps, this 'ambiguity in action' is genuinely a mixture of kindness, persuasion and coercion (Harris and Timms 1993) which are the characteristics of a system operating a care/control continuum (Boswell 1985) along which staff have to place themselves at any given time.

Within this complexity, Section 53 offenders still have a head start at the punishment end of proceedings, if only because they are labelled from day one as 'offenders' and, therefore, marked out as different, perhaps tougher, perhaps more to be feared, than their co-habitees in local authority care.

Regimes at secure units and Youth Treatment Centres, though they may differ and may not always fit the particular needs of the young offender, nevertheless place emphasis on treatment and education as an integrated part of their welfare task within the constraints of secure containment. When long-term Section 53 offenders reach the age of 16 they will transfer to a Young Offender Institution, a regime for which they are likely to have had little preparation. Many have described their transfer experiences as a real culture shock (Boswell 1991). Hitherto, they have received the benefit of welfare considerations, almost without being aware of it. Because of the lack of information both for staff and inmates as to the nature and meaning of a Section 53 sentence, it is unusual for the young person to have had it explained that when they enter the prison system it is to serve the punishment element of their sentence.

During their sentence in a YOI treatment opportunities for Section 53s are more fortuitous than integral, and education programmes tend to cater for the shorter-term inmate. Access to them is often constrained by limited resources. This is liable to constitute severe frustration for someone who has been carefully helped to understand their violent behaviour and motivated to open up their educational horizons whilst in the child care system. Family visits are also less frequent than in child care secure accommodation and overnight facilities rarely available. Despite the fact that one of the determining factors in placement is intended to be proximity to the offender's home area, this does not often work out in practice for long-termers, some of whose families have to travel extensively to make a two-hour visit. As with education, the family contact is available but not actively promoted as it would be in the child care system. These very significant changes are important when considering the effect upon a 16-year-old teenager of the transition from secure care to prison custody whilst similar transition is going on for that person from the state of childhood/adolescence to adulthood.

Similarly, as the long-term Section 53 offender moves on to the adult prison system, the 21-year-old young adult edges even closer to the punishment end of the treatment/punishment continuum. This is not to say that welfare considerations will cease but that, proportionately, they will be even less in evidence than in the YOI system, perhaps dependent upon individual prison officer or probation officer attention or the good fortune to be linked with an interested psychiatrist. (For example, until relatively recently, a consultant psychiatry service at Parkhurst Prison offered intensive ongoing therapy to violent prisoners on the closed unit). The long-term Section 53 offender will not be reclassified as an adult prisoner but neither will males, at any rate, be treated or even recognised as being any different to other long-termers. (Because the number of females is small – 30 as at 30.9.97 – their custodial history is more likely to be known to staff). That is to say that the fact that they may have spent a part of their pre-pubescence, adolescence and mid- to late-teens in custody will not win them any specialised attention or treatment in the adult setting. Involved professionals should be aware that, essentially, Section 53 offenders have to be highly self-motivated if they are to demonstrate, through attention to their own improvement via education or attendance at, for example, AA (Alcoholics Anonymous), drugs or sex offender groups, their ability and commitment to change and to cease violent offending. This is quite a tall order alongside the (in many ways more demanding) process of psychological survival in a total institution with rigid male mores and the additional nagging uncertainty of no fixed release date (Cohen and Taylor 1972).

The Section 53 offender transferred to the adult prison system will not end his or her prison career in the closed conditions in which s/he, in all likelihood, began it. A test of ability to cope in Open Prison conditions over a 2- or 3-year period is a normal Parole Board requirement prior to release. Offenders will need to demonstrate that they can use limited degrees of freedom responsibly and maturely. Oddly, for those who began their career in the child care system, this will, in some ways, be like coming full circle, perhaps with the benefit of maturity and hindsight. Nevertheless, the foregoing paragraphs serve to show the difficulty for them of moving up and down the treatment/punishment continuum and of knowing what is available to and expected of them in a range of settings and situations. Equally, staff in different settings, faced with the welfare/justice dichotomy, are likely to experience some considerable dilemma in balancing the two elements appropriately within these settings and situations. This dichotomous area clearly needs reflective attention from involved professionals if the roots of violent offending are to be even modestly understood and thereby addressed during the course of a long career in custody.

RESEARCH AND THEORETICAL UNDERPINNINGS

If professionals are to work to comprehend and address violent offending in the young, they need to be furnished with relevant theoretical perspectives and research findings. General theories of deviance and delinquency, such as class conflict, 'anomie', sub-cultural behaviour, peer group pressure, social interaction and labelling, are well documented in criminological and sociological text books (e.g. O'Donnell 1992). They are often presented as mutually exclusive, however, and this can be unhelpful when trying to make sense of a very specific problem like youth violence, which often contains elements of all these explanations together with strong psychological factors converging upon the developmental stage of adolescence. Thus it is extremely important to look to relevant research findings for guidance as to the areas which should be afforded the most attention when working with these young people.

A study of one-third of the Section 53 population in the early 1990s found that 72 per cent of the sample had experienced one or more kinds of abuse (emotional 28.5%; physical 40%; sexual 29%; organised 1.5%) in their earlier lives and 57 per cent had experienced significant loss via bereavement or separation from someone important to them (Boswell 1995). The total number experiencing one or both phenomena was 91 per cent; the total experiencing both was 35 per cent – suggesting that the presence of a double childhood trauma may be a potent factor in the backgrounds of violent young offenders. The study fleshed out the progression from trauma to violence with case studies of children who were beaten, buggered, locked in dark cellars, tortured and humiliated. Many of those who had become violent had also become disturbed and/or depressed. The fact that slightly more than 95 per cent of the Section 53 population is male accords with the Diagnostic and Statistic Manual of Mental Disorders (DSM – IV) framework which shows externalised disruptive behaviour disorders to be much more common in boys than girls, whilst internalised anxiety and repressive disorders (which may include self-harm) are either equally likely or more common amongst girls (American Psychiatric Association 1994). Here gender-based predisposition and cultural behaviour conditioning may well be a key factor.

Whilst some other studies have forged modest links between early traumatic experiences and later violent/abusive behaviour (Wolfe 1987; Rutter 1989; Dodge, Bates and Pettis 1990; Shepherd 1993), it has always proved problematic to establish cause. For example, a review of the empirical evidence that 'violence begets violence' showed that childhood abuse or neglect increased the risk of later violent criminal behaviour but that other variables intervened to determine alternative outcomes (Widom 1989). These variables are sometimes known as 'protective factors' and may include, for example, biological predisposition, environmental factors or a new and significant attachment figure which can mitigate against earlier traumatic experiences in some cases (Garmezy 1981). Clearly, also, not all Section 53 offenders will have experienced childhood trauma, and all those children who have, will not become violent offenders. However, it is significant that many members of the 1995 Section 53 survey had done so, that most had not been effectively helped to think through, interpret or resolve the traumatic event(s) which had occurred in their earlier lives and that such help could have provided a protective factor which may have made a difference to their later behaviour. It is also significant that such findings as are available on early traumata are rarely cited when a violent young offender hits the headlines, as was seen in the Bulger case – hence their emphasis in this section.

Perhaps this situation should not be a matter for surprise given that the 'battered child syndrome' was only identified just over three decades ago (Kempe *et al.* 1962), despite well-known incidents of physical child abuse over the centuries. If it is right to suggest that physical violence between family members is a normal part of family life in most societies (Gelles and Straus 1979), perhaps there is a reluctance on the part of most people – researchers, criminal justice professionals and journalists alike – to acknowledge the threat that this 'normality' poses to all members of society as potential victims and offenders. Certainly, the file search for the Section 53 study showed that questions which might have helped to establish whether or not there were links between childhood trauma and later violent offending did not, for the most part, appear to have been posed by criminal justice professionals in any systematic fashion. An interesting parallel is to be found in a study of 105 hospitalised psychiatric patients, 51 per cent of whom were found to have been sexually abused in childhood or adolescence (Craine *et al.* 1988). In the majority of these cases hospital staff were unaware of the sexual abuse and only 20 per cent of the abused patients believed that they had received adequate treatment for their abusive experiences. Likewise, 69 per cent met the criteria for PTSD (post-traumatic stress disorder) but had not been identified as such. A study of children who had killed parents and were admitted to a special hospital also referred to the fact that 'the unexpectedly low incidence of disclosure (of sexual abuse) raises the question of whether therapists are sufficiently sensitive to such issues' (Brufal 1994, p.11). Similarly, as Yule (1993) points out in a critique of issues and findings relating to childhood abuse, 'One reason why professions did not believe that children were subject to physical or sexual abuse, or suffered from PTSD, was simply that they never asked them!' (p.165).

The growing body of work on post-traumatic stress disorder (Pynoos *et al.* 1987; Scott and Stradling 1992) confirms that children suffer the after-effects of traumatic stress in a similar way to adults. The set of criteria commonly used to establish whether an individual is suffering from post-traumatic stress disorder (American Psychiatric Association 1994) has been linked with a set of early maladaptive schema (Young 1990) to produce a continuum between major childhood trauma and psychological morbidity in later life. Of note in relation to the 1995 Section 53 study are those maladaptive schema that include subjugation, vulnerability to harm, emotional deprivation, abandonment and loss.

This overall view is supported by Robert Johnson (1993), consultant psychiatrist, whose report to the Reed Committee describes his work with seriously violent adult prisoners suffering from the 'buried terror syndrome' induced by child abuse. The terror experienced by these men (one of whom, for example, was regularly used by his mother at the age of five as a human shield against his drunken father, who would beat them both with chair legs) became deeply buried for fear that its bringing back to the surface would lead to its re-enactment. (This process is often known as a state of denial). Any likelihood of this happening would precipitate an extreme, and probably violent, reaction based on the man's fundamental terror. The psychiatrist's job was sensitively and carefully to identify the terror and to show that it was now obsolete, a process which ultimately led to a recovery from violent manifestation. However, many of these men had spent decades in institutions without the questions being asked that could bring them to an understanding of their violent behaviour.

GOOD PRACTICE WITH SECTION 53 OFFENDERS

The foregoing sections highlight the complexity of legislation, penal policy and aetiology which surround 10 to 17-year-olds convicted of grave, usually violent, crimes. It is clear that the level and quality of intervention by social work and criminal justice professionals within this complexity can significantly impact upon the personal development, custodial careers and safe resettlement of those Section 53 offenders incarcerated for long periods. The three particular stages where the quality of professional contact is crucial are those of pre-sentence, custodial through-care and post-release supervision.

Pre-sentence contact

During the phases of first court appearance, pre-sentence report preparation, conviction and sentence it is particularly important that lawyers, social workers and probation officers understand the circumstances under which a Section 53 sentence may be passed and what it will mean in practice for the young offender who, in turn, should be properly informed and prepared for this eventuality. This awareness, together with knowledge or research findings about this group, which includes a high prevalence of background abuse and loss and the potential for racism (at 30.9.97, 35% of Section 53 offenders were black), is crucial in contributing to the articulacy and credibility of representations to sentencers. The offence of murder aside, it is possible to argue for alternative sentences where these are feasible, especially in a penal climate where the 'prison works' philosophy shows no sign of abating. Sentencers, too, should be clear that Section 53 is by no means the 'welfare' measure for young people that is sometimes portrayed. The population breakdown shows that children and adolescents serving lengthy, determinate or indeterminate sentences have a high chance of ending up in the prison system in adulthood (Boswell 1996). It is, therefore, incumbent upon those whose profession enables them to influence the sentencing process to ensure that they have brought together every piece of evidence (including, notably, the offender's own account of the period between early childhood and the violent offence) to make an accurate assessment of why this offence was committed. This needs to be clearly linked with a sentencing proposal which addresses and seeks to eradicate the underlying reasons for the violent offending whilst providing an acceptable level of protection for the public.

Pre-sentence report writers should be aware that reports will follow the Section 53 offender to the establishment in which they are held and to the central filing system located at prison service headquarters. They are very likely to be referred to at subsequent review and parole processes. Information in them should, therefore, be selected with the offender's longer-term career in mind and with a conscious avoidance of the onset of a labelling process.

Custodial through-care

Young people who have received long sentences (in the case of the James Bulger killers, longer than they had yet lived) cannot, for the most part, comprehend the length of time in custody that lies ahead of them. In secure units and YOIs they are subject to annual long-term Training Board reviews (which, in adult prisons, become F75 reviews) helping to determine sentence career plans – though institutional staff often say that they do not know whether they should be preparing a plan to help them adjust to adult prison or to assist rehabilitation in the community (Boswell 1991). The membership of these review boards is multi-disciplinary; the differing degrees of staff knowledge about the offender and the young lifer system itself can have a profound impact upon the review of a young person whose sentence stretches out indefinitely. Guidance to supervising probation officers suggests that effective post-release supervision depends on the building up of a trusting supervisory relationship through visits and letters over a long period (Home Office Parole Unit 1991). This allows for the supervisor to work at shoring up family and community support systems, helping the young offender to understand the reasons for his or her violent offending and contributing to the building up of strategies to avoid it in the future – thus endeavouring to increase the chances of successful rehabilitation on release. This supervision is in a unique 'bridging' position to inform review and parole processes and to act as a crucial conduit of information between establishment and home base. It can often be through the development of this trusting long-term relationship that supervisors learn of traumatic childhood experiences and the chain of events which have led towards the violent offence. It is important, however, that they familiarise themselves with the features of traumata such as abuse (see, for example, Wolfe 1987) and post-traumatic stress disorder (see Scott and Stradling 1992) so that when, for example, an offender starts to tell them about recurrent nightmares or flashbacks, they recognise this as a symptom of PTSD and, rather than let it pass, pursue it via sensitive questioning.

Overall, what seems important during the custodial careers of this group of offenders is that criminal justice professionals adopt what has been termed elsewhere a 'welfare-conscious justice model' (Boswell 1990), in which the growing young adult is communicated with as responsible and accountable rather than as a helpless victim. At the same time, however, a systematic and consistent career plan addresses problems and forces external to, but influential upon, the offending and makes provision for interventions such as counselling following child abuse and educational and social skills development opportunities. This requires recognition of the ambiguous nature of the system in which professionals play an influential part and the need to be able to step back and identify for themselves, and the offender, their position along the welfare/justice continuum at any given time.

Post-release supervision

It is normal practice for a probation officer to supervise Section 53 offenders on release, though other professionals may also be involved in the supervision plan. National Standards (Home Office 1995) require the supervising officer to ensure the protection of the public, the prevention of reoffending and successful rehabilitation in the community. In the case of long-term offenders on discretionary release, breach of licence conditions, and/or any evidence to suggest the licensee is likely to reoffend, put the safety of the public at risk or bring the licence into disrepute, are reported direct to the parole unit. Section 53 offenders subject to Life Licence are placed on probation service high-risk offender registers so that their progress will be reviewed every quarter by senior management. The supervising probation officer submits periodic reports to the DSP2 division of the prison department, in which any significant difficulties should be noted. These should include the areas of alcohol, drugs, sexual relationships, bizarre or abnormal sexual interests, inability to handle social situations, social isolation and repetition of the circumstances and/or pattern of behaviour leading to the original offence. Supported by senior management, the probation officer has the power to recommend either consideration of recall or immediate recall on public safety grounds. Probation officers also have power to recommend cancellation of the supervision requirements of a Life Licence (which, nevertheless, remains in force for life), usually after a period of about 5 years, following consistent compliance and good behaviour by the offender.

Clearly, the probation officer's control over the potential for both freedom and captivity is very considerable. The professional supervisory relationship must be able to acknowledge this openly and to be absolutely clear with the offender what is expected of him or her in terms of behaviour on licence. It also needs to hold the tension between concern for the individual offender and the protection of the public. Here good listening and gentle probing skills are needed to make ongoing, accurate assessments of risk whilst simultaneously working to reduce it via appropriate intervention skills, which, for offenders who have been in custody since their teens, may well include combinations of counselling/peer group work/education and social skills development and other focused injections which enable the offender to compensate for the deficit in a normal adolescent development at liberty.

POINTERS FOR THE FUTURE

This chapter has sought to demonstrate the crucial importance of a sound knowledge base for professionals called upon to work with Section 53 offenders at key stages in a long-term custodial career. Only by operating with clarity within legislative, penal policy and research-based frameworks can they offer an informed and balanced service to this group of offenders and to the general public. Ideally, however, good professional practice extends beyond a focus on one particular individual to a more comprehensive approach to the phenomenon of which that individual is a part. Most professionals, at some point, have the opportunity to influence crime prevention, criminal justice policy, custodial career management and public understanding.

In respect of crime prevention, education and publicity are needed at community level to encourage both children and adults to recognise and report incidents of abuse. Parent support and parenting classes (some, interestingly, now springing up in YOIs and adult prisons) can help present and future parents avoid the pitfalls of abusive or damaging parenthood. Criminal justice policy might afford some attention to the rest of Europe, where 14 years is the average age for criminal responsibility, and to the need for a single institution to house Section 53 offenders throughout their custodial career, thus eradicating inconsistency and disruption and ensuring that individual treatment or education needs are not only identified but implemented and sustained. Finally, criminal justice professionals are well-placed to interact with the public to provide serious, rather than salacious, information about young people who commit grave crimes and to emphasise the importance for community safety of replacing condemnation with an understanding of young, violent offending. Through a variety of local and national fora they can involve the public in discussing the action that each sector can appropriately take to minimise the risks of this happening in their communities.

In order that it may receive serious treatment by policy makers, the media and the wider public, the question 'Why do children and young people commit violent and murderous crimes?' must continue to be avidly pursued by criminal justice professionals in order that answers to the further question of prevention can start to emerge. Only when such specialist knowledge is more widely available can it be clearly and widely communicated, and the public at large take its own responsibility for the sustained reduction of a problem which, as the James Bulger case demonstrated, touches and challenges our society at a most profound level.

REFERENCES

American Psychiatric Association (1994) *Diagnostic and Statistical Manual of Mental Disorders*, 4th edn. (DSM-IV). Washington, DC: APA.

Boswell, G.R. (1985) *Care, Control and Accountability in the Probation Service.* Social Work Monographs, Norwich: University of East Anglia.

Boswell, G.R. (1990) *Justice Versus Welfare: Is Welfare a Dead Duck?* Unpublished paper to Suffolk Probation Service Staff Conference, 30 November.

Boswell, G.R. (1991) *Waiting for Change: An Exploration of the Experiences and Needs of Section 53 Offenders*. London: The Prince's Trust.

Boswell, G.R. (1995) *Violent Victims: The Prevalence of Abuse and Loss in the Lives of Section 53 Offenders*. London: The Prince's Trust.

Boswell, G.R. (1996) *Young and Dangerous: The Backgrounds and Careers of Section 53 Offenders*. Aldershot: Avebury.

Brufal, T. (1994) 'Homicide within and beyond the family: a comparative examination of the childhood experiences of matricidal men.' *Special Hospitals Research Bulletin*, 3, (1), 8–12.

Cohen, S. and Taylor, L. (1972) *Psychological Survival: The Experience of Long-Term Imprisonment*. Harmondsworth: Penguin Books Limited.

Craine, L.S., Henson, C.E., Colliver, J.A. and MacLean, D.G. (1988) 'Prevalence of a history of sexual abuse among female psychiatric patients in a state hospital system.' *Hospital and Community Psychiatry*, 39, 300–304.

Dodge, K.A., Bates, J.E. and Pettis, G.S. (1990) 'Mechanisms in the Cycle of Violence.' *Science*, 250, 1678–1683.

Garmezy, N. (1981) 'Children under stress: perspectives on antecedents and correlates of vulnerability and resistance to psychopathology.' In A.I. Rabin, J. Arnoff, A.M. Barclay and R.A. Zucker (eds) *Further Explorations in Personality*. New York: Wiley.

Gelles, R.J. and Straus, M.A. (1979) 'Determinants of violence in the family: toward a theoretical integration.' In W.R. Burr, R. Hill, F.I. Nye and I.L. Reiss (eds) *Contemporary Theories about the Family*. New York: Free Press.

Harris, R. and Timms, N. (1993) *Secure Accommodation in Child Care: Between Hospital and Prison or Thereabouts?* London and New York: Routledge.

Home Office (1995) *National Standards for the Supervision of Offenders in the Community*. London: Home Office Probation Service Division.

Home Office Parole Unit (1991) *Letter to Chief Probation Officers on the Treatment and Through-Care of Section 53 Offenders, 21 February*. London: Home Office.

Howard League for Penal Reform (1993) *Dying Inside: Suicides in Prison*. London: Howard League.

James Smith, D. (1994) *The Sleep of Reason: The James Bulger Case*. London: Century.

Johnson, R. (1993) *Intensive Work with Disordered Personalities 1991–1993*. Unpublished report to the Reed Committee, January.

Jones, K. and Fowles, A.J. (1984) *Ideas on Institutions: Analysing the Literature on Long Term Care and Custody*. London: Routledge and Kegan Paul.

Kelly, B. (1992) *Rhetoric and Practice in a Locked Institution for Children*. London: Routledge.

Kempe, C.H., Silverman, F., Steele, B., Droegmueller, W. and Silver, H. (1962) 'The Battered Child Syndrome.' *Journal of the American Medical Association*, 181, 17–24.

Liebling, A. (1992) *Suicide in Prison*. London: Routledge.

O'Donnell, M. (1992) *A New Introduction to Sociology*. Walton-on-Thames: Edinburgh: Quarry Bay: Victoria: Ontario: Thomas Nelson and Sons Ltd.

Pynoos, R.S., Frederick, C., Nader, K., Arroyo, W., Steinberg, A., Eth, S., Nunez, F. and Fairbanks, L. (1987) 'Life threat and post-traumatic stress in school-age children.' *Archives of General Psychiatry*, 44, 1057–1063.

Rutherford, A. (1986) *Growing out of Crime: Society and Young People in Trouble*. Harmondsworth: Penguin Books Ltd.

Rutter, M. (1989) 'Intergenerational continuities and discontinuities in serious parenting difficulties.' In D. Ciccheti and V. Carlson (eds) *Child Maltreatment Theory and Research on the Causes and Consequences of Child Abuse and Neglect*. New York: Cambridge University Press.

Scott, M.J. and Stradling, S.G. (1992) *Counselling for Post-Traumatic Stress Disorder*. London, Newbury Park and New Delhi: Sage Counselling in Practice Series.

Sereny, G. (1974) *The Case of Mary Bell*. London: Arrow Books Ltd.

Shepherd, S. (1993) *Prevalence of Sexual Abuse amongst Juvenile Prisoners*. Report to Home Office.

Widom, C.S. (1989) 'Does violence beget violence? A critical examination of the literature.' *Psychological Bulletin*, 106, (1), 3–28.

Wilson, P. (1973) *Children who Kill*. London: Michael Joseph.

Wolfe, D.A. (1987) *Child Abuse: Implications for Child Development and Psychopathology*. New York: Sage.

Young, J.E. (1990) *Cognitive Therapy for Personality Disorders: A Schema-focused Approach*. Sarasota, F.L.: Professional Resource Exchange.

Yule, W. (1993) 'Children as victims and survivors.' In P.J. Taylor (ed) *Violence in Society*. London: Royal College of Physicians.

CHAPTER 3

The Assessment and Management of Violent Offenders

Hazel Kemshall

INTRODUCTION

Recorded crime fell by around 9 per cent in England and Wales in 1997 (Povey, Prime and Taylor 1998), reflecting an unprecedented fall in burglaries and theft (*The Guardian* 1998a). However, violent crime continued to rise – with a 1.7 per cent overall rise, including a 5.8 per cent rise in offences against the person and a 6.8 per cent rise in sexual assaults (Povey, Prime and Taylor 1998; *The Times* 1997). Home Office officials attributed the fall in property crime to a period of relative economic prosperity and the rise in violent crime to increased alcohol consumption. Whilst the general decrease in crime was positively received by the Home Office Minister Alun Michael, he warned against complacency over the rise in violent offences (*The Guardian* 1998a).

The Minister's comment reveals an underlying societal and governmental concern with violent offences against the person, even in a time of general crime reduction. Soothill (1993), for example, has noted how serial sex killing is the moral panic of the 1990s, although the concern is out of proportion to the amount of offences actually committed (an average of 2.3 homicides per year). However, media coverage of notorious cases throughout the 1990s – such as the Jamie Bulger murder, the Hamilton murders at Dunblane and the West case – and the increased demonisation of sex offenders (for example, Sydney Cooke (*The Sun* 1998) have contributed to the amplification of public perceptions of violence risk (Kasperson 1992; Kemshall 1997; Sparks 1992). This has most often exhibited itself in local resistance to the siting of offender hostels, the release and accommodation of sexual and violent offenders in the community and the management of such offenders on community or post-release supervision. This has raised significant issues for practitioners, managers and policy makers in the reliable identification of those persons most likely to commit violent offences and for their subsequent effective management both within institutions and in the community.

This chapter is not concerned with the extreme acts of violence which attract public and media notoriety but with the range of physical and psychological acts of violence which the probation service has an increasing role in identifying and effectively managing. The starting point for defining violence is section 31 (1) of the Criminal Justice Act 1991, which defines a violent offence as one: 'which leads, or is intended to lead, to a person's death or to physical injury to a person, and includes an offence which is required to be charged as arson (whether or not it would otherwise fall within this definition)' (From Wasik and Taylor 1991, p.20).

However, psychological trauma as well as physical injury has been emphasised – for example, by the Butler Committee (1975) and, more recently, by the Protection of Harassment Act 1997 in which an 'aggravated indictable offence involving the fear of violence' (section 4) was created (Lawson-Cruttenden 1997). In this chapter violence is understood as the potential, threat or use of force which is likely to result in either physical or psychological harm. In addition, the chapter draws upon research literature and tools aimed at male violence, recognising that most violent offences against the person are committed by males (Home Office 1997a). Female violence is reviewed by Rumgay (Chapter 6) and the link between male violence, gender and socialisation is explored by Buckley (Chapter 5).

THE PROBLEMS OF PREDICTION

The reliable identification, classification and assessment of violent offenders has long taxed researchers and practitioners alike (Monahan 1981, 1993). This has resulted in a growing preoccupation with the prediction of 'dangerous offenders', those capable of inflicting significant harms upon others. However, prediction is not without difficulty, particularly where it is associated with preventative sentencing or extended incarceration. The Floud Committee (1981) noted the high error rates involved in such prediction and the famous Baxstrom case illustrated the difficulty in the use of prolonged detention on the grounds of preventing future dangerous acts (Walker 1996). In essence, the precautionary principle can result in an unacceptable number of false positives, resulting in legal, moral and ethical objections. Conversely, the penalties for failing to predict violence in individual cases can be great for practitioners, agencies and victims alike.

Prediction studies have also had their difficulties, not least because the prevalence of such offences is low (Monahan 1981; Walker 1996). The statistically based methodology of actuarial prediction is undermined in the case of low-frequency offences and false positives increase. Whilst actuarial methods can produce percentages or probabilities, particularly through using past behaviour as an indicator of future behaviour, probability scores cannot be taken as a definite indicator that a particular individual will reoffend violently. Heyman (1997) has described such probability reasoning as a mechanism to attribute the '...aggregate properties of a category to individuals within that category...' (p.8), thus reducing the uncertainty of risk. This systematic flaw of probability reasoning is more commonly known as the 'statistical fallacy' (Dingwall 1989). In this methodology the reduction of false negatives is achieved at the cost of false positives and considerable net-widening. The choice between false negatives and false positives is essentially a political and moral one. In criminal justice this is most often expressed as a balance between the preservation of offender rights and the protection of the public. Recent legislation, such as the Crime Sentences Act (1997), which emphasises precautionary sentencing, and the pursuit of effective predictive tools for offence recidivism (for example, Home Office 1997b) illustrate the present state of this balance.

In effect, rights have been subsumed to protection.

Possibilities of prediction

Brooks (1984) noted that the term 'dangerousness' was open to ambiguity and misinterpretation. He usefully suggested that attention to the nature, extent and frequency of likely harms was more useful. However, this does not immediately resolve the issue of how harmful an act has to be to justify preventative sentencing, for example. As Walker (1996) expresses it: 'what sorts of violence are "very serious"?' (p.10). The Criminal Justice Act 1991, in section 2 (2) (b), enabled a court to pass a sentence longer than that commensurate with just deserts for violent and sexual offences. However, subsequent appeal court cases (for example, Drabble 1996 and Nicholls 1996 in *Justice of the Peace* 1996) and criticism of discretionary sentencing illustrated the difficulty in applying the harm principle to sentencing. The discretionary principle was severely undermined by the mandatory provisions of the Crime Sentences Act 1997, which placed sentencing obligations upon the judiciary in certain cases. This represents a significant shift from judicial power to judicial duty and reflects, in part, both political and societal concerns with the identification and control of violent offenders (Thomas 1998).

Other criminal justice personnel within the prison and probation services also have obligations to assess and manage violent offenders. Such offenders are defined by the Criminal Justice Act 1991 (Wasik and Taylor 1991) and practitioners have an obligation to assess such offenders at time of sentencing, during community supervision and for parole release. How to predict, and with what levels of accuracy, are key issues for criminal justice workers and managers.

Whilst violence assessments are notoriously difficult to accurately perform (Lidz, Mulvey and Gardner 1993; McNeil and Binder 1987; Monahan and Steadman 1994), Monahan and Steadman (p.2) have argued that separating such assessments into three distinct parts is helpful:

- the 'risk factors' used to predict violence
- the type of violence and likely harm anticipated
- the probability that the violent act will actually occur.

In addition, they argue that both harm and probability should be understood as points on a continuum, rather than as dichotomous variables, and that assessors have to assess the degree of harm and the extent of probability. Both these factors are subject to a number of 'it depends' and can fluctuate over time. This type of assessment requires extensive knowledge of both the actuarial factors and clinical cues associated with violent behaviour and a structure to assist with the analysis of these variables in order to facilitate reliable decision making. In addition, Towl and Crighton (1997) have noted that there is also a subtle distinction between the prediction of risk probabilities for groups within the population and the assessment of the predisposing hazards and situational triggers which result in individual acts of harm. It is the latter which crucially concern criminal justice personnel.

Limandri and Sheridan (1995) have argued for an interactive approach stating that: 'predictions can be made more accurately when evaluators take into account such interactive factors as gender, marital state, concomitant use of disinhibiting agents, and availability of victims and weapons' (p.10).

Whilst earlier research concentrated upon the identification of personality traits associated with violent behaviour (Blackburn 1971, 1975; McGurk 1978; Megargee 1966), other commentators have emphasised the interactional nature of violence assessments (Borum 1996; Howells and Hollin 1989; Litwack 1994; Megargee 1976; Menzies *et al.* 1994; Mulvey and Lidz 1995; Novaco 1976; Shaw 1996; Scott 1977) and the combination of demographic and contextual factors. In essence, this combines actuarial indicators with case-based clinical cues within an assessment framework which emphasises the assessment of:

- predisposing hazards
- offender motivation
- access and proximity to victims
- and the conditions and opportunities under which harmful behaviours take place.

The key issue for criminal justice personnel is how to combine these factors into a structured and reliable assessment which can have routine applicability in the field. An adaptation of Scott's (1977) interactive model provides a useful starting point. The key components of such assessments would be:

- the key demographic factors about the offender (for example, age, gender and the presence or absence of the main violence predictors)
- attention to antecedents and past behaviour (for example, past history of violence)
- conditions, circumstances and situational triggers under which harmful behaviour has occurred in the past
- past and present motivations to harmful behaviours
- presence or absence of internal inhibitors and of pro- or anti-social values
- present conditions, circumstances, triggers (for example, is the past repeating itself?)
- availability of and preparedness to use a weapon
- access and proximity to past or potential victims
- the type of social interaction likely between offender and potential victim (for example, is this a long-standing violent relationship? Is this offender in a position of trust which has been violated in the past?).

(Megargee 1976; Monahan 1981; Monahan and Steadman 1994; Mulvey and Lidz 1984; Novaco 1978, 1994; Scott 1977)

A number of these factors are present in the following case study:

Case study of 'E'

Age: 22.

Offence: Inflicting Grievous Bodily Harm (GBH), section 20 wounding.

Sentence: Two-year Probation Order plus condition of attendance at Violent Offender Group.

Previous offending and disposals: 1993, Affray, £300 fine.

An acquaintance made some derogatory remarks about his girlfriend whilst at the bar of a club. E. walked away at this time, but when the other man left E. followed him hoping for an apology. When this was not forthcoming, E. lost his temper. Two other men tried to restrain him but he broke free and attacked the victim. He accepted that he had drunk five pints of lager before the attack.

E. was in full-time employment; his employer wrote in his support that he displayed no aggressive tendencies at work. E's initial supervision plan proposed that he examine how he could moderate his behaviour when angry, and to examine why he gets so angry, supported by his attendance at the violent offender group.

In addition, a review of the relevant literature suggests that the following indicators have utility in predicting violence:

1. A history of violence as the best predictor of future violence (Convit *et al.* 1988; McNeil, Binder and Greenfield 1988; Monahan 1981, 1984; Walker 1996).

2. Substance misuse as an associated, although not as a definite causal factor (Dobash and Dobash 1979; Genders and Morrison 1996). Genders and Morrison, in their study of section 18 and section 20 woundings in the West Midlands area, found that offenders were predominantly young white men with a mean age of 25 and that 41 per cent of section 18 woundings and 29 per cent of section 20s were pub-related 'in that they occurred inside or within the vicinity of public houses, discos or night clubs...' (p.40), (as, for example, in the case of 'E').

   Whilst a causal relationship is difficult to prove, Walmsley (1986) suggested that fights are more likely to occur in locations where young men gather and that alcohol may be an associated factor in terms of life-style and disinhibition. Genders and Morrison also found that alcohol was significant in offences which did not occur in pub locations – for example, in 54 per cent of the section 18s and in 40 per cent of section 20s. This is especially so in incidents of domestic violence – for example, where men return from public houses and assault female partners.

3. Mental illness (Robins and Regier 1991). However, this association is noted to be highly complex. Mulvey (1994) has noted that the absolute risk of violence amongst the mentally ill, as a group, is very small and that only a small proportion of the violence in our society can be attributed to persons who are mentally ill. Drummond, Sparr and Gordon (1989) found that differing illnesses were

associated with differing types and levels of violence, and Mulvey (1994) found that a combination of mental illness and substance abuse was more likely to result in a violent act.

However, Mulvey concludes that '...the current state of the research provides very few leads about exactly what should be made of this association. We lack tested theoretical propositions about how mental illness and violence might be related, and we have little solid information about the actual magnitude of the association' (pp.667–668).

Ryan (1996) has also reminded us that of those few homicides committed by mentally ill persons: 'males tend to kill adults who are known to them and females are most likely to kill their children. It is rare for homicides to occur at the hands of mentally ill people who are unknown to the victim' (p.100).

INTERACTIVE VIOLENCE ASSESSMENT FRAMEWORK

An interactive assessment framework focusing upon the use of the most reliable indicators can do much to rebut Monahan's contention that '...it is empirically impossible to predict violent behaviour' (1981, p10) and that clinicians should avoid prediction at all costs.

Within probation, the interactive assessment framework could improve the quality of pre-sentence report risk of harm assessments by presenting sentencers with the most relevant risk indicators for that particular offender, how they interact and the circumstances in which they are likely to occur. In addition, such assessments could assist with the correct targeting of interventions. It is recognised that violent offender groups have less impact upon offenders whose violence is instrumental – that is, used in the commission of other offences, such as robbery.

With their emphasis upon anger management and self-risk management, violent offender groups are better suited to those offenders for whom violence is a learnt and habitual response to dispute resolution or to gaining control in social interactions (Holt 1997).

Best practice for violence assessment

Megargee (1976) has defined violence as '...acts characterised by the application of overt threat of force which is likely to result in injury to people' (p.12). Whilst Megargee's definition focuses upon physical injury, the Butler Committee (1975) noted the importance of significant psychological trauma. More recent legislation (the Criminal Justice Act 1991; Crime Sentences Act 1997) has recognised sexual offending as a form of violence, not least due to the severe psychological impact it can have. Workers are required, therefore, to assess the potential occurrence and likely impact of a range of harmful behaviours from a range of offenders in various contexts and settings.

Workers have to be concerned with:

- the nature and type of harm likely
- how probable such an occurrence actually is
- the impact likely, and upon whom
- the consequences of the behaviour should it take place.

Workers must also balance rights against protection and achieve high standards of reliability without net-widening but within a climate where one individual error can be severely censured. It is, therefore, essential that workers are aware of and systematically apply the most reliable indicators of future violent behaviour. This will need to be combined with investigative clinical interviewing in order to establish individual motivations, intentions and triggers. This approach has been promoted by Weist's (1981) technique of 'getting the offender to walk the therapist through the crime' and is common to much offence analysis work.

More recent research by Steadman *et al.* (1994) into the use of the MacArthur Risk Assessment Scale has suggested that consideration of risk factors across the four domains of dispositional, historical, contextual and clinical enhances the accuracy of practitioner predictions of violence risk. This approach represents an important attempt to integrate disparate risk factors into an empirically grounded framework for violence risk assessment (Borum 1996). Whilst based upon a longitudinal study of 1000 patients admitted to civil psychiatric hospitals, its applicability to a general offender population for use in criminal justice will require further evaluation. This illustrates a significant gap which has existed between predictive research on violence amongst an almost exclusively mental health population and the development of empirically proven violence assessment tools for use in the criminal justice field.

Reliable methods are crucial in an area in which practitioners and their agencies may be exposed to legal repercussions (Carson 1996), and in which obligations to protect third parties from potential violence may apply in *Tarasoff* situations (Monahan 1993; Tarasoff 1976). *Tarasoff* has placed upon American clinicians an obligation to take reasonable steps to protect the potential victim in those circumstances in which the clinician knows, or could reasonably know, that a person for whom they have responsibility could carry out a harmful act.

In England Carson (1996) has helpfully identified those circumstances in which a 'duty of care' applies and legal consequences for negligence in the face of risk may apply.

In these situations it is imperative that individual clinical decision making achieves high standards and produces decisions which are defensible in the light of subsequent public scrutiny and hindsight bias (Carson 1996; Kemshall 1996a). Borum (1996) has argued that this can be achieved by improving assessment tools, producing practice guidelines and developing relevant training programmes.

ASSESSMENT TOOLS

Violence prediction and individual clinical assessment have been plagued by unreliability (Monahan 1981). Current literature, particularly in the mental health field, suggests that 'using structured data-gathering methods can lead to a more comprehensive and a potentially less selective examination' (Borum 1996, p.948).

A number of assessment tools currently exist, covering prediction of dangerousness, violence, partner abuse, sexual abuse, in-patient violence and violence by mentally disordered offenders in the community (Borum 1996). The tools range from checklists for clinical interviewing to actuarial predictors of risk and multi-variate analysis based in statistical methods. Significant issues exist in the use of such instruments in the field. In some instances predictive ability remains weak and is not worth the effort of resource-intensive structured interviewing to apply it. Webster *et al.*'s (1994) Violence Prediction Scheme has a claimed classification accuracy of 75 per cent in follow-up studies. However, it is based upon a sample who had a significant history of violence and generalisation to others in the general population should be treated with caution (Borum 1996). In essence, the tool can predict well in those instances where patterns of behaviour are already established and predictable. However, as Borum (1996) states, the tool has conceptual clarity, is clearly rooted in empirical literature and is easily and reliably operationalised by staff in the field. The HCR-20 (Webster *et al.* 1995) is another development and forms a systematic model for assessing violence risk. The assessment combines historical factors that have a track record in predicting risk, with clinical variables such as 'insight, attitude, symptomatology, stability and treatability' (Borum 1996, p.949) supported by attention to case management plans, motivation to change and individual coping mechanisms.

In selecting from the range of instruments on offer, criminal justice personnel will have to consider the following:

- applicability to the client group under assessment
- resource implications of the instrument and its general efficiency
- how user friendly it is to staff and the likelihood that it will be used with integrity
- validity of the instrument and the amount of false negatives and false positives likely to occur through the use of the instrument.

Webster *et al.* (1995) have argued that to be useful, an assessment tool must meet at least the following requirements:

- accessibility to practitioners, particularly across multi-agency settings
- organised around a few well-researched and well-understood ideas
- rooted in empirical research
- proven validity through testability
- integrated within current agency policies and procedures rather than as an 'add on'
- resource efficient.

This provides a useful checklist for agency managers and policy makers in the selection of assessment tools.

PRACTICE GUIDELINES

Tarasoff liability, blame and censure have significantly focused the attention of assessors upon the defensibility of their decisions. As both Carson (1996) and Monahan (1993) have reminded us, assessors are not expected to achieve 100 per cent accuracy, rather they are subsequently judged on the reasonableness of the decision. In essence, judgments of reasonableness are based upon whether a body of peers would have made a similar decision and whether all reasonable steps were taken. In these circumstances standard protocols to guide practice judgment are essential to ensure consistency, reliability and validity. In addition, such protocols enable practitioners to demonstrate how decisions are made, and that they were made according to the best available methods and the best of current knowledge (Borum 1996; Carson 1996; Kemshall 1996b; Petrila 1995).

Such protocols or practice guidance should be understood as minimum standards for decision making.

Monahan (1993) has presented a number of pointers to assist practitioners in meeting the minimum requirements to avoid *Tarasoff* liability. His central point is the adequate collection of relevant information. He helpfully distinguishes between a never-ending investigative exercise and what would be seen to be 'practically reasonable' in the circumstances. Other research, for example Appelbaum (1985), Borum, Swartz and Swanson (1996); Monahan and Steadman (1994); Mulvey and Lidz (1984), has demonstrated that 'substantial consensus could be reached about the core data that clinicians should reasonably attempt to gather and consider to make a professionally adequate determination of risk' (Borum 1996, p.953).

Following Monahan (1993), minimum standards for violence risk assessment should comprise:

- appropriate collection and use of information, including questioning of significant others and detailed investigative interviewing of the offender
- estimation of likelihood and impact based upon an assessment grounded in the evidence
- communication with relevant others
- appropriate levels of knowledge and skill within the work-force, including actuarial, clinical and legal knowledge

- case management plans well matched to the violence risks identified, appropriately resourced and delivered with integrity
- a recognition that risk indicators can be dynamic, as well as static, and are liable to change over time (Limandri and Sheridan 1995). This requires frequent assessments and interventions well matched to the risk indicators identified in order to maximise effectiveness. This is particularly important in targeting suitable offenders and selecting between those who might benefit from alternative interventions.

However, it is important to recognise the limits upon the achievement of these minimum standards which will necessarily impinge upon practitioners. There will be differing constraints in differing settings in which practitioners are required to address a range of violence risks. In preparing pre-sentence reports, for example, probation officers must address the risk of serious harm to the public, often in circumstances of partial information, time constraint and within the rules of evidence. In residential settings the immediacy of harm to potential victims and concerns about *Tarasoff* liability may naturally result in higher levels of practitioner caution and less attention to the possibility of false positives.

STAFF TRAINING REQUIREMENTS

In order to meet the minimum requirements for defensibility, staff involved in assessments of violence risk will need training in the following:

- theories of violent behaviour – for example, Gunn (1973), Megargee (1976) and Novoco and Welsh (1989)
- empirical research into both the clinical and actuarial factors for the reliable assessment of violent behaviour
- the personality and situational factors most often associated with violent behaviour and, most importantly, how they interact
- effective responses for the management of violent behaviour, particularly the potential contribution of clinical psychology and cognitively based interventions' (Kemshall 1996b, p.29).

Such training will need to focus upon both the development of knowledge and appropriate skills. As assessment and management is increasingly a multi-agency responsibility, training across disciplines is also recommended. Such training will need regular up-dating to keep abreast of the growing research in this area and should be evaluated in order to establish its subsequent impact upon the practice of practitioners in the field.

THE MANAGEMENT OF VIOLENT CASES

The range of potential violence facing practitioners in their case management is extensive. In these circumstances Brooks' (1984) advice to concentrate upon the assessment and reduction of likely harms is helpful. The key principle in the management of violence cases should be harm reduction and victim protection.

Evaluative studies of intervention strategies have mostly occurred within psychiatric residential hospitals (Hare 1991; Rice 1997; Rice, Harris and Cormier 1992; Webster *et al.* 1994) or the case management of mentally ill persons in community (Dvoskin and Steadman 1994; Estroff *et al.* 1994). Bush's (1995) work on teaching self-risk management to violent offenders represents an example of a cognitive-behavioural approach to work with violent offenders. Mental health residential studies have indicated that some interventions can have unintended consequences – for example, the exacerbation of violence risk in some individuals (Rice 1997) and particularly, therapeutic programmes targeted at psychopaths.

Rice has argued that the poor outcomes for treated psychopaths was due to their raised self-esteem fuelling their aggression. In addition, psychopaths tended to be 'false compliers', learning to fake empathy and to deceive others (Harris, Rice and Quinsey 1994). This suggests that interventions must be well targeted at specific groups and well matched to violent risks and behaviours identified.

In terms of psychopaths, Rice (1997) suggests that they are considered as a distinct group and goes on to hypothesise that it '...may not be a mental disorder at all, but instead an evolved "cheater" life strategy that contributed to fitness in ancestral environments' (p.419).

Such cheating behaviour may be better controlled by reducing the pay-off for cheating or limiting opportunities to successfully cheat. Whilst such a hypothesis may be contentious, it does illustrate that, in terms of effective treatment, it literally is 'horses for courses'.

Bush (1995) has proposed some cognitively based intervention principles for work with violent offenders:

- violence is learnt behaviour, and can be unlearnt
- patterns of violence and criminal behaviour are embedded in habits of thinking (Andrews 1990; Bush 1995)
- such thinking patterns can place offenders 'at risk' of reoffending
- offenders can be facilitated to uncover and understand their own thinking patterns
- thinking patterns can be changed through cognitive-behavioural programmes
- control of thinking patterns can be taught
- alternative pro-social thinking can be taught and rehearsed
- relapse prevention can be taught and reinforced.

These principles must also be supported by a genuine desire to change. Dobash *et al.* (1996), in their evaluation of group work programmes, noted that this client group were more likely to benefit from interventions if they recognised the need to change. Holt (1997), in an evaluation of a violent offender group programme, found that around 50 per cent of referrals were refused due to lack of motivation.

Such principles are illustrative of the 'What Works' school and have gained much currency with policy makers and managers keen for criminal justice results (HMIP 1998). Whilst 'What Works' has much to commend it, there is a danger that the 'quick fix' of easily replicated techniques is being overstated. The efficacy of such techniques owes much to the highly controlled residential settings within which it has been predominantly used and transferability to community use is not without difficulty, not least the levels of resource and agency and management support required to make such interventions work (HMIP 1998). In addition, the 'What Works' school has been greatly influenced by the results of meta-analysis, a technique of 'aggregation and side-by-side analysis of large numbers of experimental studies' (McGuire 1995, pp.7–8). This technique has been subject to recent critical scrutiny by Losel (1995), amongst others. There is a growing recognition that the criteria at the heart of such quantitative analyses are open to subjective bias and that the original studies contain differing methodologies, outcome criteria and goals which are largely overlooked by the process of meta-analysis (Copas 1995). Pawson and Tilley (1994) have taken particular issue with meta-analysis of group work programmes, stating that the dynamic and interactive process of group work is reduced to the evaluation of objectives, content, level of contact and frequency of groups programmes. They criticise the selection of static input factors and state that '...social programmes are the product of skilled action and negotiation by human agents and are not reducible to the facticity of a given event' (p.297).

However, the work of Bush (1995), amongst others, suggests that those involved in the case management of violent offenders need to adapt practice to these principles and techniques in order to increase the effectiveness of case interventions. A number of specific techniques have now become well established. For example:

- developing victim empathy in offenders
- re-running the events and circumstances of the offence, for example through psychodrama, and offence analysis based upon Weist's original technique (Weist 1981; Priestley *et al.* 1984)
- the exploration and deconstruction of the rationalisations and self-justifications used to continue violent behaviour
- explorations of masculinity, male socialisation, power and assertiveness
- rehearsing of alternative behaviours and responses.

This is illustrated by the case of 'A':

Case study 'A'

Age: 50.

Offence: Assault Occasioning Bodily Harm (section 47 Offences Against the Person Act 1861).

Sentence: Two-Year Probation Order plus attendance at the Violent Offenders Group.

Previous Offences: None.

A's offence involved an assault on his wife, who is partially sighted. The Pre-Sentence Report stated that the attack was a 'particularly vicious and frightening experience' for her and for their three children who were in the house at the time. Mrs A. confirmed that this was not an isolated incident and that violence had been part of their marriage for some time, not often as serious as this assault but, nevertheless, ongoing. She subsequently refused to live with him and he went to live initially in hostel accommodation.

The assessment drew attention to the following risk indicators:

- A's stress, which he believed caused some kind of blackout with consequent loss of control
- the circumstances of the offence and, in particular, the impact upon the children
- an acceptance by A that he needed to change
- masculinity – A talked about his desire for power and control. His anger fed his violence
- lack of awareness of own feelings and lack of empathy with others.

The group worker summary of the intervention noted:

> A was the oldest in the group and highly motivated to change, although he began full of justifications. His sculpts were frightening and powerful, in the course of which he achieved emotional engagement with the brutalisation he'd experienced as a child and, later, disclosing further violence against his partner. He was able to confront his image, never having seen himself as the projector until his VOG experience. All his justifications were repeatedly questioned until he felt unable to be angry enough to hit her. He then became more keen to see how difficulties could be resolved without violence. Despite feeling very alone and isolated from his family, he could acknowledge how they felt about his return. Even when six months had passed, he still kept in touch.

In addition to their responsibilities as report writers, supervisors and, in some instances, group workers, probation officers are increasingly becoming case managers. Dvoskin and Steadman (1994) argue that case managers are, in effect, risk managers, required to manage 'the risks faced by the client and the risk the client could possibly pose to the community' (p.680). Case managers are required to manage a wide range of risks and, in this context, the risk posed by potential violence. Whilst Dvoskin and Steadman review intensive case management for the reduction of violence by mentally ill persons in the community, their general points do have wider applicability. They argue that intensive case management should comprise:

- regular monitoring, particularly to note changes in and to take action on the individual and situational factors which result in violence
- assist clients to gain insight into high-risk situations and how to cope with them
- clear case responsibility vested in one person
- continuity of case management
- speedy access to relevant support services
- limited case loads to enable intensive work
- appropriate authority and power to limit risky behaviours (for example, recall to prison) and to enforce requirements which diminish risk.

Dvorskin and Steadman provide empirical results to illustrate the effectiveness of intensive case management in reducing violent behaviour amongst high-risk mentally ill persons in the community. Presumably, their case principles could be applied in other settings, such as probation, and with other violent persons. However, they note that intensive case management is not a panacea: 'It will fail if appropriate treatment and human services are not available in the community...The brokering and linkage of roles of case management mean little if services are not available in the community to be brokered or linked' (p.684).

More recently, the effective management of violence risk in the community has been pursued through inter-agency approaches (Home Office 1997). However, this is not without difficulties, as a recent Home Office Special Conference explored (Home Office 1997). Most pressing of these are constraints upon the disclosure of information across agency boundaries; differing responsibilities and legal powers across agencies; lack of partnership and commitment in community management resulting in 'pass the parcel' situations; difficulties in agreeing common language, desirable principles, assessment methods and resources for risk management. Indeed, Prins (1995) has argued that inter-agency work is rarely multi-disciplinary – that is, rarely does it attain the status of genuine collaboration across disciplines to provide a sum greater than its parts. The Sex Offenders Act, which came into force on 1 September 1997, requires sex offenders to register their details and whereabouts with the local police, and recent cases of public reaction to sex offenders (*The Guardian*, 24 April) have required greater inter-agency co-operation to manage community risks. The ability of the agencies involved to develop effective protocols and to maintain public confidence in harm management strategies has been severely tested.

CONCLUDING COMMENTS

Gunn (1996) has suggested that it is time to get serious about dangerousness. This is especially timely as courts in the United States and, more recently, in England are prepared to sentence on the basis of prevention (Litwack 1994). Crucial to such preventive decisions are assessments of potential harm or dangerousness. However, most commentators agree that the validity of assessment methodologies is not yet at a sufficient level to support the political agenda of prevention (Grisso and Appelbaum 1992; Litwack 1994). This raises numerous ethical and moral issues which are, in large part, side-stepped by policy makers and politicians in the implementation of precautionary based risk management systems. The language and methodologies of violence risk prediction do not always sit comfortably with legal requirements or clamours for public safety.

Whilst the MacArthur Risk Assessment Scale offers some important new insights into the assessment of dangerousness, Litwack (1994) notes that its utility is more likely to be in assisting release decisions rather than in increasing the reliability of preventive sentencing or in increasing the effectiveness of community supervision. How individual assessors form their clinical judgments in predicting violence risk is still largely under-researched (Litwack 1994; Mulvey and Lidz 1995) and the gap between research-based instruments and practically useful tools remains. This suggests that it is time to pull back from preventative legislation, precautionary risk management systems and uncritical promises of public safety in favour of a more considered investigation into the possibilities and limits of violence assessment and its attendant management issues. The price of ill-considered action and developments may well be an increased potential for an inexorable net-widening as those held accountable for assessment and prediction resort to ever more precautionary techniques and invasive systems of information collection to deliver safety. This will be both resource intensive and potentially challenging to traditional notions of justice. The real task for criminal justice personnel may not be the development of ever more violence predictor models but the initiation of an informed debate about the levels of safety and protection which can and should be offered.

ACKNOWLEDGEMENT

My thanks are extended to Paul Holt for comment on this chapter and for the provision of the case study material. However, the views expressed are entirely my responsibility.

REFERENCES

Tarasoff v. Regents of the University of California. (1976) 131 Cal. Rptr. 14, 551, p.2d 334.

Andrews, D. (1990) *The Role of Antisocial Attitudes in the Psychology of Crime.* Paper presented to the Canadian Psychological Association, Ottawa.

Appelbaum, P. S. (1985) 'Tarasoff and the clinician: problems in fulfilling the duty to protect.' *American Journal of Psychiatry*, 142, (3), 425–429.

Blackburn, R. (1971) 'Personality types among abnormal homicides.' *British Journal of Criminology*, 11, (1), 14–31.

Blackburn, R. (1975) 'An empirical classification of psychopathic personality.' *British Journal of Psychiatry*, 127, 456–460.

Borum, R. (1996) 'Improving the clinical practice of violence assessment.' *American Psychologist*, 51, 9, 945–956.

Borum, R., Swartz, M. and Swanson, J. (1996) 'Assessing and managing violence risk in clinical practice.' *Journal of Practical Psychiatry and Behavioural Health*, 4, 205–215.

Brooks, A.D. (1984) 'Defining the dangerousness of the mentally ill: involuntary commitment.' In M. Craft and A. Crafy (eds) *Mentally Abnormal Offenders.* London: Balliere Tindall.

Bush, J. (1995) 'Teaching self-risk management to violent offender.' In J. McGuire (ed) *What Works: Reducing Reoffending: Guidelines from Research and Practice.* Chichester: John Wiley.

Butler Committee, Home Office and Department of Health and Social Security (1975) *Committee on Mentally Abnormal Offenders. Cmnd. 6244.* London: HMSO.

Carson. D. (1996) 'Risking legal repercussions.' In H. Kemshall and J. Pritchard (eds) *Good Practice in Risk Assessment and Risk Management, Volume 1.* London: Jessica Kingsley Publishers.

Convit, A., Jaeger, J., Lin, S. P., Meisner, M. and Volavka, J. (1988) 'Predicting assaultiveness in psychiatric in-patients: a pilot study.' *Hospital and Community Psychiatry*, 39, 4, 429–434.

Copas, J. (1995) *Some Comments on Meta-Analysis.* University of Warwick.

Dingwall, R. (1989) 'Some problems about predicting child abuse and neglect.' In O. Stevenson (ed) *Child Abuse: Professional Practice and Public Policy.* Hemel Hempstead: Harvester Wheatsheaf.

Dobash, R., Dobash, R., Cavanagh, K. and Lewis, R. (1996) *Research Evaluation of Programmes for Violent Men.* The Scottish Office Central Research Unit.

Dobash, R.E. and Dobash, R. (1979) *Violence against Wives.* New York: Free Press.

Drummond, D.J., Sparr, L.F. and Gordon, G.H. (1989) 'Hospital violence reduction among high-risk patients.' *Journal of the American Medical Association*, 261, 17, 2531–2534.

Dvoskin, J.A. and Steadman, H.J. (1994) 'Using intensive case management to reduce violence by mentally ill persons in the community.' *Hospital and Community Psychiatry*, 45, 7, 679–684.

Estroff, S.E., Zimmer, C., Lachicotte, W. and Benoit, J. (1994) 'The influence of social networks and social support on violence by persons with serious mental illness.' *Hospital and Community Psychiatry*, 45, 7, 669–679.

Floud, J. and Young, W. (1981) *Dangerousness and Criminal Justice.* Howard League for Penal Reform. London: Heinemann.

Genders, E. and Morrison, S. (1996) 'When violence is the norm.' In N. Walker (ed) *Dangerous People.* London: Blackstone Press.

Grisso, T. and Appelbaum, P.S. (1992) 'Is it unethical to offer predictions of future violence?' *Law and Human Behaviour*, 16, 621–633.

Guardian (1998a) 'Warning despite record fall in crime.' 8 April, p.8.

Gunn, J. (1973) *Violence in Human Society.* Newton Abbot: David and Charles (Holdings) Limited.

Gunn, J. (1996) 'Let's get serious about dangerousness.' *Criminal Behaviour and Mental Health*, 51–64.

Hare, R.D. (1991) *The Hare Psychopathy Checklist-Revised.* Toronto, Ontario, Canada: Multi-Health Systems.

Harris, G.T., Rice, M.E. and Quinsey, V.L. (1994) 'Psychopathy as a taxon: evidence that psychopaths are a discrete class.' *Journal of Consulting and Clinical Psychology*, 62, 387–397.

Her Majesty's Inspectorate of Probation (1998) *Strategies for Effective Offender Supervision.* London: Home Office.

Heyman, B. (ed) (1997) *Risk, Health and Health Care: A Qualitative Approach.* London: Edward Arnold.

Holt, P. (1997) *Managing Risk and Evaluating Effectiveness: The Experience of One Violent Offenders' Group in the West Midlands.* Unpublished dissertation submitted for M. Soc. Sc. Department of Social Policy and Social Work, Birmingham University.

Home Office (1997a) *Criminal Statistics England and Wales: Supplementary Tables 1996 Volume 2: Proceedings in the Crown Court.* London: Home Office.

Home Office (1997b) 'Information on the tools available and under development to assist chief Probation Officers to decide their strategies.' Part One of Management and Assessment of Risk in the Probation Service. London: Home Office/Association of Chief Offers of Probation.

Howells, K. and Hollin, C. (eds) (1989) *Clinical Approaches to Violence.* Chichester: John Wiley and Sons.

Kasperson, R.E. (1992) 'The social amplification of risk: progress in developing an integrative framework.' In S. Krimsky and D. Golding (eds) *Social Theories of Risk.* Westport, USA: Praeger Publishers.

Kemshall, H. (1996a) *Risk Assessment and Risk Management Senior Manager Workshops*. Home Office Probation Training Section/Association of Chief Officers of Probation.

Kemshall, H. (1996b) *Reviewing Risk: A Review of Research on the Assessment and Management of Risk and Dangerousness: Implications for the Policy and Practice in the Probation Service*. London: Home Office.

Kemshall, H. (1997) 'Sleep safely: crime risks may be smaller than you think.' *Social Policy and Administration*, 31, 3, 247–259.

Lawson-Cruttenden, T. (1997) 'Harassment and domestic violence.' *Journal of Family Law*, 429–431.

Lidz, C.W., Mulvey, E.P. and Gardner, W. (1993) 'The accuracy of predictions of violence to others.' *Journal of the American Medical Association*, 269, 8, 1007–1011.

Limandri, B.J. and Sheridan, D.J. (1995) 'The prediction of intentional interpersonal violence: an introduction.' In J. Campbell (ed) *Assessing Dangerousness: Violence by Sexual Offenders, Batterers, and Child Abusers*. Interpersonal Violence: The Practice Series. London: Sage.

Litwack, T.R. (1994) 'Assessments of dangerousness: legal, research and clinical developments.' *Administration and Policy in Mental Health*, 21, 5, 361–377.

Losel, F. (1995) 'The efficacy of correctional treatment: a review and synthesis of meta-evaluations.' In J. McGuire (ed) *What Works: Reducing Reoffending: Guidelines from Practice and Research*. Chichester: John Wiley.

McGuire, J. (ed) (1995) *What Works: Reducing Reoffending: Guidelines from Research and Practice*. Chichester: John Wiley.

McGurk, B.J. (1978) 'Personality types among normal homicides.' *British Journal of Criminology 18*, (1), 146–161.

McNeil, D.M. and Binder, R. (1987) 'Predictive validity of judgments of dangerousness in emergency civil commitment.' *American Journal of Psychiatry*, 144, (2), 197–200.

McNeil, D.M., Binder, R. and Greenfield, T.K. (1988) 'Predictors of violence in civilly committed acute psychiatric inpatients.' *American Journal of Psychiatry*, 61, 1, 38–45.

Megargee, E.I. (1966) 'Undercontrolled and overcontrolled personality types in extreme antisocial aggression.' *Psychological Monographs*, 80, (3), 1–21.

Megargee, E.I. (1976) 'The prediction of dangerous behaviour.' *Criminal Justice and Behaviour*, 3, 3–22.

Menzies, R.J., Webster, C.D., McMain, S., Staley, S. and Scaglions, R. (1994) 'The dimensions of dangerousness revisited.' *Law and Human Behaviour*, 18, 1, 1–28.

Monahan, J. (1981) *The Clinical Prediction of Violence*. Beverley Hills, CA: Sage.

Monahan, J. (1984) 'The prediction of violent behaviour: towards a second generation of theory and policy.' *American Journal of Psychiatry*, 141, (1), 10–15.

Monahan, J. (1993) 'Limiting therapist exposure to Tarasoff liability: guidelines for risk containment.' *American Psychologist*, 48, 242–250.

Monahan, J. and Steadman, H. (1994) *Violence and Mental Disorder: Developments in Risk Assessment*. Chicago: University of Chicago Press.

Mulvey, E.P. (1994) 'Assessing the evidence of a link between mental illness and violence.' *Hospital and Community Psychiatry*, 45, 7, 663–668.

Mulvey, E.P. and Lidz, C.W. (1984) 'Clinical considerations in the prediction of dangerousness in mental patients.' *Clinical Psychology Review*, 4, 379–401.

Mulvey, E.P. and Lidz, C.W. (1995) 'Conditional prediction: a model for research on dangerousness to others in a new era.' *International Journal of Law and Psychiatry*, 18, 2, 129–143.

Novaco, R.W. (1976) 'The function and regulation of arousal anger.' *American Journal of Psychiatry*, 133, (10), 1124–28.

Novaco, R.W. (1978) 'Anger and coping with stress.' In J.P. Foreyt and D.P. and Rathjen (eds) *Cognitive Behaviour Therapy*. New York: Plenum Press.

Novaco, R.W. (1994) 'Anger as a risk factor for violence among the mentally disordered.' In J. Monahan and H.J. Steadman (eds) *Violence and Mental Disorder: Developments in Risk Assessment*. Chicago and London: University of Chicago Press.

Novaco, R.W. and Welsh, W.N. (1989) 'Anger disturbances: cognitive mediation and clinical prescriptions.' In K. Howells and C. Hollin (eds) *Clinical Approaches to Violence*. Chichester: John Wiley.

Pawson, R. and Tilley, N. (1994) 'What works in evaluation research?' *British Journal of Criminology*, 34, 3, 291–306.

Petrila, J. (1995) 'Who will pay for involuntary civil commitment under capitated management care? An emerging dilemma.' *Psychiatric Services 46,* 1045–1048.

Povey, D., Prime, J. and Taylor, P. (1998) *Notifiable Offences England and Wales, 1997*. Home Office Statistical Bulletin. London: Home Office.

Priestley, P., McGuire, J., Flegg, D., Hemsley, V., Welham, D. and Barnitt, R. (1984) *Social Skills in Prison and the Community: Problem-Solving for Offenders*. London: Routledge and Kegan Paul.

Prins, H. (1995) 'Risk assessment: seven sins of omission.' *Probation Journal*, 42, 4, 199–201.

Rice, M.E. (1997) 'Violent offender research and implications for the criminal justice system.' *American Psychologist*, 52, 4, 414–423.

Rice, M.E., Harris, G.T. and Cormier, C.A. (1992) 'An evaluation of a maximum security therapeutic community for psychopaths and other mentally disordered offenders.' *Law and Human Behaviour*, 16, 399–412.

Robins, L. and Regier, D. (eds) (1991) *Psychiatric Disorders in America: The Epidemiological Catchment Area Study*. New York: Free Press.

Ryan, T. (1996) 'Risk management and people with mental health problems.' In H. Kemshall and J. Pritchard (eds) *Good Practice in Risk Assessment and Risk Management*. London: Jessica Kingsley Publishers.

Scott, P. (1977) 'Assessing dangerous in criminals.' *British Journal of Psychiatry*, 131, 127–142.

Shaw, R. (1996) 'Supervising the dangerous in the community.' In N. Walker (ed) *Dangerous People*. London: Blackstone Press.

Soothill, K. (1993) 'The serial killer industry.' *Journal of Forensic Psychiatry*, 4, 2, 341–354.

Sparks, R. (1992) *Television and the Drama of Crime*. Buckingham: Open University Press.

Steadman, H.J., Monahan, J., Appelbaum, P.S., Grisso, T., Mulvey, E.P., Roth, L.H., Robbins, P.C. and Klassen, D. (1994) 'Designing a new generation of risk assessment research.' In J. Monahan and H.J. Steadman (eds) *Violence and Mental Disorder: Developments in Risk Assessment*. Chicago: University of Chicago Press.

Sun (1998) 'Cooke riot: Police station petrol bombed as mob try to lynch child killer.' 24 April, p.1, p.9.

Thomas, D.A. (1998) 'The Crime (Sentences) Act.' *Criminal Law Review*, 83–92.

The Times (1997) 'Rising violence defies general fall in crime.' 15 October, p.3.Towl, G.J. and Crighton, D.A. (1997) 'Risk assessment with offenders.' *International Review of Psychiatry*, 9, 187–193.

Walker, N. (ed) (1996) *Dangerous People*. London: Blackstone Press.

Wasik, M. and Taylor, R.D. (1991) *Blackstone's Guide to the Criminal Justice Act*. London: Blackstone Press.

Webster, C.D., Eaves, D., Douglas, K. and Wintrup, A. (1995) *The HCR-20 Scheme: The Assessment of Dangerousness and Risk*. Burnaby, British Columbia, Canada: Simon Fraser University and Forensic Psychiatric Services Commission of British Columbia.

Webster, C.D., Harris, G.T., Rice, M.E., Cormier, C. and Quinsey, V.L. (1994) *The Violence Prediction Scheme: Assessing Dangerousness in High Risk Men*. Toronto, Ontario, Canada: Centre of Criminology, University of Toronto.

Weist, J. (1981) 'Treatment for violent offenders.' *Clinical Social Work Journal*, 9, 4, 271–281.

FURTHER READING

Guardian (1998b) 'These women have found their cause, but they're not sure what it is.' Decca Aitkinhead, 24 April, p.20.

Home Office (1997c) *Inter-Agency Work with Dangerous Offenders: Sharing Information to Manage Risk*. Conference report. London: Home Office Special Conference Unit.

Justice of the Peace (1996) 'Sentencing news.' Issue 3, July, 9–10.

McNeil, D.M. and Binder, R. (1994) 'Clinical assessments of the risk of violence among psychiatric inpatients.' *American Journal of Psychiatry 148*, 1317–1321.

CHAPTER 4

Working with Men who are Violent to Partners – Striving for Good Practice

David Morran and Monica Wilson

THEORY AND PRACTICE

The problem of men's abuse of women has periodically been the subject of reform movements over the last two centuries in both the US and the UK. Over 30 years ago it once again became the focus of activists who, in seeking to eliminate this horrific problem for women and children, have since striven to provide refuge and services for abused women while simultaneously campaigning for social, legal and institutional reforms that empower women (Dobash and Dobash 1979, 1992; Schechter 1982). Much has been achieved over the last three decades, despite the enormous obstacles of denial and inertia that activists and their allies faced in achieving a recognition of the scale and importance of the issue, and the need for real social change to eliminate the problem. Much still remains to be done.

In more recent times a new element has arisen in this area of work – namely the challenging of abusive men, including the development of programmes for violent men. Beginning in the US and Canada, they have now taken root in the UK and are the object both of high hopes and great suspicion (Dobash and Dobash 1992; Hague and Malos 1993). For practitioners in social work and probation, they appear to offer something potent in the stead of previously powerless methods of practice. For some activists working with the survivors of men's violence, they are potentially dangerous, competing for scarce resources with women's services, offering false hope to women and new excuses to men (Hart 1988; Wilson 1996). In developing work with men, therefore, serious account must be taken of the potential dangers to women and children and the pitfalls for those doing the work. This chapter is intended to offer some guidance for good practice and for minimising those dangers and pitfalls based on our experience in developing and running the CHANGE men's programme in Central Scotland,[1] and on the findings of a research study into its effectiveness (Dobash *et al.* 1996).

Our understanding of men's violence to women has been informed by three decades of activists' campaigning, extensive academic research and listening to women's (and, in some cases, men's) own accounts. However, there is as yet, no universally accepted agreement about why men are violent to women partners. Different theories have been in vogue at different times. This is a crucial element in terms of informing practice since differing causal assumptions about men's violence give rise to different strategies to combat it (Adams 1988, Dobash and Dobash 1992: Fawcett *et al.* 1996). Pahl pointed out as long ago as 1985 that the emphasis on the nature of the problem being that of 'battered wives' rather than 'violent husbands' shifted attention away from perpetrators and that long-term solutions would need to address the problem more accurately as that of 'violent husbands' (p.5).

Causal theories concerning men's violence to women have developed differently in the US and the UK. In the former more micro-analytic theories which see both the cause and solution as rooted in individuals and individual change have predominated in informing practice. In the UK more macro-level theories have prevailed. Dobash and Dobash (1992) explain this difference in the historically much greater emphasis on the politics of the mind and emotions in the US, as opposed to the UK historical legacy of an emphasis on social and material conditions in politics.

Theories which explained men's violence in terms of the pathologies of either the men or women concerned were briefly in vogue in the UK in the 1970s and early 1980s (Smith 1989). Men who used violence were described as neurotic, mentally ill or

1 CHANGE was funded from 1989–1996 by the Urban Programme and sponsored by Central Regional Council Social Work Department.

disturbed; female victims were similarly labelled, implying that they invited the violence upon themselves. Implicit in these pathological explanations is the notion that solutions lie in treating 'sick' individuals rather than addressing the need for wider social or institutional changes. Their brief flowering gave rise to some strange and novel suggestions about how abused women should be treated (Dobash and Dobash 1992). However, basing a general theory of men's violence on the pathology of either victim or perpetrator fails to stand up in the face of the evidence. The logical extension of this theory, given our current knowledge of the prevalence of the problem, is that there is a massive epidemic of mental illness (Fields 1994). Nonetheless, individualistic explanations remain seductive to practitioners as they seem to offer scope for action. All we need do is identify the 'sick' individuals and treat them to solve the problem. When working with individual, or groups of, violent men it can become very easy to lose sight of the larger understanding of the problem and concentrate on the individual's traits. As detailed below, many of men's own accounts of their violence (when they are not blaming their partner) conform to ideas of irrational, out-of-character actions that they cannot understand and from which they may seek to be 'cured'.

Other theories which have been propounded for explaining men's violence to women have taken a family-based view. Family systems theory, which views violence as a dysfunctional element in the family system, implies the need for intervention on a family level rather than focusing on the man. A wider societal view has been adopted by those who view the problem in terms of social structural features, which indicts society for its unequal distribution of life's 'good things' leading to men 'taking out' their frustration on women partners. Social learning theory, which views violence as learned and reinforced behaviour requiring cognitive and behavioural intervention to end it, has informed many intervention programmes, particularly in the US (Adams 1988; Bograd 1988; Smith 1989; Stordeur and Stille 1989).

A broader approach still is that taken by what has been termed the 'pro-feminist' perspective (Dobash and Dobash 1979, 1992; Hague and Malos 1993; Schechter 1982). This views violence to women as occurring in historical and cultural as well as personal contexts. As the United Nations Beijing Declaration of 1995 states:

> Violence against women is a manifestation of historical unequal power relations between men and women and one of the crucial social mechanisms by which women are forced into a subordinate position to men. (United Nations 1996, p.75)

When implementing interventions with men, this model of work recognises the need to provide basic cognitive and behavioural skills for abusers about caretaking and communication skills but, in addition, 'sees it as just as essential to challenge the sexist expectations and controlling behaviours that often inhibit men's motivation to learn and to apply such skills consistently in a non-controlling manner' (Adams 1988, p.192).

The problem of women abuse 'cannot be eradicated as long as men have the power in the family and in society' (Russell 1988, p.8). Solutions to the problem of violent men, therefore, must incorporate challenging the social context in which their violence occurs (Dobash and Dobash 1992; Morran and Wilson 1994, 1997).

The pro-feminist perspective sees men's abuse of, and violence towards, women as intentional behaviour (Dobash and Dobash 1992; Yllö and Bograd 1988). By placing domestic violence in its historical and cultural context, a pro-feminist perspective offers a broad theory of the problem which can account for the question 'Why do men beat their wives/partners?' (Bograd 1988, p.13). The seeds of wife beating lie in the historical subordination of women to male authority and control. This subordination was institutionalised in the structure of the patriarchal family and supported by economic and political institutions, and by a belief system which made women's subordination seem natural, morally just and sacred (Buzawa and Buzawa 1990; Dobash and Dobash 1979).

Adopting a pro-feminist perspective requires that intervention strategies for solving the problem of domestic violence should involve all those organisations and individuals concerned (Edelson and Tolman 1992). Effective intervention needs to put the safety of women and children at the forefront of its agenda. It must incorporate ways of challenging community tolerance for domestic violence by questioning social attitudes to the problem. It requires challenging both individual offenders and the way domestic violence is treated by the various social institutions involved. Principally, these will be institutions of the criminal justice system: the police, courts and probation/social work. In order to highlight the criminal and unacceptable nature of men's violence to women, a pro-feminist perspective would suggest that any work aimed at changing men's violence would best operate as a sanction of the justice system. At the same time, it is crucial that refuge and support services for women are maintained and that women are consulted by those undertaking intervention work with men (Morran and Wilson 1997; Pence and Paymar 1990).

ACCOUNTABILITY TO WOMEN

Any work with abusing men should be informed by the experiences of women survivors, both in terms of content and approach and in terms of the safety of individual women. The first objective – informing content and approach – involves keeping a clear and stated perspective. As previously noted, when working with individual violent men, it can be difficult to maintain clarity of perspective and workers can be drawn into individualistic explanations. Opening practice to the scrutiny of peers, while sometimes difficult and risky, is important; as is good and informed supervision. Working closely with organisations for survivors, such as Women's Aid, can also provide a useful check that the approach is consistent and content is not collusive. This will not always be easy as there will often be tensions between the agenda of survivors and their advocates and the perceptions they may hold about the appropriateness of working with men (Wilson 1996).

If women's safety is the primary object of any intervention, as it should be, strategies for achieving it require to be developed prior to any intervention with men taking place. This involves giving clear messages to women partners that there can be no promises that men *will* change, ensuring that she has information about, and access to, services which meet her needs and keeping her informed both about the nature of the intervention work and the man's participation in it. Clear guidelines about confidentiality are very important: women must feel able to give honest accounts of past and current abuse in the knowledge that this will not be shared with men unless they specifically ask for this, and even then workers must make judgements about how safe it is to do so. In our experience this is a very difficult area of practice as workers may be privy to accounts of continuing abuse which men are not disclosing. The following case study, based on one of the most difficult situations we faced, illustrates this point.

Case study

John was a young man of 23 who was referred to the men's programme following violence in his current relationship with a woman. He had been referred two years previously when he was in a previous relationship. He was then assessed as unsuitable on the basis of denial, refusal to accept responsibility and unwillingness to change. It was with some hesitation that staff agreed to accepting him but at his assessment interviews he stated that he now realised he must do something to change his violent behaviour. Our information was that this was the fourth woman to whom he had been violent.

John's partner, Lily, had been contacted and visited at the assessment stage when she had given a detailed account of his violence, which was much more extensive that he was admitting to. Lily was clearly terrified of John but wanted him to participate in the programme. She was told in clear terms that staff had grave doubts about the likelihood of his benefiting from the programme. She was put in touch with a worker from the local Women's Aid group, who visited her and also liaised with the programme staff. Lily made regular phone contact with programme staff herself, who visited her at home, often hearing details of continuing verbal abuse and threatening behaviour and, eventually of physical violence, which she asked to be kept in confidence. Lily's greatest wish was that he would leave her. She was scared to leave him as he had threatened to kill her whole family if she ever did.

From the outset, John's demeanour on the programme was that of a remorseful man who was taking the work seriously. He disclosed enough about his behaviour to appear as if he was doing the work but the extent of his disclosure did not match up with what programme staff knew and were hearing from his partner. This made working with him in that group extremely difficult as staff were unable to challenge his assertions that he was no longer violent and that he was changing. As the work progressed, the reports received from Lily became more troubling and arrangements were made for her to go into the local refuge at any time. As advised, she did call the police after one violent incident but John had left the scene before they arrived and they did not pursue the matter. During all this time, programme staff's concerns about John were shared with Lily, with the worker from Women's Aid and with the social worker holding the probation order. All concerned searched for ways of holding John to account without compromising Lily's safety. None was found.

One night, John turned up to the programme in a brand new car. Lily had been persuaded to sell her house 'so that we could get somewhere together that did not remind John of her former husband'. John said it was 'our' new car, but Lily did not have a driving licence.

Shortly thereafter, John crashed 'their' new car, writing it off, and was charged with drunk driving and police assault. He was remanded in custody. Lily had to vacate her house and moved into a refuge. John's contact with the programme ceased; his probation was breached and he was given a custodial sentence. Lily was re-housed by the local council and she also ceased contact.

WORKING DIRECTLY WITH MEN

Before discussing issues relating to intervention with men, it is necessary to acknowledge that for an, as yet undetermined, proportion of men who are violent to their partners, nothing is likely to work in terms of changing their behaviour. The seriousness, frequency and sophistication of their violence, their casual attitude to punishing and terrorising women, the justifications they employ, the rights to which they feel they are entitled and the tacit approval they receive from wider society all conspire to make them highly unlikely to cease their violence and abuse.

Direct work with men who have been identified or convicted of violence against partners is still highly contentious in terms of the ethical dilemmas it raises, the approaches adopted by practitioners and its effectiveness. There is, however, both a growing 'expertise' within the probation service and among various voluntary agencies working in this field (Scourfield 1995; Lees and Lloyd 1994). There is also a body of evidence from research and practice which highlights examples of responsible and effective work (Dobash *et al.* 1996; Edelson and Tolman 1992; Morran and Wilson 1997; Pence and Paymar 1990). While the authors' own experience was of working with men who had been *convicted* of violence against their partner, it is acknowledged that practitioners may find themselves working with men who come from a range of referral sources and, accordingly, the themes explored below are not intended to relate solely to a criminal justice-based approach.

CONTRADICTORY ATTITUDES TOWARDS VIOLENCE

Men often exhibit a range of confused and, sometimes, contradictory attitudes towards their relationships with women generally (Morgan 1992; Seidler 1994) and this would seem also to bear on their views about violence against women. While the vast majority may appear to condemn 'men who hit women' and dissociate themselves from this type of act, many still subscribe more or less overtly to the view that in certain types of situation – for example, where women are seen as feckless, flirtatious or unfaithful, or where they have been found wanting as wives or mothers – 'any man' would do the same thing. Thus women who do not fulfil the 'reasonable' demands which society traditionally places on wives may be held to a greater or lesser extent to have brought the violence on themselves (Hearn 1993; Morran and Wilson 1997).

Practitioners need to be aware of this double standard. While almost all men will seek to justify their behaviour, some will be aggrieved and defensive that they and not their partner are the focus of the practitioner's attention, while others will cling to the belief that they are not 'really' violent, that in fact they are somehow victims of circumstance. The latter group's underlying beliefs about women's deservedness of punishment in certain situations subverts the otherwise reasonable attitudes and behaviour to which they apparently subscribe. It will, in many instances, mean that such men find it difficult to understand or get in touch with their violence, seeing it as something which only surfaces in extreme situations, as something which *happens* to them rather than something for which they are responsible.

Where the practitioner is a man, he will need to acknowledge that he may share some of these contradictory beliefs and confusing feelings. Working with male violence and its underlying attitudes means exploring fundamental aspects of personal intimate relationships. These may not be as straightforward as he would like.

Women practitioners will also find themselves confronting their own contradictory attitudes, beliefs and feelings about themselves as women and relationships with men. In addition, they will often find themselves the object of men's underlying misogyny (Wilson 1996).

RISK ISSUES

Although the assessment of risk is a daily activity for most social work practitioners, it has been noted – for example, by Kemshall (1996) in relation to probation practice – that this is often unsystematic and that workers bring their own values, knowledge and experience to this task. This is equally the case in relation to assessment of risk concerning 'wife assault' (Saunders 1995).

While tools such as the Conflict Tactics Scale (Straus 1979) and the Hostility Toward Women Scale (Check and Malamuth 1983) have been developed, these have generally focused on the extent, range and different types of violence, aggression and hostility among identified violent men in order to more fully understand the range of 'tactics' employed and, therefore, increase understanding of the predictability of violence. These may serve more as, what Saunders (1995) defines as, 'risk markers'. They point to general factors in these men's lives, such as violence in family of origin; class; alcohol abuse; 'behavioural deficits'; violence toward children; anger; stress; depression and low self-esteem.

As assessment tools, however, they relate more to what have been described as 'generally predictive' rather than 'specific' risk factors (Brearley 1982). They are also assessment tools which are usually developed once work has actually begun with a male violent offender. They are arguably less likely to be useful to a practitioner who is required to make an assessment about the appropriateness of working with someone who is violent. It may be more helpful to focus on some of the urgent and pressing difficulties which men present to those carrying out such assessments.

ASSESSMENT

Any assessment should begin by focusing on the violence and the context in which it occurred. Practitioners need to encourage the man to consider whether there may be a pattern to his use of violence and whether it also relates to other forms of behaviour which may be violent or abusive. Issues of frequency and severity need to be considered and, where possible, cross-referenced with the partners' accounts. This is crucial, as many men are likely still to be living with or in regular contact with their partners. The degree to which the man accepts responsibility for his violence and the extent to which he is motivated to examine and change his behaviour needs to be considered. His own agenda, either of avoiding custody or retrieving his relationship is also an inescapable component of the assessment process. The most important factor in the assessment is the safety of the woman to whom the man has been violent. It is crucial that practitioners need to be aware that as his relationship with his partner is variable and may change from week to week, so may be the risk which he presents in these changing circumstances (Morran 1996; Morran and Wilson 1997).

ETHICAL DILEMMAS

The difficulties of assessing and predicting risk and the consequences of getting it wrong pose a number of ethical and practical dilemmas. In some instances, for example, men who appear motivated to change will subsequently prove highly resistant to doing so, but it may be difficult to prove that this constitutes non-compliance. It may also be difficult to confront them with the fact that the worker is aware of their continuing violence, as the case study illustrates. In some assessment discussions it may be that a partner is enthusiastic that workers agree to 'help' her partner while the practitioner him/herself may feel that the man is obviously unsuitable or too dangerous. This poses a dilemma about refusing to work with men for whom it is evident that no other meaningful intervention is likely to occur. While violent assault of a partner does, in some instances, result in imprisonment, this, and the temporary comparative safety it offers to women, may only pertain in a minority of cases. In most instances courts still respond by imposing disposals such as fines, which do not challenge the man's behaviour in any meaningful way and, in fact, serve effectively to punish the whole family. While this may be frustrating, practitioners should not be drawn into recommending intervention simply due to the inadequacy of other sentencing options. This would be irresponsible.

Both at the assessment stage and beyond, when work is actually underway, practitioners may frequently find themselves grappling with these kinds of dilemma. Are they being responsible by engaging with particular men despite concerns about the propriety or the effectiveness of doing so and, given that the man's partner or future partner may be lulled into a sense of false hope, or worse, placed at further risk?

DIFFICULTIES IN UNCOVERING THE ISSUE WITH MEN

Our experience in assessing men's violence was, at least partially, assisted by the fact that men were referred for an offence involving violence. For many practitioners, however, violence may only be an issue they encounter or confront with other offending or problematic behaviour in a man's life. In either instance he is likely to present a complex set of defences and excuses similar to those 'techniques of neutralisation' (Sykes and Matza 1957), which all of us adopt to rationalise behaviour about which we may feel uncomfortable or guilty.

The most difficult of these rationalisations is denial, where men either reject responsibility for the offence or, indeed, deny the offence completely. For us, the issue of men's denial was the main reason for assessing men as being unsuitable for intervention. Similarly, men will also minimise their violence and its impact on partners in order to escape practitioners' attempts to engage with them.

PROVOCATION

As previously noted, a man may take the view that he is not usually violent, that he has responded to a situation where he has reached the end of his tether or that he has reacted in an explosive way to some extremely provocative event or set of circumstances. In this kind of situation the man wants to assure the worker that it is the woman who is the problem, that her behaviour is of concern, not his.

In effect, the man is blaming the woman (Adams 1998; Dobash and Dobash 1979; Hearn 1993; Morran and Wilson 1997).

Most practitioners would reject the excuse of provocation and would advocate instead that one is responsible for one's own behaviour, but this is a goal to be aimed for and not necessarily something which can be expected of men at the outset. The issue of provocation is, in fact, likely to be around for much of the time that one works with violent men. This is not difficult to understand. It both diminishes blame and seems to make some sense of the, sometimes, bitter give-and-take of personal relationships.

While workers may want to challenge men's views that they are provoked by partners, they may find themselves settling for the more limited goal of encouraging men to see that 'provocation', as they define it, need not lead inevitably to violence. Needless to say, men's reasons for citing provocation may range from situations which might disturb us all – such as imagined or real infidelity, say, to the most basic of traditional male expectations of wifely services: 'My dinner was burnt!'

STRIVING FOR EFFECTIVE PRACTICE

There is a need for more and longer term research into the effectiveness of direct work with men who are violent to women partners; namely, whether it results in a reduction or cessation of violent activity or further offending. Research into voluntary interventions, particularly in the US and Canada, has often been problematic, due, in part, to high attrition rates, which has made follow up difficult (Dobash and Dobash 1992). The effectiveness of court-mandated work with men has been more adequately addressed. Hamberger and Hastings (1993) provide a useful overview of a number of North American evaluations which do suggest a number of positive trends. They conclude, rather gloomily, however, that due partly to a variety of methodological short-comings, 'not much' is known about the longer term effects of treatment on wife assault.

More recent UK research indicates that court-mandated intervention in the form of men's groupwork programmes resulted in a significant proportion of participants reducing their violence and associated controlling behaviour. The study also drew substantially on women's views of their partners' behaviour during and post programme completion. These women's accounts indicated a significant improvement in the quality of their lives and their relationships (Dobash *et al.* 1996).

Based on the findings of this research, a framework for delineating 'the process of change' which men undergo has been proposed (Dobash *et al.* 1996, p.110):

- men need to see that change is possible
- men come to see change as desirable
- men need to have reasons to change (which may include an awareness of costs and benefits)
- men change from object to subject (they develop an awareness of their own behaviour and choices)
- men move from external constraints to internal controls
- men shift their language and thinking to expand their emotional and cognitive landscape
- men achieve changes through talking, listening, learning and thinking
- men identify specific elements of change in both behaviour and attitudes.

Consistently within the literature there appears to be an increasing consensus that the most credible, accountable and effective of interventions share a number of features, beginning with the fact that the man's violence is the problem in question and that he resorts to that violence in order to obtain or maintain personal power within a relationship. There is also an understanding of violence as being physical, sexual and psychologically abusive behaviour, an analysis of violent or abusive incidents, the recognition and tracking of moods and emotions, the examination of male socialisation and attitudes to women and the development of a range of cognitive skills and techniques for increasing control over one's own well-being and behaviour (Adams 1988; Dobash and Dobash 1992; Scourfield, 1995; Sonkin, Martin and Walker 1985; Stordeur and Stille 1989).

It would seem also that work conducted in group programmes has lent itself more easily to evaluation and research. It needs to be borne in mind that, for a variety of reasons, group work approaches may not be appropriate or possible for many practitioners nor suitable for many individuals. In the wider criminological literature pertaining to the effectiveness of group work approaches with offenders it was found that for the less serious or experienced offender, groups could have a contaminating effect which could actually increase the risk of further offending (McIvor 1992). Care needs to be taken that men are not similarly contaminated by attending group-based violence programmes. There is undoubtedly much valuable one-to-one work taking place between practitioner and offender in this field, although there is clearly a need for further evaluation of this activity.

ANGER

A number of elements in intervention techniques merit further attention and debate. These relate primarily to focusing on men's anger and their (in)ability to communicate with their partners. While anger management techniques can be useful for working with some men, it is important to bear in mind the accounts of many women who have borne violence as well as frequent observations from research and practice that many violent men need not be angry when they are being violent to their partners; their violence is more often to do with power and control (Dobash and Dobash 1979; Pence and Paymar 1986; Morran and Wilson 1997). It is a matter of concern that interventions (such as those sometimes conducted by psychologists within a number of prisons) may adopt anger management strategies without necessarily asking why, if anger is the problem, it should be 'appropriately' directed against women.

Similarly, men's apparent inability to communicate has often been thought to be a predisposing factor in their violence. Indeed, when we asked men with whom we were working to tell us what they were learning and what was changing about their behaviour, they often cited the fact that they found they were talking to their partners much more than they had done before and that this was useful and valued. What was significant, however, was that they now thought differently about their partner and saw her as a person. It was men's reluctance to consider communicating that was a problem, not their inability to do so.

HOW LONG CAN NEW THINKING HOLD OUT?

Some final questions must remain unanswered. It is difficult for men to incorporate and hold onto new ways of thinking about themselves and how they relate to women in a non-violent and equal manner when the 'real' patriarchal world in which they live continues to perpetuate powerful images about how men and women ought to be, and where masculine attributes of toughness, aggression and even violence are still the valued norm for many. Challenging violent men means questioning almost all of the concepts on which 'masculinity' is constructed. We frequently noted, when undertaking training with probation officers for example that a large proportion of officers wanting to engage in this activity were women. Women are undoubtedly required to undertake this work and we subscribe to the idea of male and female practitioners working in tandem on this issue. However, while male practitioners will undoubtedly find it difficult at times to acknowledge and challenge behaviour which may also challenge them in a deeply personal way, it is necessary for them to begin doing so in order to begin to solve, as opposed to perpetuate, the problem.

REFERENCES

Adams, D. (1988) 'Treatment models of men who batter: a profeminist analysis.' In K. Yllö and M. Bograd (eds) *Feminist Perspectives on Wife Abuse*. London: Sage Publications.

Bograd, M. (1988) 'Feminist perspectives on wife abuse, an introduction.' In K. Yllo and M. Bograd (eds) *Feminist Perspectives on Wife Abuse*. London: Sage Publications.

Brearley, C.P. (1982) *Risk and Social Work*. London: Routledge and Kegan Paul.

Buzawa, E.S. and Buzawa, C.G. (1990) *Domestic Violence: The Criminal Justice Response*. London: Sage Publications.

Check, J.V.P. and Malamuth, N.M. (1983) *The Hostility toward Women Scale*. Conference paper presented at 91st Annual Convention of American Psychological Association, California, USA.

Dobash, R.E. and Dobash, R.P. (1979) *Violence Against Wives*. New York: The Free Press.

Dobash, R.E. and Dobash, R.P. (1992) *Women, Violence and Social Change*. London: Routledge.

Dobash, R.E., Dobash, R.P., Cavanagh, K. and Lewis, R. (1996) *Research Evaluation of Programmes for Violent Men*. Edinburgh: The Scottish Office Central Research Unit.

Edelson, J.L. and Tolman, R.M. (1992) *Intervention for Men who Batter: An Ecological Approach*. London: Sage.

Fawcett, B., Featherstone, B., Hearn, J. and Toft, C. (eds) (1996) *Violence and Gender Relations: Theories and Interventions*. London: Sage Publications.

Fields, M.D. (1994) 'Criminal justice responses to violence against women.' In A. Duff, S. Marshall, R.E. Dobash and R.P. Dobash (eds) *Penal Theory and Practice. Tradition and Innovation in Criminal Justice*. Fulbright Papers 14, Manchester University Press.

Hague, G. and Malos, E. (1993) *Domestic Violence: Action For Change*. Cheltenham: New Clarion Press.

Hamberger, L.K. and Hastings, J.E. (1993) 'Recidivism following spouse abuse abatement counseling: treatment Program implications.' *Violence and Victims*, 5, 157–170.

Hart, B. (1988) *Safety for Women: Monitoring Batterers' Programs*. Harrisburg, PA: Pennsylvania Coalition Against Domestic Violence.

Hearn, J. (1993) 'How men talk about men's violence to known women.' *Masculinity and Crime: Issues of Theory and Practice: Conference Report*. The Centre for Criminal Justice Research.

Kemshall, H. (1996) 'Risk assessment: fuzzy thinking or "decisions in action"?' *Probation Journal*, 43, 1, 2–7.

Lees, J. and Lloyd, T. (1994) *Working with Men who Batter their Partners*. London: Working With Men.

McIvor, G. (1992) 'Intensive probation: does more mean better?' *Probation Journal*, 39, 1, 2–6.

Morgan, D.H.L. (1992) *Discovering Men*. London: Routledge.

Morran, D. (1996) 'Working in the CHANGE programme: Probation-based groupwork with male domestic violence offenders.' In T. Newburn and G. Mair (eds) *Working with Men*. Dorset: Russell House.

Morran, D. and Wilson, M. (1994) 'Confronting domestic violence: an innovative criminal justice response in Scotland.' In A. Duff, S. Marshall, R.E. Dodash and R.P. Dobash (eds) *Penal Theory and Practice: Tradition and Innovation in Criminal Justice*. Manchester: Manchester University Press.

Morran, D. and Wilson, M. (1997) *Men Who are Violent to Women; A Groupwork Practice Manual*. Dorset: Russell House.

Pahl, J. (ed) (1985) *Private Violence and Public Policy*. London: Routledge.

Pence, E. and Paymar, M. (1990) *Power and Control: Tactics of Men Who Batter*. Duluth: Minnesota Program Development Inc.

Russell, D.E.H. (1988) 'Forward.' In K. Yllo and M. Bograd (eds) *Feminist Perspectives on Wife Abuse*. London: Sage Publications.

Saunders, D.G. (1995) 'Prediction of wife assault.' In J.C. Campbell (ed) *Assessing Dangerousness – Violence by Sexual Offenders, Batterers, and Child Abusers*. London: Sage Publications.

Schechter, S. (1982) *Women and Male Violence – The Visions and Struggles of the Battered Women's Movement*. London: Pluto Press.

Scourfield, J. (1995) *Changing men: U.K. Agencies Working with Men who are Violent towards their Women Partners*. Norwich: Probation Monographs, University of East Anglia.

Seidler, V. (1994) *Unreasonable Men – Masculinity and Social Theory*. London: Routledge.

Smith, L. (1989) *Domestic Violence: An Overview of the Literature*. London: HMSO.

Sonkin, D.J., Martin, D. and Walker L.E. (1985) *The Male Batterer – A Treatment Approach*. New York: Springer.

Stordeur, R.A. and Stille, R. (1989) *Ending Men's Violence: One Road to Peace*. Newbury Park, CA: Sage.

Straus, M.A. (1979) 'Measuring family conflict and violence: the conflict tactics scale.' *Journal of Marriage and the Family*, 41, 75–88.

Sykes, G. and Matza, D. (1957) 'Techniques of neutralisation: a theory of delinquency.' *American Sociological Review*, 22, 664–70.

United Nations (1996) *The Beijing Declaration and the Platform for Action.* Fourth World Conference on Women, Beijing, China, 4–15 September 1995. New York : United Nations.

Wilson, M. (1996) 'Working with the CHANGE men's programme.' In K. Cavanagh and V. Cree (eds) *Working With Men – Feminism and Social Work.* London: Routledge.

Yllö, K. and Bograd, M. (eds) (1988) *Feminist Perspectives on Wife Abuse.* London: Sage Publications.

FURTHER READING

Cavanagh, K. and Cree, V. (eds) (1996) *Working with Men – Feminism and Social Work.* London: Routledge.

CHAPTER 5

Managing Violence; Managing Masculinity

Karen Buckley

INTRODUCTION

This chapter seeks to explore the extent to which our stereotypical thinking around gender may prevent us from effectively assessing the risks of dangerous behaviour presented by men. To do this it will explore the range of dangerous behaviours committed by males and suggest that these behaviours may be wholly or partly rooted in the impact of gender stereotyping. To correctly predict the risks of violence (to the self or others), whether or not it results in offending, or, indeed, to judge how an offender may be able to make use of insights he is given, one must be in a position to view him holistically. Thus as well as looking at the impact of male behaviour on women and children, the chapter will also explore the way in which stereotypical masculinity influences men to behave in ways which are potentially or actually dangerous to themselves and to other men.

Assessing the risk of violent and dangerous acts is of critical importance in any work with offenders, not simply because of the impact of its outcomes. Increasingly, probation services, for example, are moving to target their scarce resources on the more dangerous offender, using research which suggests that this is where the input is most effective (see Underdown 1998 for examples). The prediction of risk of harm and reoffending is central to much practice and looking at the issues with clarity and without prejudiced assumptions becomes highly important in contributing to effectiveness.

The chapter will conclude with some pointers for good practice in future work, taken from a conference debate sponsored by the Nottingham Men's Health Forum, following a paper I presented on this theme. The chapter will focus on male behaviour and look at its roots in the constructs of masculinity. It will look at a range of male actions, including street violence targeted at other men; violence in the home targeted at women and children; and sexually abusive behaviours towards children, women and other men. Looking at this behaviour in total, and at its connections, it will ask why men are dangerous in order to see the nature of the risk they present.

This is not to say that women cannot behave in ways which are dangerous, and we should be alert to this potential in their behaviour, as studies like Saridjaan's (1996) on women abusers has shown. However, the focus on the impact of gender on men has validity for two reasons. First, women do not offend in anything like the numbers that men do (Home Office 1997). Second, we need to view offenders not just as individual men (or women) but in the context of their structural position in society. In this context it is helpful to use Archer's (1994) distinction between aggression and violence. Aggression, he suggests, is the feeling, and violence is the act or the outcome, and the translation from feeling to outcome will vary in presentation and impact according to the status and power, both structural and personal, of the actor. What each gender does with its feelings of violence, and the impact of any actions, will be affected by men's greater structural power.

CONSTRUCTS OF MALE BEHAVIOUR

To focus on male behaviour from a gendered perspective requires an approach which is broadly social constructionist (Hearn and Morgan 1990). On the basis of this approach, this chapter broadly works with an acceptance that, in the nature/nurture debate, it is the precepts and activities that go on within nurture that are most relevant. Whatever the contribution of nature and inheritance to the unformed male or female child, the impact of the social milieu has been demonstrated over and over again to be so culturally and historically variable as to make its impact clear (Edholm 1982).

Competing expectations of male behaviour are not necessarily mutually exclusive; few of them, however, explain the extent of the outcomes of such behaviour. That women physically give birth to children, for example, does not wholly explain the predominance of their role in child rearing. Likewise, an approach based on evolutionary psychology, as outlined by Daly and Wilson (1994), would suggest that the explanation for male violence and risk taking lies in the social demands and agendas that confronted ancestral man, with young men being the group where there was the most intense selection for confrontational and competitive capability. There is, no doubt, an historical, handed-down perspective to the formation of behaviour, but it does not account for the magnitude of risk taking amongst young men or its entirely anti-social outcomes. There is also no sense in such theories of the potential of evolutionary capacity to change. We can, apparently, grow taller and live longer but not outwit our ancestral urges. It seems that whatever inheritance we start with, we cannot overlook learned behaviour. As John Gilbert (1994) has suggested, 'We cannot ignore the way in which cultures activate competitive tendencies and create multiple arenas for conflict' (p.353).

On a similar theme, Archer (1994) observes that inter-male competition and risk taking is most pronounced amongst those who have nothing to lose. Archer emphasises here a problem for the criminal justice system in analysing risk. We are not dealing with success here, but failure. This is not to say that there is not a pattern to male behaviour, but that to understand its logic you have to have a clear understanding of its imperatives and their roots in gender construction as a social and learned phenomenon. This raises questions about how we are taught and what we are taught about gender, and also about the potential for change.

In the context of risk analysis, it seems timely to ask why it should be young men who are maximally risk-prone and vulnerable to violent death as well as its major perpetrators?

To answer these questions one needs to look broadly at the study of masculinity within sociology (see Kimmell 1990 for review). How is masculinity constructed and for what purpose? Though written twenty years ago, Brannon and Davids' (1976) constructs of stereotypical masculinity have yet to be surpassed for their accessibility. They suggest four pillars of being a stereotypical man as 'No sissy stuff ... be a big wheel ... be a sturdy oak ... and give em hell...' (p.16).

Whilst these constructs have been criticised as, perhaps, a white and heterosexist view of manhood, they have resonance as, arguably, the prevailing view. Even if your sub-culture offers you different models, these are the ones by which you will be judged. For example, black feminist writers like Wallace (1978) or Hill Collins (1990) have illustrated how, 'if you try to articulate a different and healthier way of being male (or female), this is immediately devalued by racist attacks. bell hooks (1981), for example, has described how African American patterns of child rearing, where the child is a collective responsibility not personal property, have been devalued and rewritten by racism since they act against the white notion of the family as the locus of male power or 'the Englishman's home is his castle'.

Masculinity, in this version, is a set of precepts or teachings that the individual must live up to to be a man, and it is reinforced by rewards (even if illusory ones). Men make of these rules what they can by using the tools that race, class, finance or sexuality leave open to them. They make sense of their own particular social situation and its disadvantages lest they be judged and not allowed to join the club of manhood. Thus men may appear to behave quite differently whilst still paying homage to the criteria by which they are judged as men. It is not unheard of, for example, for middle-class, well-to-do white men to see macho behaviour as the quaint prerogative of the overtly physically oppressive working class or black man. The man who rapes or physically beats women because he is damaged and seeking immediate power to show he is a man makes it just that little bit easier for 'nice' men to keep women in line.

Within our society men must always be demonstrating that they are men. The status must constantly be earned and constantly shored up. Integral to the direction of male behaviour is the way in which men engage with this process and with the beliefs that toughness and physical aggression (or 'no sissy stuff' and 'give em hell') are integral to manhood. Reviewing a range of literature, for example, Archer (1994) writes that 'violent acts usually develop from an escalating exchange of verbal aggression and minor physical acts. The exchange begins with an event which one of the protagonists perceives as an identity threat' (p.45).

Men may be promised rewards of status and power if they conform to the constructs of masculinity, but one could also argue that they are kept in line by them. Just how they are kept in line is of importance. If they do not conform to the stereotypes, they are accused of being like a woman. To bond with the gang or the fratriarchy as it has been called, a man may have to indulge in all sorts of terrifying and risky rituals just to show that he is not a sissy, not a girl, not a pouf. For example, in an examination of the Merseyside Car Offenders Project (COP), Buckley and Young (1996) found 'a high degree of influence from peer friendships and the need to maintain this to get admiration by taking risks, even life-threatening ones.' Participants saw their risky behaviour as normal, a boys thing, one of the rites of passage. Young men also became addicted to the adrenalin rush and could perceive themselves as being uncontrollable, almost taken over by macho behaviour. It seems that this becomes a perfect way of discarding responsibility for your own actions and parallels the 'she was asking for it' accounts of rape and domestic violence familiar to practitioners.

This kind of thinking provides a great challenge to workers and, indeed, requires them to work on their own perception of 'normal for boys' – for example, when earlier motor projects talked of 'engaging with the buzz' or finding alternative exciting activities to motivate offenders (or maybe interest staff). Equally, it has not been unusual to see probation officers explaining offenders' behaviour in reports in the offenders terms, giving long and verbatim accounts of why an assault had occurred, as if this somehow excused it (see Whitehead and Cordery (1992), for example, for a comparison of male probation officers and male clients using gender in confrontation). Acceptance of male behaviour has also been enhanced through distancing by class or youth – and the development of a normal, for them, culture. The COP review concluded that it was highly likely that participants were absorbing the media view and presentation of car crime and using it as a way of abdicating responsibility for their own actions.

Again, there is resonance for practitioners in the way in which sex offenders diminish their offences by blaming their victims, displaying them as provocative. This is validated in media images and literature (see Russell (1993), for a collation of evidence). Likewise, as Denney (1995) has expressed it, 'Men who are unable to exercise power in a public domain will exercise power in a private one over less powerful women, children and men' (p.67). Such violence does, however, take to the streets. Campbell (1993), analysing the estate riots of the 1990s, suggests that the young men involved, far from being starved of male role models, were actually saturated with them. The issue is, of course, what the models demonstrate. As Campbell (1993) concludes, 'For a lad whose culture celebrated a man's authority and power, and lethal weapons as the solution to social problems, the discovery of his own illiteracy or incompetence could of course carry the dread that being inside society meant being defeated' (p.96).

Stereotypical thinking around gender allows men not to take responsibility for oppressive, violent or self-destructive behaviour and allows the blaming of victims. A central theme is certainly distancing from all that is female. In facing the task of analysing risk correctly, social workers, probation officers and others have to face their own histories of collusion as workers and individuals.

In posing the question of why society chooses to set up certain behaviours as 'normal for boys', some authors, notably hooks (1981) and Hill Collins (1990), have suggested that central to Europeanised thinking is the notion of dichotomy. This involves perceiving oneself only in an oppositional context. Thus to be possessed of good and valuable qualities, a person must see themselves in contrast to bad or poor qualities in others. Such thinking fuels, or even forms, racism and sexism and leads to the development of in and out groupings, such as religious groups. It also makes the divide between the genders and the maintenance, at all costs, of appropriately gendered behaviour a priority. Those who have power take and define the good qualities, and judgements about the most risky or dangerous behaviours become focused on that which threatens the spurious normality, rather than that which causes maximum pain or damage.

GENDER STEREOTYPES AND SEXUAL OFFENDING

In any study of risk analysis the most fraught area is often that of sexual offending. In a real sense it is fraught, not because the judgements are any different, but because the stakes are high and because stereotypical thinking has historically clouded our capacities to see offending or to even believe it exists. To fully understand the subject we have to explore the connections between gender constructs and imperatives, and the acting out of sexual behaviour. David Evans (1993) has argued that gendered behaviour and sexual behaviour are taught in confused and interconnected ways, so that the two become one. Each gender has specific sexual attributes and behaviours attached to it, and Willis (1990) has demonstrated how sexual knowledge and apparent prowess are one of the ways of claiming manhood. Likewise, Smeaton and Byrne (1987) have demonstrated how men who endorse extreme masculine role attributes and values show, on the one hand, physical aggression in relationships and, on the other, a proclivity towards sexual aggression. In recent work (Buckley 1998), I tried to outline how gender stereotyped behaviour is acted out in sexuality, which, for me, begins to account for the high, almost exclusive, predominance of males in offences of rape, abuse and family violence.

Put simply, we are taught our gender roles and sexually appropriate behaviour as confused and interrelated concepts. Thus if our inter-gender relationships are suffused with anger, or seen as oppositional concepts, it is unsurprising that sexual behaviours become activities used to perpetuate this state of affairs.

Professional concern around this area highlights that we are here dealing with some of the most risky behaviour of all, because it takes risks with the emotional and mental well-being of the next generation. We are beginning to have some idea of the numbers of abused women and the damage done to them. We may, however, have little or no idea of the extent of damage done to men by men because to tell is to become a victim and, therefore, not a man.

RAPE VIOLENCE AND CHILD ABUSE

Despite pioneering studies which are beginning to explore the activities of women in these cases (Lobel 1986; Saridjaan 1996), known perpetrators in these cases are largely male. Victims are often female, though they can be male. However, as Frude (1994) points out in relation to domestic violence, 'aggressive behaviour by women is injurious in relatively few cases and much is retaliatory' (p.153).

Stark and Flitcraft (1988) demonstrate that domestic violence is the single most common source of serious injury to women, being responsible for more injuries to them than road accidents, muggings and rape combined. Whether one views domestic violence from the interactionist perspective of Frude or from the feminist/social stratification model exemplified in the work of Dobash and Dobash (1979), what is clear is that men believe they have authority and validation to act in ways which are extremely risky and dangerous to their spouses.

In similar vein, Pollard (1994) suggests that 'Most rapes are committed by "psychologically normal" males whose aggression may be both tacitly condoned by their immediate peer group, and more indirectly condoned by attitudes that are prevalent in society generally' (p.187). Petty and Dawson (1989) found repeated sexual aggression to be related to desires to be held in high esteem by acquaintances and suggest that sexual aggression may be maintained in men through peer pressure. Again, we see extremely dangerous and damaging behaviour by men as a result of understandings about how men are entitled to behave, or, indeed, how a man should behave.

Superficially, at least, the abuse of children seems contextually different to the previous categories since it appears to be socially abhorred and condemned. How, therefore, can it be validated by any social codes? What we know from the work of Finkelhor (1986) and others is that its common form is for males in a position of authority to victimise girls in subordinate positions, with male abuse of boys being far less common. Summarising recent research, Andrews (1994) writes that those most likely to be perpetrators of physical and sexual abuse will be men who are suffering stressful life circumstances and who have abusive tendencies, possibly as a result of childhood experiences or poor mental health. This may explain the likely perpetrator but not fully the choice of victim.

Lew (1990), however, extending this theme, relates it to stereotypical masculinity by outlining how the unattainable images of masculine power lead men to try to shore up their fragile selves over and over again. He thus describes the feelings of male perpetrators as:

> He feels he must achieve power so as to avoid further victimisation. In a world divided into victims and perpetrators abuse can be interpreted as power. The only way of masculinizing (empowering) himself seems to be by turning someone else into a victim... It feels like his only possibility of leaving the role of victim... (p.44).

Put simply, gender relations are taught as power relations, thus they are open to all kinds of abusive behaviour. Given their disruptive impact, which is well documented, they constitute one of the greatest risk areas that behaviour based on stereotypes of masculinity could be said to impact on. To illustrate our understanding of the impact of masculinity, a comparison with female behaviour is useful. In review, Goodwin (1994) writes that evidence from both social psychology and sociobiology suggest that men and women have different sets of responses and motives for their aggressive sides and their behaviour should be interpreted in this light. He comments: 'Women are likely to resort to aggression only once a critical level of stress has been reached: men's aggression is more instrumental and aimed at achieving a particular goal' (p.146). Viewed from this perspective, men can be seen to be educated into using aggression and consequent violence for a purpose, such as the achievement of domestic, gender-based or neighbourhood dominance. This has considerable implications for the way that we structure any work with them. It also highlights the conceptions of what workers (particularly male ones) may regard as 'normal for boys'.

MEN AS VICTIMS OF MEN

Lew (1990) has collated and documented evidence on the extent of male on male abuse. However, men are often victims of other men's actions in a variety of other settings where stereotypical male behaviour leads to unpleasant consequences. Men are also at risk of street violence. Reviewing the demographic factors which influence this, Archer (1994) observes:

> It is not just men who are more likely to commit violent acts to other men, but men of a certain age range... young men... The main reason that the streets of poor urban areas are the places where much inter-male violence occurs is because they are designed as male territory. (p.138)

In conclusion, Archer suggests that it is possible to demonstrate that same-sex physical aggression and violence is much more common between men than women and relates to beliefs about the centrality of toughness and physical aggression to demonstrating masculine status. From the perspective of this chapter, we can see that masculine stereotyped behaviour causes considerable risks to male well-being in public places. As a context of their abusive behaviour, men are more likely to find themselves being punished and policed by the state. As Hudson (1988) has outlined, the state may encourage the system of gender stratification but it certainly punishes its casualties, as the number of men in prison might evidence. Likewise, as Campbell (1993) remarks of the public reaction to young men involved in street riots, 'it was not that they lost their identity but the way they asserted it, that was the problem' (p.322).

WORKING WITH VIOLENCE

Attempting to conform to the stereotypes of masculinity clearly sets men up for a variety of behaviours which are dangerous to themselves and others. To formulate strategies to deal with them, one has to look at the way in which masculinity teaches men to behave, otherwise strategies to work with them will flounder. Masculine men are unlikely to tell of issues that 'un-man' them. Writers around abuse tell how men find it difficult to both confess what has happened to them and to present themselves as victims (Lew 1990). Thus they may not present themselves for counselling, so that those agencies, such as the probation service, where they are forced to go because of their offending may have a particular responsibility.

In this context, and pertinent to working with young men, Davidson (1998) has demonstrated that young heterosexual men were neglectful of their sexual health, viewing risk taking in this area as part of being a man. Again, the men in his sample identified this sense of not being in control of their sexual behaviour, together with an inability to un-man themselves, by seeking advice. This has implications for the dangers they present to women – for example, when their refusal to take responsibility for their behaviour leads to unwanted pregnancies or the transmission of diseases.

'Masculine' men may not have a language in which to discuss their needs. Seidler (1988), for example, has suggested that a lifetime of conformity to stereotypical masculinity may cause men to lose half their emotional life. They may be unable to express what they experience. Some of the work that has been done around thinking skills and cognitive development rings bells for those who analyse the impact of masculinity. Ross (1991) found impulsiveness, not thinking before acting, concrete as opposed to abstract thinking and an inability to comprehend the needs of others. Likewise, Gardiner and Nesbit (1996) found men being easily influenced by superficial argument, with poor levels of problem solving arising from an inability to correctly predict the consequences of behaviour. Dichotomous thinking requires simplicity of analysis and the imperatives of being seen to be a man may well override more common-sense judgements. The indoctrination of gender stereotypes (which affect the workers' thinking too) can mean that the dangerousness of behaviour is not perceived. Confrontations may occur which might have been avoided, or an offender may fail to make use of advice or learning, because this analysis has not been done.

MANAGING THE RISK OF VIOLENCE

As stated earlier, Archer (1994) makes a distinction between aggression and violence and the difference in potential outcomes from aggression between the two genders. Not only are men more likely to resort to violent acts, but the impact of these acts will be greater because of their greater structural power. When we explore and identify risk of violence, the gender of the perpetrator is a very relevant issue.

Men's roles in society have changed in the past two decades, in ways which have not always had the effect of integrating them better as citizens. Traditionally, they were integrated as employees, husbands and fathers. These roles have declined, but society's values and judgements of men have often failed to integrate this process. Traditionally, this integration perhaps mitigated against the worst impacts of stereotypical masculinity by providing men with a place of status. Also, gender stereotyping hid much of the damage that men were doing, or the risks they presented, by avoiding the exposure of domestic violence, rape or child abuse; by blaming the victims; or making it too difficult for them to complain. Faced with this knowledge, we have to ask, as professionals working with violent and abusive behaviours: what is to be done about men, in a structural as well as a case-by-case sense?

WORKING WITH VIOLENCE UNPACKING THE GENDER SCRIPT TO MOVE FORWARD

In November of 1997 I presented a paper on men and risk taking to a conference organised by the Nottingham Men's Health Forum, an inter-agency group funded by a health service grant to look at the risks men present to themselves and others. The risks presented by conforming to stereotypical behaviour were high on everyone's agenda. Participants represented a range of projects, including hostels, advice projects and voluntary and statutory agencies. The group examined how they, as workers, evaluated the risks that male clients and users presented and how their understanding of the imperatives of stereotypical masculinity enabled them to judge situations and any dangers inherent in them. It was acknowledged that risk taking might result in dangerous or violent behaviour but that it was not of itself unhealthy, nor did it automatically lead to damaging scenarios. It was, rather, the motives and understandings behind it that required exploration. Having shared tactics, the group came up with a series of pointers for improving future practice as follows:

- examine the risk: what are the motives for taking it? are they defined by stereotypical or clear thinking?
- examine the potential outcomes of risk: who might benefit? who might get hurt? what are the consequences? is there a risk of violent behaviour?
- take control: do not feel helpless in the face of gender or accept versions of behaviour based on this from those you work with

- don't disconnect: do not let men (and young men in particular) disassociate themselves from the consequences of their actions; explain their dangerous implications to them
- don't use your victim: don't blame women or expect them to sort gender issues for you or accept such behaviour from those you work with; equally, in male-on-male confrontations don't become irrational about the other parties
- develop a sense of self, rather than self as a group member, and encourage this in those you work with; much unpleasant and violent male behaviour is grounded in the need to establish the self according to group norms
- give and get feedback: getting an objective view of behaviour or of advice given is of exceptional importance
- obtain good supervision: if your agency does not offer it, use peer networks or outside groups
- network with like-minded people: this gives support and may help achieve change.

CONCLUSION

The above pointers refer primarily to male workers, but it was acknowledged that they could be helpful to women and to the necessary self-reflection that they needed to undertake in unpacking their gender roles.

Practitioners can do a number of things, as well as sharing their work techniques. They can point out areas where research is badly needed and highlight policy gaps. What these practitioners were reinforcing, and what is suggested in the body of literature quoted, is that when it comes to analysing violent behaviour, there are observable and quantifiable differences in the behaviours of the two genders. We have to examine more closely what is done to individuals in the name of building gender roles and socialising appropriate behaviour. We have to ask what we want men to be and how we might as a society get them there. Staff supervision has to be gender aware if it is to be of value in helping workers challenge and manage dangerous behaviour.

Gender roles are only one part of the puzzle of violent behaviours. They are cross-cut by the impact of disadvantage based on race, class, economics, early damage and other variables. They are, however, sufficiently significant to form the basis for a number of research-based questions and challenges to established practice and policy.

REFERENCES

Andrews, B. (1994) 'Family violence in a social context.' In J. Archer (ed) *Male Violence*. London: Routledge.

Archer, J. (1994) 'Male violence in perspective.' In J. Archer (ed) *Male Violence*. London: Routledge.

Brannon, R. and David, D. (1976) *The 49% Majority*. Reading, Mass: Addison Wesley.

Buckley, K. (1998) 'A gendered perspective.' In B. Beaumont (ed) *Work With Offenders*. London: Macmillan.

Buckley, K. and Young, K. (1996) 'Driving us crazy.' In T. Newburn and G. Mair (eds) *Working With Men*. Lyme Regis: Russell House.

Campbell, B. (1993) *Goliath: Britain's Dangerous Places*. London: Methuen.

Daly, M. and Wilson, M. (1994) 'Evolutionary psychology of male violence.' In J. Archer (ed) *Male Violence*. London: Routledge.

Davidson, N. (1998) Presentation To Nottingham Men's Health Forum. November.

Denney, D. (1995) 'Discrimination and anti-discrimination.' In T. May and A. Vass (ed) *Working With Offenders*. London: Sage.

Dobash, R. and Dobash, R. (1979) *Violence Against Wives*. New York: Free Press.

Edholm, F. (1982) 'The unnatural family.' In E. Whitelegg, M. Arnot, E. Bartels, V. Beechey, L. Birke, S. Himmelweil, D. Leonard, S. Ruehl and M. Speakman (eds) *The Changing Experience of Women*. Oxford: Blackwell.

Evans, D. (1993) *Sexual Citizenship*. London: Routledge.

Finklehor, D. (1986) *A Source Book On Child Sexual Abuse*. Beverley Hills: Sage.

Frude, N. (1994) 'Marital violence an interactionist perspective.' In J. Archer (ed) *Male Violence*. London: Routledge.

Gardiner, D. and Nesbit, D. (1996) 'Cognitive behavioural work with male offenders.' In T. Newburn and G. Mair (eds) *Working With Men*. Lyme Regis: Russell House.

Gilbert, J. (1994) 'Male violence; towards an integration.' In J. Archer (ed) *Male Violence*. London: Routledge.

Goodwin, R. (1994) 'Putting relationship aggression in its place; contextualising some recent research.' In J. Archer (ed) *Male Violence*. London: Routledge.

Hearn, J. and Morgan, D. (1990) *Men Masculinities and Social Theory*. London: Unwin Hyman.

Hill Collins, P. (1990) *Black Feminist Thought*. London: Routledge.

Home Office (1997) *Understanding the Sentencing of Women*. Research Study 170. London: HMSO.

hooks, belle. (1981) *Ain't I A Woman*. Boston: South End Press.

Hudson, A. (1988) 'Boys will be boys; masculinism and the juvenile justice system.' *Critical Social Policy*, 7, 21, 30–48.

Kimmel, M. (1990) 'After 15 years the impact of the sociology of masculinity on the masculinity of sociology.' In J. Hearn and D. Morgan (eds) *Men Masculinities and Social Theory*. London: Unwin Hyman.

Lew, M. (1990) *Victims No More*. London: Methuen.

Lobel, K. (1986) *Naming The Violence*. Washington: Seal Press.

Petty, G. and Dawson, B. (1989) 'Sexual aggression in normal men: incidence belief and personality characteristics.' *Personality and Individual Differences*, 10, 355–362.

Pollard, P. (1994) 'Sexual violence against women, characteristics of typical perpetrators.' In J. Archer (ed) *Male Violence*. London: Routledge.

Ross, R. (1991) *Reasoning and Rehabilitation of Offenders*. Conference Proceedings: What Works: Effective Methods To Reduce Offending, April, Greater Manchester Probation Service.

Russell, D. (1993) (ed) *Making Violence Sexy. Feminist Views On Pornography*. Buckingham: Open University Press.

Saradjian, J. (1996) *Women Who Sexually Abuse Children*. Chichester: John Wiley.

Seidler, V. (1988) 'Fathering authority and masculinity.' In R. Chapman and J. Rutherford (eds) *Male Order*. London: Lawrence and Wishart.

Smeaton, G. and Byrne, D. (1987) 'The effects of rated violence and erotica, individual differences and victim characteristics on acquaintance rape proclivity.' *Journal of Research In Personality*, 21, 171–84.

Stark, E. and Flitcraft, A. (1988) 'Violence amongst intimates.' In V.B. Van Hasselt, R.L. Morrison, A.S. Bellack and M. Hersen (eds) *Handbook Of Family Violence*. New York: Plenum.

Underdown, A. (1998) *Strategies For Effective Offender Supervision*. London: Home Office.

Wallace, M. (1978) *Black Macho And The Myth Of Super Woman*. New York: Dial.

Whitehead, A. and Cordery, J. (1992) 'Boys don't cry.' In P. Senior and D. Woodhill (eds) *Gender, Crime and Probation Practice*. Sheffield: Pavic Publications.

Willis, P. (1990) *Common Culture*. Buckingham: Open University Press

FURTHER READING

Buckley, K. 1994) 'Being a woman makes you sick.' In P. Senior (ed) *Mentally Disordered Offenders and Probation Practice*. Sheffield: Pavic Publishers.

CHAPTER 6

Violent Women

Building Knowledge-Based Intervention Strategies

Judith Rumgay

INTRODUCTION

The periodic 'discovery' of a new generation of violent women is greeted with a curious excitement. Whether this reaction is inspired by male relief that men no longer need bear the brunt of responsibility for society's violence or, conversely, trepidation at the prospect of a community stalked by predatory women or, perhaps, female pride in at last 'getting even' in serious crime, remains a puzzle. It is perplexing precisely because, beneath the 'impact statistics' alleging large percentage increases in female violence and the 'impact stories' about unique cases of female perpetration (Chesney-Lind, Sheldon and Joe 1996), lies a muted yet continuing truth: the female contribution to serious violent crime is small. In 1996, 935 females were sentenced in the Crown Courts for offences of violence against the person. Since 10,882 males were so sentenced, this represents a proportion of 8 per cent of women to the total (Home Office 1997). The 265 females sentenced for robbery in 1996 represents 6 per cent of the total of 4480 (Home Office 1997).

The statistical evidence for an increasing volume of female violence has been debated elsewhere (e.g. Chesney-Lind 1995a; Simon and Landis 1991; Steffensmeier 1995). The point at issue, however, for the purposes of what follows, is that interventions targeted at violent females must recognise their comparative scarcity in the population of offenders. Despite their continuing paucity, theories which postulate the 'masculinisation' (Adler 1975) of female crime in conditions of increasing sexual equality of opportunity (Simon and Landis 1991), have become popular in public consciousness. Yet any attempt to apply such theories to the experiences of women offenders will surely stretch the ingenuity of any practitioners coming into contact with them. Meaningful interventions with such women depend upon a clear view of the emerging messages of research into the characteristics of female aggression. This chapter seeks to begin to extract those messages and their potential applications to practice.

This is not an exercise in comparing male and female violence, although some comparative observations will be made where they illuminate an issue. Practice development cannot rely solely on observations of similarities and differences between the sexes but must build on a positive understanding of female aggression in its own right. This includes recognition of the perspectives of women perpetrators themselves on their violence, in order that interventions may tap the moral realities of their worlds as they experience them. This, after all, is the essential thrust of current developments in cognitive-behavioural work with male offenders. Yet, as we shall see, the moral choices of female offenders develop in relational contexts which are influenced by gender.

The chapter begins by exploring characteristics of female violence. It then considers some important aspects of the experiences of violent female offenders and explores the motivational factors which propel some women to choose violence. Finally, it discusses the implications of the emergent knowledge base for professional practice.

CHARACTERISTICS OF FEMALE VIOLENCE

That females contribute a small proportion of violent crime has been confirmed repeatedly by studies in all countries where data exists (Kruttschnitt 1993). Most studies also find little evidence of a growth in female violence; some, indeed, suggest a decline (Kruttschnitt 1993; Maher and Curtis 1995; Steffensmeier 1995). Wilczynski (1997) observes that filicide is the only category of violent crime for which the female contribution approaches equality with males. While feminist criminologists, in seeking to explain this phenomenon, have stimulated research into the contextual realities of female aggression, attention has thus far focused predominantly on the extreme phenomenon of homicide. American research has also begun to illuminate the violence of female gang members, drug users, robbers and sex workers. It is largely from these types of study, despite their specialised criminological and cultural emphases, that we must begin to derive a knowledge base on which to build interventions for female violence.

Targets of female violence

Fatal violence by women is predominantly directed at family members. The majority of victims are sexual partners (Kruttschnitt 1993; Mann 1996). The second most vulnerable targets of women's lethal violence are their children (Kruttschnitt 1993; Mann 1996), particularly those under one year of age (Wilczynski 1997). Family members other than intimate partners and children are relatively infrequent victims of female homicide (Mann 1996). This propensity for women to attack those close to them was reflected in Saradjian's (1996) study of female sexual abusers of children. Women most frequently abused their own offspring, those in close kin connection and children in their care. Women who targeted adolescents were more likely to abuse children outside the immediate family, although Saradjian noted the comparative unavailability of older potential kin victims.

Mann (1996) noted the preponderance of males among the non-family homicide victims of females. Males constituted the majority of friends and acquaintances, and all strangers killed. However, the paucity of stranger victims (23 among 296 homicides) in Mann's study in itself testified to the female preference for targeting people with whom interpersonal relationships exist. Felson (1997a) also observed that target choice for homicide, even in apparently similar motivational contexts, is mediated by gender. Examining homicides motivated by heterosexual jealousy and 'love triangles', Felson found that males predominantly targeted their male rivals while females most often killed their male partners.

Target preference in non-lethal violence also appears to be mediated by gender. The presence of weapons and/or accomplices are probably considerations in this. Baskin and Sommers (1998) reported that women's robbery victims were equally likely to be males as females when weapons were used. In the absence of weapons, women elected to rob other women. Miller (1998) similarly contrasted male robbers' preference for male victims with women's targeting of females when they were unarmed or armed only with a knife. Male targets, however, could be 'disarmed' through the adoption of sexual enticement strategies or the presence of accomplices.

Situational aspects

Women are apparently unlikely to direct their violence at multiple victims. Wilczynski (1997) reported that only 10 per cent of female child killers were violent towards another person at the time of the homicide. This compared with 30 per cent of males, who, usually in such cases, targeted their female partner. The absence of multiple or secondary victims, however, reflects a situational feature of homicide by females, which is connected to their target preferences. Women are usually alone with their victim when they kill (Mann 1996). This, in turn, arises from the prominence of domestic situations in female violence. As Felson (1997b) observed, female involvement in violence, whether as perpetrators, victims or witnesses, is 'dominated by incidents of domestic violence' (p.217).

Felson further suggested that women's chances of involvement in violence, in any active or passive capacity, outside the home are substantially reduced by their 'risk aversion', which prompts precautionary behaviours (similarly, Kruttschnitt 1993). Thus Mann (1996) found that most murders were committed in the home where the female killer and the victim lived. Similarly, although the phenomenon of elder abuse has achieved recognition more as a social than a criminological problem, it is known that physical abuse is perpetrated by females within the home (Aitken and Griffin 1996; Brownell 1996). When others are present, in occasions of female violence outside the home, as in cases of stranger killings (Mann 1996) or robbery (Baskin and Sommers 1998; Miller 1998), they may be accomplices to the offence.

Relational contexts

The situational features of female violence suggest the importance of studying the relational context in which it arises. From this perspective, acts of violence perpetrated by women, which, initially, appear to be predominantly betrayals of intimate trust, assume a very different character. Commenting on female slayings of sexual intimates, Mann (1996) dispassionately remarks:

> [T]he victims in domestic cases appear to have been more likely candidates for homicide than the nondomestic victims... [A] substantial proportion of the domestic homicide victims had previous arrest records, especially prior violent arrest records. Also they were more likely to have been drinking before their deaths. It is possible that the personal lifestyle of these victims when combined with alcohol use proved to be lethal, particularly since victim precipitation was recorded in 83.7 percent of the domestic cases. (p.82)

Indeed, 'victim precipitation' of fatal assault has been recognised as a distinctive feature of female homicide of adults (Daly 1994). In the killing of sexual intimates, such precipitation is commonly found to involve an actual or threatened attack by a man who has previously battered the woman (Campbell 1995; Daly 1994; Shaw 1991). Such evidence as exists on non-fatal violence between intimates suggests a similar theme (Daly 1994).

Several commentators have suggested that attacks by females on strangers and acquaintances may frequently be viewed in terms of victim precipitation. For example, Baskin and Sommers (1998) argued that women living in disadvantaged urban environments are 'frequently thrust in violence-prone situations in which the victim enters as an active participant, shares the actor's role, and becomes functionally responsible for it' (p.123). Similarly, Maher and Curtis (1992, 1995) reported that for drug-involved women, for whom sex work was central to economic survival, violence was usually a response to actual or threatened harm in drug-dealing or sexual situations in which they were vulnerable. While observing that strangers killed by women were generally less likely to provoke their own victimisation, Mann (1996) nevertheless found cases in which the homicides were committed against male burglars attempting entry into the women's homes and cases in which the women were rape victims who killed their attackers.

The stressful environments in which female violence erupts within close relationships is differently illustrated in studies of child abuse. Mann (1996) confirmed the presence of common factors in child abuse in the killing of young children: mothers in such cases typically provided most of the child care, had entered an early marriage, had not wanted a child, lacked parenting skills and were socially isolated. Wilczynski (1997) reported that almost all the women in a study of child homicide were the primary or sole carers of their victims, with partners being either absent or unsupportive. Wilczynski concluded that 'filicidal women tend to kill after being burdened with too much responsibility for too long' (p.104).

VIOLENT FEMALE OFFENDERS

Age distribution

Several commentators have reported that female homicide offenders tend to be older than their male counterparts (Kruttschnitt 1993; Mann 1996). The peak age for female involvement in homicide, in the late twenties and thirties, has been attributed to their concentration of numbers in intra-familial killings. Wilczynski (1997) observed a relatively even distribution across the age range of females committing child homicide, linked to neonaticides by the very young and other killings by older women. For non-lethal violence and robbery, the age distribution for women more closely resembles that for men, being most prevalent among those aged between the mid-teens and twenties (Kruttschnitt 1993). Mann (1996) also noted that female non-domestic killers were younger than their domestic counterparts.

Baskin and Sommers (1998) observed that women may initiate violent crime early or later in their criminal careers. For those who began violent offending early, this activity was part of a youthful lifestyle in which a variety of offences and other deviant behaviours, such as truancy and substance use, occurred. For late onset women, however, entry into violent crime followed a previously non-violent criminal career involving 'gender-congruent activities' such as prostitution and shoplifting. Late onset was almost entirely driven by the economic demands of a severe drug habit.

Race

American research has shown a disproportionate involvement of black women in violent crime. Indeed, it appears that black women's involvement in homicide matches that of white men (e.g. Baskin and Sommers 1998). Caution is required, however, before assuming transferability of this finding across cultures. Kruttschnitt (1993) could find no evidence of unusually high rates of violence by black women outside of the United States, in either predominantly black or predominantly white countries.

Criminal histories

It seems that women, including violent offenders, accumulate fewer convictions than do men (Daly 1994). Wilczynski (1997) reported that male child killers were considerably more likely than females to have prior criminal convictions. Not only were males more likely to have multiple previous convictions but also to have convictions for violence itself.

Histories of abuse

Research into the social histories of female offenders repeatedly confirms the extent of physical, sexual and emotional abuse in their experience (see, for example, Chesney-Lind and Sheldon 1992). The depth of deprivation and abuse appears to be particularly pronounced among those who engage in violence (Baskin and Sommers 1993; Daly 1994; Roberts 1996). Saradjian (1996) noted, among the women in her study of female sexual abusers of children, not only extreme emotional deprivation during childhood but profound and prolonged sexual abuse. Moore and Hagedorn (1996) reported that girls who became gang members were more likely to come from 'underclass' families and to have run away from home than boys, whose working class backgrounds were more conventional (see also Joe 1995). For gang girls who progressed to heroin use, there was a particularly strong likelihood that they originated in violently and sexually abusive families, with parents who were themselves alcoholic or drug users. Moreover, experiences of abuse continue in adulthood for very many of these women (see, for example, Inciardi, Lockwood and Pottieger 1993; Maher and Curtis 1992). In many qualitative studies and biographical accounts the appalling descriptions of the prior beatings sustained by women who subsequently kill their partners seem to render their final retaliation toneless by comparison (see, for example, Ahluwalia and Gupta 1997; Browne 1987).

CHOOSING VIOLENCE

Criminologists have customarily distinguished between instrumental and expressive violence. Comparing instrumental (as in robbery motivated by economic need) with expressive violence, Decker (1996) explains: 'The frequency and intensity of interactions with persons one is intimately involved with creates circumstances that lead to disputes and potentially fatal violence of an expressive nature' (p.430). A theoretical account of homicide as the enactment of a 'character contest' (Luckenbill 1977), in which antagonists, encouraged by onlookers, fight to save face in the aftermath of public insult, has become a popular explanation of expressive violence (e.g. Felson and Steadman 1983).

Certain features of female violence already described encourage an assumption that it is primarily expressive – in particular, the preference for intimate targets and the predominantly domestic settings. Reports that, uniquely in the case of violence between intimates, the frequency of female perpetration matches that of men (Steinmetz 1977/8; Straus and Gelles 1986) give further credence to an interpretation of women's aggression as primarily expressing relational frustrations. Indeed, while men may typically attribute their violence to external causes, women more readily offer internal motivations (Vivian and Langhinrichsen-Rohling 1994). For example, Wilczynski (1997) noted the tendency for male child killers to present their action as a response to a disobedient or otherwise difficult child, while females more often referred to their own state of mind at the time of the slaying. This difference persisted even among actively psychotic parents, with men reporting delusions relating to the external world, such as being watched or followed, while women became absorbed into their internal worlds and gender roles – for example, in obsessional cleaning or believing themselves to be bad mothers.

Yet recognition that many female homicides of sexual intimates represent defence against attack, notwithstanding the anger which may be released in the act, challenges the clarity of the distinction between expressive and instrumental violence. The boundaries between these two types of action is further blurred by reports, described previously, that much female street violence, while occurring in the economic context of drug and sex selling, nevertheless has a defensive element. Thus Steffensmeier (1995) has remarked that commission of a 'masculine' crime does not necessarily entail a 'masculine' involvement. Mann (1996) questioned the relevance of the 'character contest' theory to female homicide, pointing out that most perpetrators were alone with their victims, while face-saving involves public embarrassment and that even when by-standers were present they did not encourage the woman. Indeed, a social psychological perspective might suggest that awareness of gender roles, which traditionally proscribe aggressiveness in females, would be heightened in public interactions (Eagly and Steffen 1986), thus inhibiting any such 'character contest'. Women, far more frequently than men, report guilt and anxiety about aggression and believe that their aggressive behaviours may present dangers to themselves (Eagly and Steffen 1986). Thus, when aggression is optional, women are more likely than men to elect an alternative behaviour (Eagly and Steffen 1986). How, then, do some women come to choose violence?

The apparent frequency of assaults by women on sexual intimates masks a qualitative point about attacks in such relationships. Within domestic violence, the injuries inflicted by males are more likely to involve a weapon (Straus, Gelles and Steinmetz 1980), to require medical attention (Morse 1995; Vivian and Langinrichsen-Rohling 1994) and to have adverse psychological impact (Vivian and Langinrichsen-Rohling 1994) than those inflicted by females. A greater proportion of female than male homicide victims are killed by a sexual partner (Home Office 1997). What, then, would motivate a woman to use lethal force?

Moral reasoning and learned expectancies for violence

Feminist perspectives have exposed the importance of relational involvement, rather than independence, to healthy female psychological development (Gilligan 1982, 1988a; Marcia 1980). Successful adaptation to adult life changes also depends, for women, on positive re-definition of identity within a relational context (Attanucci 1988; Willard 1988). Gilligan (1988b) concluded: 'Resistance to psychological illness among adolescent girls and adult women was, thus, associated with their ability to define care in terms that reflect experiences of authentic relationship or responsive engagement with others' (p.xxxiii). Such studies reveal the significance of women's relational worlds for their framing and resolution of moral choices. Reference groups are particularly important for the development of self-efficacy in females, who rely on external feedback and acceptance for their self-evaluation and self-esteem (Douvan and Adelson 1976; Garfinkel and Garner 1982).

Unsurprisingly, therefore, females experiencing abusive relationships invest a lot of time and cognitive effort in rationalising the abuse to themselves. Such attempts to explain the apparently inexplicable, particularly when the experience of abuse plays an integral part of formative learning about relationships, may demand considerable cognitive distortions. For example, Saradjian (1996) reported that women perpetrators of child sexual abuse apparently recognised in adulthood that their own experiences had been sexually abusive. Nevertheless, they often recalled that their abuser was their sole source of affection, or believed that they had been responsible for the abuse or in love with their abuser. Saradjian argued:

> Each woman perpetrator as a child had to, at least partially, assume pseudo-adult roles in relation to her carers. These pseudo-adult roles entailed fulfilling the carer's physical needs, emotional needs and/or sexual needs. The internalised models of the relationships between children and parents that these women assimilated would therefore most likely include the belief that a child's *raison d'etre* is to serve the needs of an adult, whatever those needs may be. (p.48)

Browne (1987) similarly commented on the integration of the experience of childhood physical abuse into the relational cognitions of women who were battered as adults. Moreover, attempts to find 'reasonable' explanations of violent attacks by intimate partners continued over long periods, even among women who had not experienced childhood abuse. Such rationalisations generate adaptive behaviours, aiming to reduce the frequency and intensity of, or to survive, the assaults. While the resulting behaviours appear objectively self-defeating, they may subjectively represent real efforts at relational problem-solving (Browne 1987; Dutton 1996; Gordon 1995). These problem-solving strategies must also be interpreted within a context in which the abused female sees no prospect of escape or aid and frequently reflect the failure of efforts to secure help (Browne 1987; Dutton 1996; Gordon 1995; Saradjian 1996). As Gordon (1995) observed: 'What would it mean to resist a father with no realistic chance of escaping one's dependence on him?' (p.287). Women choosing crime may thus already hold learned expectancies about the role of violence within relationships, not least its prominence in assertions of power and coercion.

Lifestyle

The choice of forms of economic crime which carry increased likelihood of violence may be contextualised within a lifestyle holding little prospect of advancement through legitimate employment (Baskin and Sommers 1998). Involvement in sex work and drug distribution, for example, heightens risk of participation in violence (Baskin and Sommers 1998; Maher and Curtis 1995). Baskin and Sommers (1998) pointed to the particular volatility of the crack-cocaine markets in severely disadvantaged urban areas in this respect, describing confrontations between dealers, robbery of customers and sexual aggression as commonplace in such environments (see also Inciardi, Lockwood and Pottieger 1993; Maher and Curtis 1992). Engulfment in such lifestyles entails the absorption of social roles and identities which are defined by deviant activities, including violence.

Aggressive skills

Effective use of violence requires a degree of competence in its enactment. Aggressive skills are more usually acquired within the context of male social and occupational roles (Eagly and Steffen 1986). Exposure to violence as witness or victim does not necessarily offer an effective learning experience for its perpetration. Indeed, Mann (1996) noted that in many cases of homicide by females there was little evidence of expertise in the use of force or weaponry. Death, which often followed a single shot or stab, might, Mann suggested, be better explained by delay in accessing medical services.

Where willingness to use violence is part of a lifestyle choice, females are more likely to be involved in a social network in which fighting skills can be learned. For example, Campbell (1991) noted the coaching and approval available to girl gang members, alongside positive expectations that violence will be used by females in particular situations. Miller (1998) described robbery strategies in which women manipulate gender role expectations antithetical to female violence in order to enhance the element of surprise in an attack. Where violence is not an accomplishment, however, context-specific motivations may be required to account for its invocation, particularly where potentially lethal force is used.

Motivations for violence

Motivations for violent offending may not be gender-specific. For example, Baskin and Sommers (1998) reported that, for early initiates into robbery, violence was one aspect of a lifestyle choice in which the primary rewards were expressive: thrills, excitement and peer approval (also Miller 1998). Instrumental motivations appeared to be secondary, although not unimportant, considerations. However, similar offending, whether initiated or continued later in life, was promoted by the economic demands of drug addiction. Wright and Decker (1997) describe similar motivational shifts among male robbers. Within such lifestyles, also, women were prepared to invoke violence for revenge or face-saving after a perceived wrong. Indeed, in unpredictable environments violence was an established mechanism for regulating social behaviour (Baskin and Sommers 1998).

For particular offences, however, motivations may be more strongly mediated by gender. Wilczynski (1997) identified clear gender bias in the motives professed by child killers. Men were more likely to explain the homicide in terms of retaliation, jealousy and discipline, while women's accounts predominantly invoked an unwanted child, altruism or mental illness. Even apparently similar motivations showed gender differences. For example, killing a child in retaliation for anger provoked by the adult partner reflected, among men, an extension of their power and control in intimate relationships. Female retaliators appeared rather to be protesting their lack of power, including resentment of the male partner's abuse or lack of support. Alder and Baker (1997) also noted that where anger was a feature of homicide by mothers, death was not intended. In most such cases the mothers were young, unsupported, experiencing a variety of severe social, psychological and health problems and had previously assaulted the child.

Neonaticide, or killing of an infant within 24 hours of birth, appears to be almost exclusively committed by females. It seems inappropriate to represent it solely as an aggressive act. It is typically characterised by the mother's youth, her fear of disclosing the pregnancy, consequent denial of it to herself and others, failure to prepare for the birth and, subsequently, inefficient attempts to conceal the body (Alder and Baker 1997; Wilczynski 1997).

Altruism, as a motive for child homicide, may be prompted by real or imagined suffering on the part of the child and by deep feelings of inadequacy as a parent (Wilczynski 1997). Alder and Baker (1997) also reported a number of murders followed by completed or attempted suicide, in which the mother was coping alone or with an abusive partner, was experiencing multiple difficulties and usually believed that she was acting in the child's best interests.

Finally, self-defence appears to be one of the strongest motivators for female aggression (Mann 1996). This was clearly implied in the previous examination of the precursors to women's violence. It was also seen that certain lifestyles heighten vulnerability to attack, thus provoking defensive violence, notwithstanding any general acceptance of aggression as a means to achieving particular ends. For women who lack skills in violent perpetration, Browne (1987) describes the cognitive changes which promote a decision to use lethal force in a persistently abusive intimate relationship: belief that threats to kill the woman or others are sincere; expectation that death will follow another attack; recognition of abuse or endangerment of a child; and loss of hope of relief.

The conditions in which women engage in serious violence thus appear to be extreme. Female violence emerges within a context of familiarity with violence as witness and/or victim. It is often a response to strong, frequently repeated provocation which threatens personal safety. Attacks on weaker victims, particularly children, reflect profound and multiple psychological, social and economic difficulties. Where female violence reflects a lifestyle choice, that choice is made in the context of deep and chronic social and personal disadvantage. As Chesney-Lind, Sheldon and Joe (1996) remark: 'Girls' gang life is certainly not an expression of "liberation", but instead reflects the attempts of young women to cope with a bleak and harsh present as well as a dismal future' (p.203). Baskin and Sommers' (1998) study of women who initiate violent offending as a lifestyle choice must also be understood within a highly stressed environment of urban poverty in which a volatile and dangerous crack-cocaine market dominates the informal economy (also Maher and Curtis 1992). The unusual rates of violent offending by black American women appear to emerge in their disproportionate exposure to such extreme conditions (Baskin and Sommers 1998; Kruttschnitt 1993; Maher and Curtis 1992). It is sobering to note that the only other environment to be portrayed as promoting unusual levels of violence, often in previously non-violent women, is that of the prison (Mandaraka-Sheppard 1986; Stevens 1998).

TOWARDS KNOWLEDGE-BASED INTERVENTION STRATEGIES

The foregoing discussion suggests three potential foci for interventions with violent female offenders: their learned expectancies for violence; their motivational accounts of aggression; and their strategies for offence commission. However, the selection of focus and method of intervention requires individualised understanding of the historical background to, and situational context of, the offending. The intense, context-specific relational problems which underpin much serious female violence suggest that offence gravity may not necessarily be a reliable predictor of repetition. Equally, the distorted priorities of the social and economic conditions in which repeated violence has been found to emerge suggest that desistance may have as much to do with multi-faceted alterations in lifestyle (Baskin and Sommers 1998) as with management of personal aggression. This review of current knowledge about the historical, situational and motivational characteristics of female violence offers some gender-specific perspectives on the elements of meaningful intervention.

Life trajectories and criminal involvement

The 'typical' age distribution of violent crime appears to be a predominantly male phenomenon. For females, there seem to be several, offence-specific age distributions. Underlying these age variations there are different life trajectories to the choice of particular forms of violent crime and to repeated recourse to aggression. Age also reflects the different relational worlds of younger and older women, and the immediate significance of those worlds for their aggressive acts. Thus a primary focus on 'typical' violent crime, which largely concentrates on young male lifestyles, will overlook these nuances in women's pathways to violence and offer solutions which are unadapted to the social and psychological realities implied by their age status.

Situational contexts of violence

The solitary nature of much serious female violence requires us to relinquish favoured notions of aggression as a character contest fought in defence of public 'face'. Interventions which focus on non-aggressive styles of self-presentation and management of conflict in public places will have relevance only for the violent choices of some groups of female offenders. Moreover, interventions which assume that aggression concerns provocation by complete or relative strangers will overlook the salience of close relationships in the production of female violence. Interventions which emphasise independence, individuation and resistance to peer pressure will neglect the importance of relational involvement in the moral reasoning of females (Gilligan 1982, 1988a; Bardige *et al.* 1988). Thus meaningful interventions must focus on the privately negotiated relational worlds of women who elect violence as a means of regulating interactions with significant others.

Denial

Some contemporary approaches to criminal justice intervention encourage challenges to denial, which is viewed as evasion of personal choice and responsibility (see, for example, Knopp 1989; Weisner and Room 1984). Denial appears as a recurrent theme in studies of women who become involved in violence, both as perpetrators and victims: young women who kill their infants have denied their pregnancy (Alder and Baker 1997; Wilczynski 1997);

battered women deny the intensity of their partners' attacks (Petretic-Jackson and Jackson 1996). Yet to confront denial would fail, in such instances, to recognise the extent to which it has been central to coping with insoluble difficulties. Denial has been one of the problem-solving strategies through which women have coped with crisis (Wilczynski 1997). Interventions intended to alert women to the risks inherent in their situations are unlikely to rely on confrontation, which may instead achieve defensive entrenchment.

Moreover, the prominence of victim precipitation in analyses of female violence challenges an assumption that other-blaming by perpetrators must represent an evasion of personal responsibility. The therapeutic problem thus may be redefined in terms of appreciating the reality of victim precipitation in female recourse to violence without discarding personal responsibility. Challenging and confrontative approaches to apparent blame avoidance and denial of full responsibility may fail to acknowledge the interpersonal complexity of a woman's attempts at explanation.

Re-interpreted as experiences of inability to control a propulsion into violence, defined by powerlessness to influence events or the behaviour of significant others, positive approaches to denial appear to require primarily the establishment of some confidence in personal efficacy.

Anger management

Theoretical approaches to 'typical' male violence often provide accounts of episodic, situationally inspired aggressive explosions. Techniques for anger management in provocative situations, therefore, offer relevant enhancements of personal efficacy. Yet the application of such analyses and interventions to effective comprehension and modification of female aggression is questionable. For example, viewed against a background of repeated and escalating victimisation, women's homicide of their abusive male partners appears to represent less an acute failure of anger management than a chronic failure of self-protection. Even within the context of apparently situationally inspired opportunism provided by street-level sex work, Maher and Curtis (1995) observed that much female violence culminated out of a longer sequence of events which often involved victimisation or bullying by a male. Again, in such circumstances, female perpetrators seem to have been 'managing' their anger for an appreciable period of time before electing a violent response.

These observations do not imply that anger is not an issue in female aggression. They do, however, suggest a perspective which recognises that, in many instances, female violence is not an early choice. Rather, through unsuccessful attempts at non-violent resolutions of relational conflict, women may come to perceive that they have progessively eliminated the possibilities for alternative strategies, or that their victim no longer merits their tolerance.

An application of this appreciation of female anger as accruing over time and repeated provocation is suggested by Hamberger and Potente (1994), who present anger as an energy source for problem solving. Hamberger and Potente further suggest that victimised women need help to learn effective skills in positive self-assertion and self-protection rather than in self-restraint.

Responsibility

Several commentators have deplored the negation of responsibility in professional characterisations of female offenders (see, for example, Allen 1987). Yet refusal to acknowledge histories of abuse, profound social and psychological stress and situational provocation seems equally to repudiate the realities within which women choose violence. The problem for professionals working with violent women must be to reconcile appreciation of such factors with recognition of a capacity for personal responsibility.

The key to this may lie in a future-oriented approach which engages the woman in active preparation to alleviate and manage the accumulation of stressors which have facilitated her choice of violence. As Dutton (1996) remarks:

> [E]ven within the most egregious of abusive circumstances, some personal choices remain. Although some behaviors are clearly limited by obstacles and events beyond the battered woman's control, one of the goals of advocacy and mental health intervention with battered women should be to increase the range of those choices. (p.120)

Risk management

Effective risk management with violent female offenders may not take the form of proactive, professional assessment, monitoring and intervention that is represented in much of the literature (see, for example, Harris, Clear and Baird 1989; Webster *et al.* 1994). In such perspectives it is the professional's task to observe risk indicators and to exert increased surveillance and control. Meaningful risk management, however, in many female cases, may more relevantly translate into the transfer to the woman herself of effective self-monitoring, self-protection and risk-reduction skills. Self-monitoring skills include enabling the woman to recognise her own risk of harm within particular relationships and situations, and the significance of changes in victimisation, reduced tolerance level and isolation from social support networks (Campbell 1995; Petretic-Jackson and Jackson 1996). Risk-reduction skills may include strategies for non-aggressive self-assertion, enhancing personal safety and accessing appropriate support systems within a domestic environment and intimate relationship (Hamberger and Potente 1994; Petretic-Jackson and Jackson 1996).

This approach to risk management acknowledges both the reality of risks of harm in the woman's relational environment and the likelihood that the woman will be alone at the point of choosing violence. External controls on her recourse to violence are, therefore, problematic. Moreover, the approach recognises the woman as a responsible actor by requiring her to identify, regulate and reduce the stressors which promote the likelihood of her own violence. Risk management, thus, may take the practical forms of enhancing safety and self-efficacy.

This is not to argue that women should take responsibility for their victimisation experiences but rather that they may take responsibility for the legacy of those experiences in terms of their future choices. To avoid this professional challenge is to deepen the risks of both victimisation and violence, and to deny women opportunities for personal growth via the criminal justice system which are commonly offered to men. Thus, for example, Hamberger and Potente (1994) describe the decision to offer a court-ordered programme to battered women charged with domestic violence under recent mandatory arrest legislation in America:

> [M]ale batterers were often ordered to counseling with the added incentive of reduced fines or dropped or reduced charges. By not providing intervention alternatives and incentives to domestically violent women, the system was operating unfairly and sending a very negative message: Women could expect to be dealt with *more* harshly than men. (p.130)

CONCLUSION

Intervention strategies targeted at violent women must be adapted to significant historical, situational and motivational issues in female aggression. Appreciation of these factors in the emergence of women's violence also forces an appraisal of the appropriate sources, types and timing of professional intervention. For example, if battered women are likely to kill their partners after a considerable period of attempts to tolerate and moderate their victimisation, unlikely to have previous convictions for serious violence and unlikely, given the unique circumstances of their offence, to commit another homicide, *post hoc* training in anger management techniques will be simply too late. Having reached that point, more benefit may be derived from interventions aimed at alleviating the physical and psychological damage of prolonged victimisation and the trauma of offence commission. If, however, the professional objective is to prevent such an outcome of domestic violence, criminal justice agencies, such as the prison and probation services, are not themselves well placed to achieve it directly. Greater effectiveness will surely be gained from outreach and self-protection, self-efficacy and risk-reduction programmes undertaken by community organisations likely to contact abused women, including, for example, battered women's shelters and women's counselling agencies. The final message of the knowledge base collated here, then, must be to demonstrate the need for imaginative and effective multi-agency alliances and initiatives which may meaningfully integrate appreciation of the interactive nature of victimisation and violence in female aggression.

REFERENCES

Adler, F. (1975) *Sisters in Crime: The Rise of the New Female Criminal.* New York: McGraw-Hill.

Ahluwalia, K. and Gupta, R. (1997) *Circle of Light: The Autobiography of Kiranjit Ahluwalia.* London: HarperCollins.

Aitken, L. and Griffin, G. (1996) *Gender Issues in Elder Abuse.* London: Sage.

Alder, C.M. and Baker, J. (1997) 'Maternal filicide: more than one story to be told.' *Women and Criminal Justice*, 9(2), 15–39.

Allen, H. (1987) 'Rendering them harmless: the professional portrayal of women charged with serious violent crimes.' In P. Carlen and A. Worrall (eds) *Gender, Crime and Justice.* Milton Keynes: Open University Press.

Attanucci, J. (1988) 'In whose terms: a new perspective on self, role and relationship.' In C. Gilligan, J.V. Ward and J.M. Taylor (eds) *Mapping the Moral Domain.* Cambridge: Harvard University Press.

Bardige, B., Ward, J.V., Gilligan, C., Taylor, J.M. and Cohen, G. (1988) 'Moral concerns and considerations of urban youth.' In C. Gilligan, J.V. Ward and J.M. Taylor (eds) *Mapping the Moral Domain.* Cambridge: Harvard University Press.

Baskin, D.R. and Sommers, I.B. (1998) *Casualties of Community Disorder: Women's Careers in Violent Crime.* Boulder: Westview Press.

Browne, A. (1987) *When Battered Women Kill.* New York: MacMillan.

Brownell, P. (1996) 'Social work and criminal justice responses to elder abuse in New York City.' In A.R. Roberts (ed) *Helping Battered Women: New Perspectives and Remedies.* New York: Oxford University Press.

Campbell, A. (1991) *The Girls in the Gang.* Second Edition. Oxford: Basil Blackwell.

Campbell, J.C. (1995) 'Prediction of homicide of and by battered women.' In J.C. Campbell (ed) *Assessing Dangerousness: Violence by Sexual Offenders, Batterers, and Child Abusers.* London: Sage.

Chesney-Lind, M. (1995a) 'Rethinking women's imprisonment: a critical examination of trends in female incarceration.' In B.R. Price and N.J. Sokoloff (eds) *The Criminal Justice System and Women: Offenders, Victims, and Workers.* Second edition. New York: McGraw-Hill.

Chesney-Lind, M. (1995b) 'Girls, delinquency and juvenile justice: toward a feminist theory of young women's crime.' In B.R. Price and N.J. Sokoloff (eds) *The Criminal Justice System and Women: Offenders, Victims, and Workers.* Second edition. New York: McGraw-Hill.

Chesney-Lind, M. and Sheldon, R.G. (1992) *Girls, Delinquency, and Juvenile Justice.* Pacific Grove: Brooks/Cole.

Chesney-Lind, M., Sheldon, R.G. and Joe, K.A. (1996) 'Girls, delinquency and gang membership.' In C.R. Huff (ed) *Gangs In America.* Second Edition. Thousand Oaks, Sage.

Daly, K. (1994) *Gender, Crime, and Punishment.* New Haven: Yale University Press.

Decker, S. H. (1996) 'Deviant homicide: a new look at the role of motives and victim-offender relationships.' *Journal of Research in Crime and Delinquency*, 33, 4, 427–449.

Douvan, E. and Adelson, J. (1976) *The Adolescent Experience.* New York: John Wiley.

Dutton, M.A. (1996) 'Battered women's strategic response to violence: the role of context.' In J.L. Edleson and Z.C. Eisikovits (eds) *Future Interventions with Battered Women and their Families.* Thousand Oaks: Sage.

Eagly, A.H. and Steffen, V.J. (1986) 'Gender and aggressive behavior: a meta-analytic review of the social psychological literature.' *Psychological Bulletin*, 100, 3, 309–330.

Felson, R.B. (1997a) 'Anger, aggression and violence in love triangles.' *Violence and Victims*, 12, 4, 345–362.

Felson, R.B. (1997b) 'Routine activities and involvement in violence as actor, witness or target.' *Violence and Victims*, 12, 3, 209–221.

Felson, R.B. and Steadman, H.J. (1983) 'Situational factors in disputes leading to criminal violence.' *Criminology*, 21, 1, 59–74.

Garfinkel, P. and Garner, D. (1982) *Anorexia Nervosa: A Multidimensional Perspective*. New York: Brunner/Mazel.

Gilligan, C. (1982) *In a Different Voice*. Cambridge: Harvard University Press.

Gilligan, C. (1988a) 'Exit-voice dilemmas in adolescent development.' In C. Gilligan, J.V. Ward and J.M. Taylor (eds) *Mapping the Moral Domain*. Cambridge: Harvard University Press.

Gilligan, C. (1988b) 'Prologue: adolescent development reconsidered.' In C. Gilligan, J.V. Ward and J.M. Taylor (eds) *Mapping the Moral Domain*. Cambridge: Harvard University Press.

Gordon, L. (1995) 'Incest and resistance: patterns of father–daughter incest.' In B.R. Price and N.J. Sokoloff (eds) *The Criminal Justice System and Women: Offenders, Victims, and Workers*. Second edition. New York: McGraw-Hill.

Hamberger, L.K. and Potente, T. (1994) 'Counseling heterosexual women arrested for domestic violence: implications for theory and practice.' *Violence and Victims*, 9, 2, 125–137.

Harris, P.M., Clear, T.R. and Baird, S.C. (1989) 'Have community supervision officers changed their attitudes toward their work?' *Justice Quarterly*, 6, 2, 233–46.

Home Office (1997) *Criminal Statistics England and Wales: Supplementary Tables 1996 Vol. 2: Proceedings in the Crown Court*. London: Home Office.

Inciardi, J.A., Lockwood, D. and Pottieger, A. (1993) *Women and Crack-cocaine*. New York: Macmillan.

Joe, K.A. (1995) '"Ice is strong enough for a man but made for a woman": a social cultural analysis of crystal methamphetamine use among Asian Pacific Americans.' *Crime, Law and Social Change*, 22, 3, 269–289.

Knopp, F.H. (1989) 'Northwest treatment associates: a comprehensive, community-based evaluation and treatment program for adult sex offenders.' In P.C. Kratcoski (ed) *Correctional Counseling and Treatment*. Second Edition. Prospect Heights: Waveland Press.

Kruttschnitt, C. (1993) 'Violence by and against women: a comparative and cross-national analysis.' *Violence and Victims*, 8, 3, 253–270.

Luckenbill, D.F. (1977) 'Criminal homicide as a situated transaction.' *Social Problems*, 25, 176–186.

Maher, L. and Curtis, R. (1992) 'Women on the edge of crime: crack cocaine and the changing contexts of street-level sex work in New York City.' *Crime, Law and Social Change*, 18, 3, 221–258.

Maher, L. and Curtis, R. (1995) 'In search of the female urban "Gangsta": change, culture, and crack cocaine.' In B.R. Price and N.J. Sokoloff (eds) *The Criminal Justice System and Women: Offenders, Victims, and Workers*. Second edition. New York: McGraw-Hill.

Mandaraka-Sheppard, A. (1986) *The Dynamics of Aggression in Women's Prisons in England*. Aldershot: Gower.

Mann, C.R. (1996) *When Women Kill*. Albany: State University of New York Press.

Marcia, J. (1980) 'Identity in adolescence.' In J. Adelson (ed) *Handbook of Adolescent Psychology*. New York: John Wiley.

Miller, J. (1998) 'Up it up: gender and the accomplishment of street robbery.' *Criminology*, 36, 1, 37–66.

Moore, J.W. and Hagedorn, J.M. (1996) 'What happens to girls in the gang?' In C.R. Huff (ed) *Gangs In America*. Second Edition. Thousand Oaks: Sage.

Morse, B.J. (1995) 'Beyond the conflict tactics scale: assessing gender differences in partner violence.' *Violence and Victims*, 10, 4, 251–272.

Petretic-Jackson, P. and Jackson, T. (1996) 'Mental health interventions with battered women.' In A.R. Roberts (ed) *Helping Battered Women: New Perspectives and Remedies*. New York: Oxford University Press.

Roberts, A.R. (1996) 'A comparative analysis of incarcerated battered women and a community sample of battered women.' In A.R. Roberts (ed) *Helping Battered Women: New Perspectives and Remedies*. New York: Oxford University Press.

Saradjian, J. (1996) *Women who Sexually Abuse Children: From Research to Clinical Practice*. Chichester: John Wiley and Sons.

Shaw, M. (1991) *Paying the Price: Federally Sentenced Women in Context*. Ottawa: Solicitor General Canada.

Simon, R.J. and Landis, J. (1991) *The Crimes Women Commit, The Punishments They Receive*. Lexington: MA, Lexington Books.

Steffensmeier, D. (1995) 'Trends in female crime: it's still a man's world.' In B.R. Price and N.J. Sokoloff (eds) *The Criminal Justice System and Women: Offenders, Victims, and Workers*. Second edition. New York: McGraw-Hill.

Steinmetz, S.K. (1977/78) 'The battered husband syndrome.' *Victimology*, 3/4, 499–509.

Stevens, D.J. (1998) 'The impact of time-served and regime on prisoners' anticipation of crime: female prisonisation effects.' *The Howard Journal of Criminal Justice*, 37, 2, 188–205.

Straus, M.A. and Gelles, R.J. (1986) 'Societal change and change in family violence from 1975 to 1985 as revealed by two national surveys.' *Journal of Marriage and the Family*, 48, 465–480.

Strauss, M.A., Gelles, R.J. and Steinmetz, S.K. (1980) *Behind Closed Doors: Violence in the American Family*. New York: Doubleday/Anchor.

Vivian, D. and Langhinrichsen-Rohling, J. (1994) 'Are bi-directionally violent couples mutually victimized? A gender-sensitive comparison.' *Violence and Victims*, 9, 2, 107–124.

Webster, C.D., Harris, G.T., Rice, M.E., Cormier, C. and Quinsey, V.L. (1994) *The Violence Prediction Scheme: Assessing Dangerousness in High Men*. Toronto: University of Toronto, Centre of Criminology.

Weisner, C. and Room, R. (1984) 'Financing and ideology in alcohol treatment.' *Social Problems*, 32, 2, 167–184.

Wilczynski, A. (1997) *Child Homicide*. London: Greenwich Medical Media.

Willard, A. (1988) 'Cultural scripts for mothering.' In C. Gilligan, J.V. Ward and J.M. Taylor (eds) *Mapping the Moral Domain*. Cambridge: Harvard University Press.

CHAPTER 7

South-Asian Young Women's Experiences of Violence and Abuse

Umme Farvah Imam

INTRODUCTION

Over the past few decades the women's movement world-wide has raised the issue of violence against women on a global level. There has been a profusion of research and knowledge which has contributed significantly to our understanding of women's experiences as victims and survivors of male violence. In Britain research has primarily been dominated by Western feminist theory, which has proved inadequate and inappropriate in considering the experiences of black[1] women in general and South-Asian women in particular (Mama 1988). There is a paucity of research on the experiences of young South-Asian women and girls, and little attention is given to the significance of racism, ethnicity, patriarchal and religious systems which compound their experience of abuse and violence. Myths and stereotypes about young Asian women, the media preoccupation with arranged/forced marriages (*The Guardian*, 25 March 1996) and 'culture conflicts' and 'clashes' contribute to racialising the discourse on these young women (Ahmed 1986; Ahmad 1990; Mama 1988; Anthias and Yuval-Davis 1992). Anecdotal and practice evidence suggests that South-Asian women and girls experience specific problems in relation to domestic and family violence (Guru 1986) in addition to the

1 I use the term 'black' to refer to all non-white people who suffer discrimination and oppression based on skin colour in Britain and who use it as a 'term of political self-description and cultural counter-assertion' (Cambridge 1996).

patriarchal racism (Brah 1992) they experience as members of black communities in Britain.

This chapter draws from an exploratory study which was aimed at identifying the key issues that were significant in the abuse of young South-Asian women living in Britain. The research came as a result of work with South-Asian women generally and with young women specifically, in both youth work and refuge settings. The issues raised in developing work with young women, their over-representation in refuges and the demand and establishment of several single women's hostels specifically for young women of South-Asian heritage (source: personal contacts, communication with South-Asian refuges), both locally and nationally, highlighted the need to identify the factors that were critical and distinctive in their experiences. An understanding of these specific issues is essential in order to inform the development of appropriate and effective policy and practice responses. Group work and interviews with young women, practitioners and research participants in the study reveal a complex web of interacting influences at the individual, family, communal and societal levels which make their experience of abuse and control significantly different from both white and male counterparts. The analysis is based on participants' perceptions of the ways in which the power relations within the wider society complicate the issues and limit their choices and opportunities for contesting and challenging their situations. I consider how race, gender, ethnicity and social class interact to shape these experiences and argue that this complexity needs to be examined through a polycentric understanding of their historical, social, cultural and political realities (Brah 1992).

TERMINOLOGY

I use the term 'South-Asian' to refer to women of Bangladeshi, Indian and Pakistani heritage, including those who have come to Britain via East Africa. South-Asian women in Britain are an extremely diverse group whose individual experiences are shaped by their age, gender, class/caste, religion, cultural practices and traditions, and rural-urban origins, as well as their common experience of colonialism, racism and similar patriarchal systems (Brah 1992).

Even at an exploratory level, the wide range of experiences reported as coercive, dominating or abusive throws up interesting issues for the terminology and definitions currently in use to describe abuse of women in the family. The term 'domestic violence' or its American equivalent, 'woman abuse', are limited as they refer to abuse in intimate relationships and do not cover the range of experiences reported. Liz Kelly (1988) provides useful terminology to examine the 'continuum of sexual violence' perpetrated against women by men. She widens her definition to include any physical, visual, verbal, or sexual act that is experienced by the woman or girl, at the time or later, as a threat, invasion or assault, that has the effect of hurting her or degrading her and/or takes away her ability to control intimate contact (Kelly 1988, p.41).

However, the fact that she is exploring the continuum of 'sexual violence' against women and girls and her predominantly white sample inevitably limits its application to young women of South-Asian heritage. The terms currently in use to name abuse of women and girls are problematic as they all imply sexual relationship (past or present) between the abuser and the abused. In considering the abuse of young South-Asian women it is important to recognise two factors: that the abuse may or may not be sexual – it is, nevertheless, a violation of their person and that the abuser need not necessarily be male – and white women (racial abuse) or other black women (power relations based on age and/or relationship and tradition) could be perpetrators of abuse and violence.

Other terms, which, on face value, seem relevant, become inappropriate when applied to South-Asian women as they have been conceived entirely from Western-centric perspectives. One such example is the term 'family violence'. Richard Gelles and Moray Strauss are the most prominent proponents of the family violence approach (Gelles 1985, 1993; Gelles and Strauss 1988; Strauss 1980; Strauss and Gelles 1986). This social structural approach to violence in the family identifies the source of violence in the ideology of the modern nuclear family. Rooted in Western perspectives on the individual and family, it is limited in its relevance to people who do not share the ethos and values of individualism. South-Asian people belong to collectivistic cultures where the individual is seen as interdependent and related to others and not autonomous and separated from others (Imam 1999). Robinson (1995) contends that it is extremely difficult to understand the lifestyles of black people using theories developed by whites to explain whites. What is needed is a framework which is reflective of the social, political and psychocultural systems they inhabit.

THE EXPLORATORY STUDY

Methodology

Work with young South-Asian women in youth work and refuge settings highlighted several issues and concerns which are quite specific to their experience and distinct from those of their peers – both male and white. In order to establish these, their range, significance and relative importance, it was essential to adopt a qualitative approach which would provide a knowledge and awareness of these factors drawn from the young women's perspectives. Kelly (1988) asserts that it is important not to pre-determine the meaning of events for women and that it is only by understanding women's experiences of violence and abuse from their own perspectives should we endeavour to categorise and classify. In order to establish the factors and issues significant in their abuse, ten women were contacted through refuges and hostels who had sought help from welfare agencies due to abuse either within the family and community or wider society. Informal interviews were used to identify and understand how the women made sense of their experiences, the meanings they ascribed to them and the ways in which they accepted, negotiated and/or contested their situations. The sample, though small, was representative of the different Asian communities in Britain and included Pakistani (Muslim), Bangladeshi (Muslim), Indian (Sikh), Kenyan (Hindu) and Kenyan (Muslim) women. The majority of the women were born in Britain (8), one had migrated from the Indian sub-continent following marriage to a British citizen and another had emigrated from East Africa as a child. Seven women were single and, of the other three, two were in the process of leaving their husbands. The ages of the women ranged from sixteen to twenty-five years.

The recognition that some of the issues emerging from these interviews were significant to young South Asian women generally highlighted the need to explore these with a general sample. This was done through organising focus groups for young women in both youth group and social settings. The aim was to include women from the three major communities – Bangladeshi, Indian and Pakistani – in order to draw out the commonalties and differences in experiences. The three focus groups were drawn from these communities and 26 young women participated. These focus groups were not entirely representative of the diverse configurations within these communities in relation to class, disability or sexual orientation. For example, they did not include any women who were second migrants (from East Africa) and the focus group including women of Indian origin consisted predominantly of women from Sikh communities.

The range of experiences reported

Of the ten women interviewed, experiences of violence and control were considerably diverse. These included: domestic violence; rape by a white male; sexual abuse by a distant cousin; sexual abuse by brother-in-law (husband's brother); physical and emotional abuse by males in the family – father, brother, uncle, father-in-law; physical abuse by women in the family – mother-in-law, mother, sister; white peers, husband's white girlfriend; sexual harassment and threats to single woman living alone by both white and black males.

The focus groups threw up some interesting issues that had not emerged as clearly from the interviews. Primarily, they revealed perceptions of male and family domination; distinct gender roles and differentiation in parental attitudes and behaviour towards male and female young people; a strong sense of obligation to the family for emotional and financial resources; the significance of arranged marriages and fear of forced marriages; religious and cultural practices. The experiences of coercion, domination and control established a complex pattern of inter-connections between age, gender, ethnicity, class, patterns of migration, religion and cultural practices and the intersections of these with racism and patriarchal dominance in the wider society.

PATRIARCHAL RACISM AND ABUSE IN PUBLIC SPACES

An analysis of the experiences of abuse and violence reported by the young women indicates the impact of wider societal influences and structures on individual experiences. The complex interconnections between racism and patriarchal relations in society at large and the cultural norms and traditions of particular families and communities emerge as distinctive features of their experience. The experiences reported illustrate the ways in which race and gender interact to compound the abuse they suffered as women.

Most members of the focus group and interviewees highlighted the interaction of race and gender with specific reference to abuse in public places. With reference to women generally, Hanmer and Saunders (1984) demonstrate how fear of violence in public places restricts women's movements outside the home and results in greater dependency on men, thus exposing them to male assault within the home and by known men. In relation to South-Asian (and other black) women the public/private dichotomy is neither as clear cut nor completely reflective of their experiences of living in a racist society. The young women participants reported that fear of violence in public places was more of a reality and an issue with reference to their race rather than gender – the majority of young women in both samples (with the exception of two) reported that danger in public places was perceived generally due to their 'race', where they were more likely to face abuse, both verbal and physical, from white women and men. Cultural restrictions were the main reason given: they would rarely be out unaccompanied or apart from a group and, therefore, less vulnerable to sexual abuse in public places. The exceptions to this were those young women who were being harassed by young South-Asian men from fundamentalist religious groups that were hounding them to return to families. Some women also spoke about young men from their communities who took it upon themselves to control women's movements in public places – for example, colleges and universities. A young Muslim woman described how she had to stop going to college and take up a distance-learning course due to harassment by these students, who felt that she was contravening religious and communal prescription.

Perceptions of parental control over movements outside the home acknowledged that their personal safety, in addition to gender issues, may prompt such control. However, they also expressed their concerns of how this fear of racial and sexual crime outside the home could be/was used to restrict and 'control' them generally. Stanko (1988) maintains that 'the myth of the safe home helps to maintain and reproduce society's binders, obscuring many of women's widespread experiences of male violence within the home' (p.75). She goes on to explain how criminologists create the public-private dichotomy which links public spaces with danger and private spaces with safety. For South-Asian women, in addition to white 'society's binders', their freedom of movement was further curtailed by their ethnicity, which, for most, seemed to bring about greater restrictions through confining and isolating them within the home and family. They were thus more vulnerable to violation and abuse, primarily from men in the home and family but also, in some cases, by other women.

Most of the participants in the focus groups reported both verbal and physical abuse in school, college and youth club settings by white males and, more significantly, by white females. In the case of the latter, it was experienced as more emotionally and psychologically debilitating as it was continuous, usually taking place over a prolonged period and not restricted to specific incidents like the former. Two interviewees reported physical/sexual abuse in a public place. The first, a twenty-year-old woman of Pakistani origin, was beaten up by her husband in a shopping centre when he caught up with her after she had escaped from his cruelty and taken shelter in a refuge in another town. She was then dragged to his car in full view of other shoppers. The security guards at the shopping centre and a policeman all stood by and watched the happenings without any attempt to intervene or assist the woman, despite the fact that her companions from the refuge appealed to the policeman and the security guards for help.

This example illustrates the interplay between cultural racism and sexism. The police and security guards will often intercede in fights between males in public places. In this case non-intervention may be due to the fact that it was a South-Asian woman being physically assaulted by a South-Asian man.

The second example is of a young woman who had left home due to physical abuse by her father, who was against her pursuing her studies in college and who was arranging her marriage in Pakistan. The experience of Samia, who was raped by a white fellow student, is given below.

Samia (Pakistani Muslim), nineteen years of age, had left home at eighteen due to 'parental control' and the refusal of her family to let her go into further education and pressure to get married. She spent a few days with a white school friend who had gone to university in another town. Fear of her family tracing her prompted her to find accommodation in a hostel for young people in a neighbouring city, which had an extremely low South-Asian population. She enrolled at a local college and developed a network of friends, predominantly white, in the college and hostel. One evening, following a night out with a group of young people, she was assaulted in a park (taking a short-cut to her hostel) by one of the white men in the group, who followed and raped her. She left the hostel the following day to go into an Asian women's refuge in yet another town.

Samia talked at length about the ten months she spent in the hostel. Although there was support from the workers and some of the residents, she felt tremendous pressure from her friends of both sexes to have sexual relationships. The dilemma for her was that if she did not go out with the others, she would be extremely isolated. As she wanted to enjoy herself and socialise with the others, she thought that there would be safety in numbers and, therefore, would go out in a group with other young people from the hostel and from college:

> I didn't think that this could happen in broad daylight… I had often taken that short-cut, and though initially I felt apprehensive when I was crossing one particular place due to the thick bushes, this was usually when it was late… I didn't even think that he would be waiting there for me that day…

When interviewed, Samia was living in a refuge and trying to come to terms with her experience. She had often thought about going back to the family once she had completed college but, after her ordeal, she felt that she could not possibly face her parents and family, although she felt that the support of her family and friends would have undoubtedly helped her in coping with her experience. There was also an element of self-blame for defying her parents and seeking to be independent – she had paid a very high price for that independence. Being with other women from a similar cultural background was helping her in re-building her self-worth and coping effectively with her abuse. Sometime in the future, when she felt that she had the emotional resources to deal with the situation and was not feeling as 'vulnerable and defiled', she would think of returning to her family.

Parallels to Samia's experience can be found in those of black women fleeing domestic violence. Fleeing from one form of abuse (sexual abuse) to face another (racial abuse) often forces them back into the oppressive situation they had initially sought to escape. In Samia's case, escape from inflexible parental attitudes and oppressive cultural situations exposed her to further oppression and sexual exploitation.

CULTURAL SEXISM: ABUSE IN COMMUNAL AND PRIVATE SPACES

Despite differences due to community, class/caste, different trajectories of migration and religion, South-Asian women share common cultural traditions in relation to family values (Bhopal 1996). Their stories of surviving abuse, parental control, negotiating cultural and religious rules, contesting, challenging and accommodating ethnocentrism in families and communities are extremely similar. The most distinctive feature of their experience, which underpinned the different variations in individual experiences, was the overarching influence of patriarchy.

Patriarchal traditions and structures

Black feminists (for example, Carby 1982; Parmar 1982; Anthias and Yuval-Davis 1992) have challenged feminist theory for its postulation of the unitary nature of women's experience of oppression. This has meant that, in recent years, analyses of patriarchy, the family and sexuality have become more inclusive of race and ethnicity (Walby 1990). The concept of patriarchy has been contested on the grounds that it is limited in explaining women's oppression – in particular, the way in which it has been theorised excludes the experiences of black and Third-World women. Adrienne Rich extends her definition to include non-white women and, in light of the young women's experiences, this seems quite comprehensive in explaining their oppression:

> Patriarchy is the power of the fathers: a familial-social, ideological, political system in which men – by force, direct pressure, or through ritual, tradition, law, and language, customs, etiquette, education and the division of labour, determine what part women shall or shall not play, and in which the female is everywhere subsumed under the male. It does not necessarily imply that no woman has power or that all women in any given culture may not have certain powers. (Rich 1977, p.57 cited in Kelly 1988, p.21)

The power of the fathers and male elders within the wider family was perceived to be a major factor in the abuse they experienced – ranging from coercion and control in family and other social settings to more severe forms of physical abuse. Ritual and tradition were also high on the list of factors that were significant in their abuse. In particular, the dowry system, arranged marriages and the concept of *izzat* were cited as prime examples of the exertion of patriarchal power and control.

ARRANGED MARRIAGES

Arranged marriages have attracted much media attention, usually being sensationalised as forced marriages. The custom of arranged marriages has to be understood in the context of South-Asian cultural values, family structures and traditions (Bhopal 1996). South-Asian researchers have demonstrated that, generally, young people accept arranged marriages (Anwar 1998; Bhopal 1996; Brah and Minhas 1985).

Although the majority of the participants accepted the custom of parents and relatives choosing their partners for marriage, one-third of the focus group participants felt that the tradition was oppressive as women were forced to agree with parental decisions. They gave examples of family and friends who had had no say in the choice of their partners. Brah (1992), reporting her findings in relation to young South-Asian women's attitudes to arranged marriages, maintained that the majority of her sample group accepted the practice and expected to have a say in choosing their partner. Anwar (1998) proposes that class is an important factor in the acceptance of arranged marriages by young people. He reports greater acceptance of arranged marriages among young people from middle-class families than working-class young people. This is ascribed to greater communication and discussion between parents and young people and flexibility in parental attitudes.

The members of the focus group echoed some of these findings. In all three focus groups the majority of young women (19 out of 26) anticipated arranged marriages, which they clearly distinguished from forced marriages. All of these young women were confident that they would have a choice in choosing their future partners. Some gave examples from their own experience when they had rejected men suggested or introduced by the family. Nevertheless, those that had rejected potential partners reported feeling pressured by other family members to acquiesce. One of the interviewees, who had left home and was living in a specialist hostel, had been forcibly married to a much older relative in Pakistan at sixteen. Whilst in Pakistan, she had been sexually abused by her husband's younger brother.

DOWRY

The dowry is an important element of the arranged marriage and remains the most common cause for harassment of daughters-in-law by the new family, significantly by the women. This is a traditional Indian practice and involves the giving of gifts by parents to the bride, usually in return for her giving up all rights to immovable property and the parental estate (Kishwar and Vanita 1984). Although there are great variations amongst different communal groups, it generally includes both personal gifts to the bride and gifts to the new family. Despite inexhaustible campaigning by women's groups and subsequent anti-dowry legislation in India, dowry giving and receiving is on the increase (Bhopal 1996). Based in Hindu traditions, it is present with variations in all South-Asian communities which ascribe similar terms to it – *daaj* (Punjabi), *dahej* (Hindi), *jahez* (Urdu) and *joutuk* (Bangla). Of particular significance is its prevalence in South-Asian Muslim communities: Indian, Pakistani and Bangladeshi. This is because it is in direct contradiction to the Islamic practice where the groom is required to provide a gift of money to the bride (over which she has complete control and which she retains in the event of divorce). This gift, or *mehr*, which is an essential part of the marriage contract, has become a tokenistic gesture for South-Asian Muslims who give much greater significance to the tradition of dowry – gifts from the bride's parents – which they have adopted from Hindu traditions.

Most of the participants in the focus groups discussed the prevalence of dowries within the different communities and how it was, often, a source of abuse for women following marriage. They discussed how the dowry had become a status symbol with parents vying to provide gold, houses, cars, etc, to negotiate marriages with higher status families.

Both Sikh and Muslim women felt that they would have greater personal control over the dowry compared to the Hindu women. Two of the married young women interviewed identified the lack of an adequate dowry as the main cause of abuse. Both these women were Muslims (Pakistani and Bangladeshi), which indicates the salience of patriarchal systems over religion. They reported regular physical and verbal abuse – particularly by the women in the family, sisters-in-law and mother-in-law.

Research on dowry in the British context is quite limited. Bhachu (1988, 1996) demonstrates how wage-earning Sikh women have been able to negotiate higher dowries and gain greater personal control over them. With respect to other communities, there is a real dearth of knowledge and understanding of the ways in which the dowry system impacts upon women's status and conditions within the household. Further work is needed to analyse this practice within the context of other South-Asian patriarchal systems as they interface with Western systems and structures.

IZZAT OR HONOUR

This is a powerful patriarchal concept used culturally to control women's freedom and sexuality. In different contexts it may mean reputation, respectability or honour (Bhopal 1996; Imam 1994). Although both men and women in the family and community should share responsibility for upholding family/community honour, it is women's actions and transgressions that invariably bring disrepute or *badnaami* (infamy). The example given below is significant as it also demonstrates how young women contest and challenge their situations.

Kulbir (Indian), was married at seventeen to a British citizen. The marriage broke up after three years when she left home because of domestic violence and, finally, physical abuse by her husband's white mistress. 'My mother-in-law insists that by leaving home and coming to the refuge I have brought shame to my family... what about *Manjit* (husband)? I said, does he not bring dishonour by living with a *gori* (white woman) openly in the community?'.

Most of the young women interviewed and those in the focus groups – across the different communities – felt that common cultural norms about modesty and respectability established control not only over sexual activities and relationships but more generally in terms of their movements and social relationships outside the home/community. The only exception was when this happened on social or communal occasions at weddings or places of worship. There were, however, differences in experiences: those who came from middle-class families and urban origins reported more liberal parental attitudes whilst those who came from families that originated from rural India, Pakistan and Sylhet reported more conservative attitudes. In the case of the latter, young women from families of Indian origin reported comparatively greater freedom and more liberal attitudes than their Muslim counterparts. Several young women from these groups thought that these norms were not as fixed and rigid as they had been 'even ten years ago'.

Sukhi, a sixteen-year-old young woman from a Sikh family, shared her experience and understanding of these restrictions: 'I had to help out in the shop... it was difficult to go out with my friends. Sometimes, I would go out with a group of friends (female) on a Saturday evening but had to come home by ten... It wasn't fair – some of them could stay out later'. Others pointed out the greater freedom their male counterparts enjoyed and how they faced little restrictions within and outside the home. They challenged parental assertions that the restriction on movement outside the home were due to concerns for their safety, pointing out the overwhelming evidence that young men were, generally, the victims of racial attacks and murder.

The family and kinship networks

Although patriarchal ideology places women within the home and family, for South-Asian (and other black) women this is not essentially the primary site for their domination and subordination as it also provides support and refuge from racism and oppression (Brah 1992; Anthias and Yuval-Davis 1992; Imam 1994). These and other qualitative differences in how the family is experienced have underpinned black feminist challenges of white counterparts for their reductionist conceptualisation of the family as a primary site for women's subjugation (Knowles and Mercer 1990; Brah 1992: Anthias and Yuval-Davis 1992). As Avtar Brah (1992) points out: 'When women (South-Asian) acknowledge the importance of family life they do not, however, necessarily accept as legitimate the hierarchical origination of the household or the exercise of male power' (p.71).

Although the great majority of South-Asian families in Britain live in modern nuclear two-generational households, the extended family and kinship networks are extremely significant (Modood, Beishon and Virdee 1994). In the British context the extended family has been seen to be problematic and it is only recently that the strengths of black families have been highlighted (Ahmad 1990; Robinson 1995). Robinson (1995) cites Martin and Martin's (1978) definition to draw out the distinctive features of the extended family:

> a multigenerational, interdependent kinship system which is welded together by a sense of obligation to relatives, organized around a dominant figure; extends across geographic boundaries to connect family units to an extended family network; and has a built in mutual aid system for the welfare of its members and the maintenance of the family as a whole (p.1)

Therefore, in spite of the fact that the households may be nuclear, the family may extend across several households. There is potential for both support and abuse within the structure. The dominant figure, generally male, may also be female. In fact, women as elders enjoy high status and respect (Ahmed 1986) and may also be instrumental in exerting coercive power over younger women to maintain patriarchal dominance. Another factor which has potential for the abuse of younger women is the importance given to the maintenance of the family unit, which, along with *izzat*, exerts a powerful influence on women in the family. When family honour is at stake, the inevitable result will be the collusion of the wider family in the abuse of young women.

The majority of participants reported both support and control, affection and abuse in the way they experienced the family and kinship:

> My grandmother always stuck up for me. She sometimes stopped my dad from hitting me. He could push mum away but he had to lay off when *ma ji* (paternal grandmother) intervened and told him off... (Asha, 19-year-old woman of Kenyan Hindu origin)

The example above demonstrates not only support and censure of abuse in the family but also the dynamics of age and gender within the family. The grandmother, as an elder, had the power to admonish and challenge abusive behaviour. Unfortunately, 'Westernisation' and 'modernisation' is eroding the few family values which could offer women control and support within the family.

Extended family and kinship networks not only widen the potential for abuse from several males/elders but also highlight the availability of young women to men who may not be related but nevertheless have access to women by nature of their membership of communities. From the focus groups, some examples emerged of young women being abused by distant cousins, father's cousins and distant relatives. The case of Samia, cited earlier (sexually abused by her husband's younger brother), highlights this vulnerability, which is made more profound by the fact that women are silenced by cultural norms about *izzat* and forced to preserve and maintain family and kinship structures. The kinship networks have been also been significant in tracking women who have fled from abuse in the family – the 'bounty hunters' are often part of the *biraderi* and feel responsible for protecting the honour of the clan.

ISSUES OF GENDER IN THE ABUSE OF YOUNG WOMEN

In recent years black feminists have challenged the assumptions of the 'masculinity' of the abuser in relation to domestic violence (Mama 1988; Guru 1986; Ahmed 1986). Female members, on the basis of age and/or relationship with the abused, have equally been cited as perpetrators of both physical and emotional abuse against other women. They also highlight the collusion of female members of abuse within the family:

> It was my mother who did not want me to go to college. She would constantly wind my dad up and I would be locked up in the house. (Momtaz, 17-year-old young woman of Bangladeshi origin)

Other participants cited mothers-in-law, mothers, sisters and sisters-in law as perpetrators of physical and emotional abuse. The majority of interviewees (7) named female relatives as carrying out both controlling and dominating behaviour as well as physical and emotional abuse. However, like their parallels in the abuse and sexual abuse of women, women's power and control is somewhat limited due to their gender and they are always less powerful than their male counterparts. A better understanding of these factors and the ways in which they impact on individuals is needed in order to consider their implications in understanding the abuse of young women and also the ways in which they shape the help-seeking process.

Religion and fundamentalism

Religion and tradition are used universally to control and subjugate women and exert a powerful influence through maintaining the social and cultural subordination of women. Despite diversity in religious norms relating to women's roles and position in communities, custom and practice among Hindus, Muslims and Sikhs in South-Asian, communities tends to be more dominated by common cultural traditions than religious prescription. The prevalence of dowry amongst Bangladeshi, Indian and Pakistani Muslim communities both in Britain and in the Indian sub-continent and the continued subordination of women, despite the egalitarianism between sexes and castes, that was fundamental to the Sikh religion are some examples of the ways in which culture prevails over religion.

Amongst the participants, the responses of the young Muslim women were the most wide-ranging in terms of how religion was experienced – ranging from 'liberating' to 'dominating'. The first category of response came from young women who were practising

Muslims and took pride in the assertion of their 'religious' identities. For these women, this was a response to the racism they experienced in wider society and a counter-assertion of the ethnicity which was denigrated by the dominant majority (Afshar 1989). Only two of this group of six women wore *hijaab* (veil), the others felt that, in doing so, they were accepting male domination and prescription of women's role. In the second group, none wore *hijaab* and (3 out of 8), although from Muslim families, did not identify themselves as Muslims.

Generally, the Hindu and Sikh women reported more liberal attitudes by parents and communities, although religion was given greater significance by the Sikh women. There were also differences between the groups in relation to class, with those from middle-class families reporting greater 'Westernisation' and liberalism. These findings support those of other research in this area (for example, Modood, Beishon and Virdee 1994; Anwar 1998), with Muslims giving greater importance to their religion than the other religious groups. Some women who felt confined by the orthodoxy, particularly amongst the Sikhs and Muslims, did not self-identify as Sikhs/Muslims. The Muslim women (Pakistani and Bangladeshi) talked about stricter parental control on both personal relationships and marriage. One young Muslim woman, interviewed in a refuge, had been referred by an Islamic organisation in the south of England. Religion was extremely important to her and she spoke of the support the organisation had offered by identifying an Asian women's refuge which would provide both safety and the opportunity and support for practising her religion. This is an interesting example because in the past religious leaders and groups have denied the need for women's refuges. Recently, there has been a shift in the community responses to refuges and shelters set up for women fleeing violence and abuse. Over the past decade, leaders in the South-Asian communities have moved from a position of opposing refuges and shelters to actively seeking funding and providing housing for women escaping violence (Anthias and Yuval-Davis 1992). Clearly, the agenda is very different and the objective is to reinforce traditional gender roles and counsel women back to the home and family, and the abuse. Black feminists and women activists have challenged the agencies and organisations that sanction this and point out the 'racialisation' of welfare for abused women. One of the most powerful ideologies that has maintained stereotypes of South-Asian communities, generally, and South-Asian women in particular, has been that of multiculturalism. It has underpinned race relations between the State and black communities and is based on the assumption that all minority communities are homogenous (Anthias and Yuval-Davis 1992). Focused entirely on ethnicity and culture, it accepts cultural diversity and the need for communities to govern themselves according to cultural and religious values. However, the systems and structures established to maintain race relations have promoted male dominance through the appointment and recognition of male community leaders reinforcing male power and control within communities (Anthias and Yuval-Davis 1994).

CONCLUSION

The dominant discourses on young South-Asian women and their roles in the family and community – the exclusive focus on cultural conflicts, identity crises and inter-generational conflicts – indicates the limited understanding of their lives in Britain. Little recognition is given to ways in which the dominant majority contributes to the abuse and control of the young women through the cultural racism (Ahmed 1986) and maintenance of myths and stereotypes. The 'culture deficit' model promotes the image of young South-Asian people 'caught between two cultures' – the superior and progressive Western culture and the inferior and backward minority culture. Young people's internalisation of these images and representations alienates them from the support of their communities and does not necessarily bring about acceptance and assimilation into the wider society. Little recognition is given to the fact that they grow up in both cultures and actively act within and between these rather than being forged by one or other or the conflict and clashes between them. Underlying the culture-conflict hypothesis are assumptions that minority cultures are static and permanent, not fluid, dynamic and changing like the dominant majority culture. These cultural assumptions and stereotypes inevitably influence the thinking and responses of those whom young South-Asian women contact for help.

At the communal and family level, male hegemony is reinforced by both religious and cultural traditions as well as by the dominant society. The particular ways in which these are articulated needs to be explored in greater depth in order to support young women in South-Asian communities.

Our understanding of abuse in the lives of young South-Asian women is extremely limited. Some studies that have been undertaken highlight the emotional and psychological costs of abuse and violence to individuals and the social costs to communities and societies. For example, there is some evidence that disproportionate numbers of young South-Asian women suffer from eating disorders (Ahmad, Waller and Verduyn 1994) – the most significant contributory factor reported is perception of maternal control and dominance. The significantly higher rate of suicide among 16 to 25-year-old South-Asian women – three times the national average (Raleigh 1990; Raleigh *et al.* 1996) – needs to be analysed in greater depth to draw out practice strategies and policy development which is aimed specifically at meeting the needs of young women of South-Asian heritage.

REFERENCES

Afshar, H. (1989) *Three Generations of Women in Bradford.* Paper presented at the Conference of Socialist Economists.

Ahmad, B. (1990) *Black Perspectives in Social Work.* Birmingham: Venture.

Ahmad, S., Waller, G. and Verduyn, C. (1994) 'Eating attitudes among South-Asian schoolgirls. The role of perceived parental control.' *International Journal of Eating Disorders*, 15, 1, 91–97.

Ahmed, S. (1986) 'Cultural racism in work with Asian women and girls.' In S. Ahmed, J. Cheetham and J. Small (eds) *Social Work with Black Children and their Families.* London: B.T. Batsford.

Anthias, F. and Yuval-Davis, N. (1992) *Racialised Boundaries – Race, Nation, Gender and Class and the Anti-racist Struggle.* London: Routledge.

Anwar, M. (1986) 'Young Asians between two cultures.' In V. Coombe and A. Little (eds) *Race and Social Work.* London and New York: Tavistock.

Anwar, M. (1998) *Between Cultures. Continuity and Change in the Lives of Young Asians.* London and New York: Routledge.

Bhachu, P. (1988) 'Home and work: Sikh women in Britain.' In S. Westwood and P. Bhachu (eds) *Enterprising Women: Ethnicity, Economy and Gender Relations.* London and New York: Routledge.

Bhachu, P. (1996) 'The multiple landscapes of Asian women in the diaspora.' In V. Amit-Talai and C. Knowles (eds) *Re-situating Identities: The Politics of Race, Ethnicity and Culture*. Toronto: Broadview Press.

Bhopal, K. (1996) *Gender, 'Race' and Patriarchy – A Study of South-Asian Women*. Aldershot: Ashgate.

Brah, A. (1992) 'Women of South-Asian origin in Britain.' In P. Braham, A. Rattansi and R. Skellington (eds) *Racism and Anti-racism: Inequalities, Opportunities and Policies*. London: Sage/OU.

Brah, A. and Minhas, R. (1985) 'Structural racism or cultural difference: Schooling for Asian girls.' In G. Weiner (ed) *Just a Bunch of Girls*. Milton Keynes.

Cambridge, A. (1996) 'The beauty of valuing black cultures.' In V. Amit-Talai and C. Knowles (eds) *Re-situating Identities: The Politics of Race, Ethnicity and Culture*. Toronto: Broadview Press.

Carby, H. (1982) 'White women listen. Black feminism and the boundaries of sisterhood.' In Centre for Contemporary Studies *The Empire Strikes Back*. London: Hutchinson.

Gelles, R. (1985) *Intimate Violence in Families*. Beverly Hills: Sage.

Gelles, R.J. (1993) 'Through a sociological lens: Social structure and family violence.' In R. Gelles and Loseke (eds) *Current Controversies in Family Violence*. Newbury Park: Sage.

Gelles, R.J. and Straus, M.A. (1988) *Intimate Violence: The Causes and Consequences of Abuse in the American Family*. New York: Simon & Schuster.

Guru, S. (1986) 'An Asian women's refuge.' In S. Ahmed, J. Cheetham and J. Small (eds) *Social Work with Black Children and their Families*. London: B.T. Batsford.

Hanmer, J. and Saunders, D (1984) *Well Founded Fear*. London: Hutchinson.

Imam, U.F. (1994) 'Asian children and domestic violence.' In A.E. Mullender and R. Morley (eds) *Children Living Domestic Violence: Putting Men's Abuse Of Women on the Child Care Agenda*. London: Whiting and Birch.

Imam, U.F. (1999) 'Youth workers as mediators and interpreters – working with black young people.' In S. Banks (ed) *Ethical Issues in Youth Work*. London: Routledge.

Kelly, L. (1988) *Surviving Sexual Violence*. Oxford: Polity/Blackwell.

Kishwar, M. and Vanita, R. (eds) (1984) *In Search of Answers. Indian Women's Voices from Manushi*. London: Zed Books.

Knowles, C. and Mercer, S. (1990) 'Feminism and anti-racism.' In A. Cambridge, and S. Feuchtang (eds) *Anti-Racist Strategies*. Aldershot: Avebury Press.

Martin, E.P. and Martin, J.M. (1978) *The Black Extended Family*. Chicago: University of Chicago Press.

Modood, T., Beishon, S. and Virdee, S. (1994) *Changing Ethnic Identities*. London: PSI.

Parmar, P. (1982) 'Gender, race and class – Asian women in resistance.' In Centre for Contemporary Studies *The Empire Strikes Back*. London: Hutchinson.

Raleigh, S. (1996) 'Suicide patterns and trends in people of Indian sub-continent and Caribbean origin in England and Wales.' *Ethnicity and Health 1*, 1, 55–63.

Raleigh, S., Bulusu, L. and Balarajan, R. (1990) 'Suicides among immigrants from the Indian sub-continent.' *British Journal of Psychiatry 156*, 46–50.

Robinson, L. (1995) *Psychology for Social Workers: Black Perspectives*. London: Routledge.

Stanko, E.A. (1988) 'Fear of crime and the myth of the safe home – a feminist critique of criminology.' In K. Yllö and M. Bogard (eds) *Feminist Perspectives on Wife Abuse*. London: Sage.

Straus, M.A. (1980) 'A sociological perspective on the causes of family violence.' In M.R. Green (ed) *Violence in the Family*. Boulder: Westview.

Straus, M.A. and Gelles, R.J. (1986) 'Societal changes and change in family violence from 1975 to 1985 as revealed by two national surveys.' *Journal of Marriage and the Family*, 48, 465–79.

Walby, S. (1990) *Theorising Patriarchy*. Oxford: Basil Blackwell.

FURTHER READING

Amos, V. and Parmar, P. (1981) 'Black girls in Britain.' In A. McRobbie and T. McCabe (eds) *Feminism for Girls: An Adventure Story*. London: Routledge and Kegan Paul.

Choudry, S. (1996) *Pakistani Women's Experience of Domestic Violence*. Research Study 43. London: HMSO.

hooks, b. (1991) *Yearning: Race and Gender in Cultural Politics*. London: Turnaround.

Mama, A. (1988) *The Hidden Struggle: Statutory and Voluntary Sector Responses to Violence Against Black Women*. London: LRHU/Runnymede Trust.

Mama, A. (1995) *Race, Gender and Subjectivity*. London: Routledge.

Millet, K. (1971) *Sexual Politics*. London: Hart Davis.

Sehgal, G. and Yuval Davis, N. (eds) (1992) *Refusing Holy Orders: Women and Fundamentalism in Britain*. London: Virago.

Van Dijk, T.A. (1993) *Discourses and Racism. London:* Sage.

Wilson, A. (1978) *Finding a Voice*. London: Virago.

Yllö, K. (1993) 'Through a feminist lens.' In R. Gelles and D. Loseke (eds) *Current Controversies in Family Violence*. Newbury Park: Sage.

Yuval-Davis, N. (1994) *Fundamentalism, Multiculturalism and Women*. London: Sage/OU.

CHAPTER 8

Linking Thoughts to Actions

Using the Integrated Abuse Cycle

Colin Hawkes

INTRODUCTION

The problem of how to obtain accurate and reliable information from young people who are believed to pose a risk of significant harm from sexual or physical abuse is one which exercises many professionals involved in child protection work.

This chapter will consider the development and clinical use of the integrated abuse cycle (Vizard *et al.* 1996) in the assessment of sexually abusing and sexually aggressive children by the Young Abusers Project. A brief description of the Project and the context within which it works is followed by an exploration of the problems encountered in carrying out psychiatric or specialist social work assessments.

The main body of the chapter will focus on the integrated abuse cycle and how to use it in interviewing a variety of children, with clinical examples of aspects of the techniques referred to. Finally, the chapter will discuss the use of the cycle in other work settings and with other client groups.

THE YOUNG ABUSERS PROJECT

The Young Abusers Project was established in 1992 with the aim of providing a national community-based service for assessing and treating young people with sexually aggressive or sexually abusive behaviour. The Project is part of Camden and Islington Health Trust, is financially and managerially supported by the NSPCC and is classified as operating at the fourth tier of the National Health Service by virtue of the complex multidisciplinary and forensic work undertaken.

The staff group is led by a Clinical Director, Dr Eileen Vizard, a Consultant Child and Adolescent Psychiatrist, and is composed of experienced and highly skilled practitioners from different backgrounds, including clinical psychology, child psychotherapy, social work and probation. The Project practice is genuinely co-operative and all assessments are carried out by small teams of three workers.

The client group, which is predominantly male, has dropped in age with successive years, from 16.8 years in 1992 to 11.7 years in 1996. More than 900 referrals and enquiries have been made and in excess of 190 children assessed. The youngest child seen at the Project was seven years old and the eldest, an exception to the normal upper age limit of 19 years, a young man of 22 years with a severe learning disability.

Although the Project has continued to offer a national service, most referrals have been of children from the south-east of England, in particular from Greater London, and the ethnic make-up has come to reflect the ethnic diversity of this region with an increasing proportion of non-white children assessed.

Each year the Project undertakes the assessment of a number of children who have carried out the most serious violent acts, including murder and abduction. In most instances the assaults have been sexual in nature, although this is not always the case. The majority of assessments in this category have been forensic, with children facing charges of murder or rape, but some of the assailants have been too young to be dealt with within the criminal arena.

All of the Project's work is underwritten by a commitment to child protection, which governs both policy and practice. This means that assessment and treatment are provided, in co-operation, as far as is possible, with social work departments, professional carers and, where appropriate, the families of the children concerned. In keeping with most other specialist agencies the Project operates on the basis of open confidentiality – that is, clinical details are confidential unless child protection concerns arise, which are then reported and investigated. These issues are thoroughly explained to the children and professionals involved at the outset of the assessment process.

In essence, the Project takes the view that although the behaviour of some very young children who are or have recently experienced sexual victimisation may be correctly described as 'abuse reactive', those who continue to behave in a sexually aggressive or harmful way towards others do so in an increasingly conscious way. If this developmental problem is not accurately identified and addressed at an early stage, in our experience, there is a significant risk that it will persist, become addictive in nature and resistant to intervention as the child grows older. The issue of how to describe these behaviours and the children who display them is a subject for debate elsewhere. However, it is crucially important that dangerous and disordered sexual acts are distinguished from normal developmental sexual experimentation. Effective techniques to achieve reliable assessment will prevent potentially harmful labelling of children without problems, in addition to helping recognise those in need of help and treatment.

THE PROCESS OF ASSESSMENT

The four components of assessment are: professionals meeting; psychiatric assessment interview; psychological assessment; comprehensive report. (Vizard *et al.* 1996). In order to meet the constraints of time and cost, the process of assessment is a relatively intense one. The first step is the collection of information and the identification of the professionals involved. A meeting of professionals then takes place, at which a variety of issues relating to the individual child and to child protection are addressed. It is at this stage that efforts are made to achieve joint instruction by the different legal representatives involved, particularly when a criminal trial is in the offing. Where this is achieved, the risk of future conflict and splitting within the professional network is reduced.

The child is then interviewed by a team of three workers, two in the room and one providing live supervision by way of a video and radio link. This initial two-hour interview is followed, when appropriate, by a second session in which family members or carers participate. The referring professional plays an active and important role in beginning the assessment interview and in being present at the conclusion to join in making any comments which can be addressed to the child. This joint activity helps reliable and honest communication about sexual issues which are often not made explicit to children and their families.

Following the assessment a full psychiatric report is prepared.

PROBLEMS ENCOUNTERED IN ASSESSMENT

The aim of assessment is to obtain accurate information on which to base decisions about a number of factors. Most referrers to the Young Abusers Project seek opinions on the degree of risk of significant harm from sexual abuse posed to and by children and advice on accommodation and treatment options. Difficulties in carrying out assessment stem from the complex causes of problematic sexual behaviour, and these problems are themselves confused or masked by systemic issues. In particular, we have noted the frequency with which the principles of Criminal Justice and those reflected in the Children Act of 1991 are perceived to be at odds. Children who are subject to Care Orders or who are on Child Protection Registers by virtue of their sexually abusive behaviour are entitled to have all their needs met, including the right to therapeutic treatment, even if, or when, they become child defendants in criminal trials.

The provision of treatment requires assessment and the process of questioning and exploration necessary in carrying out this assessment is often seen by defence solicitors and others as contrary to the best interests of a child awaiting trial for allegations of a sexual nature. As a consequence, children with seriously disordered and dangerous behaviour are often left unassessed and untreated for lengthy periods. When such children arrive for assessment they may have been instructed to give 'no comment' interviews, which means that their problems remain unassessed and that help is not given.

Although the Project, unsurprisingly given the child protection and child developmental backgrounds of staff members, believes that early and thorough identification of the problem is to the advantage of all concerned, this chapter does not examine the rights and wrongs of this dilemma. The pragmatic approach which we have adopted to deal with the problem is outlined later.

Other systemic problems emanate from distortions in the professional network. For instance, distortions which result from the impact of powerful family members who wish to maintain the *status quo*, with abused or abusing children remaining at home together with untreated Schedule I offenders or vulnerable potential victims. In this situation it is difficult for professionals to take a more directly protective role, perhaps requiring going to court to obtain a Care Order, when the ethos within which they work is one of partnership with parents in terms of the Children Act 1989. The Project policy of not offering treatment until the sexually abusing family member is removed is not always understood or appreciated at the outset of assessment, particularly if the abuser is a younger child.

Other familiar problems are met in the interview room when the child attends for assessment. These may be a consequence of genuine difficulties in comprehension or communication resulting from brain damage, intellectual impairment, cognitive distortions resulting from chronic problems in their upbringing, hearing or speech problems, the age of the child concerned, cultural or racial difference or from mental health problems. On the other hand, the child may seek to deny involvement or responsibility in order to avoid the consequences. These problems are usually identified in advance at the meeting of professionals and from documentary sources and practical steps are taken to address them. For instance, it may be advisable to include a staff member with particular skill in working with learning disabilities or to equip the room with age-appropriate toys with which to help engage the child.

THE INTEGRATED CYCLE IN THE ASSESSMENT INTERVIEW

Assessment interview outline

The first stage of the assessment interview is *clarification and rapport building*. The therapists begin with brief introductions and explanations which acknowledge the situation of the child concerned and, as far as possible, help to put them at their ease. The referring worker, who has been prepared for the task, then gives an outline, in clear and explicit terms, of the concerns which have led to the child being referred to the project and the worries which are held for the future.

The child's reaction to this list of concerns is then sought and, if they are able to admit to a shared worry about their abusive behaviour, it may be possible to move immediately to stage two: *mapping the abuse – the fantasies, strategies and behaviours.* If the child is too anxious or defensive, it may be necessary to achieve a more empathic atmosphere by looking at the background and experiences of the child, perhaps through the construction of a family tree, before moving on to stage three: *the future – placement, treatment and personal change.*

The information obtained from stage two provides a basis for the child, together with the professionals, to consider future developments and to speculate together about how to meet child protection and child needs.

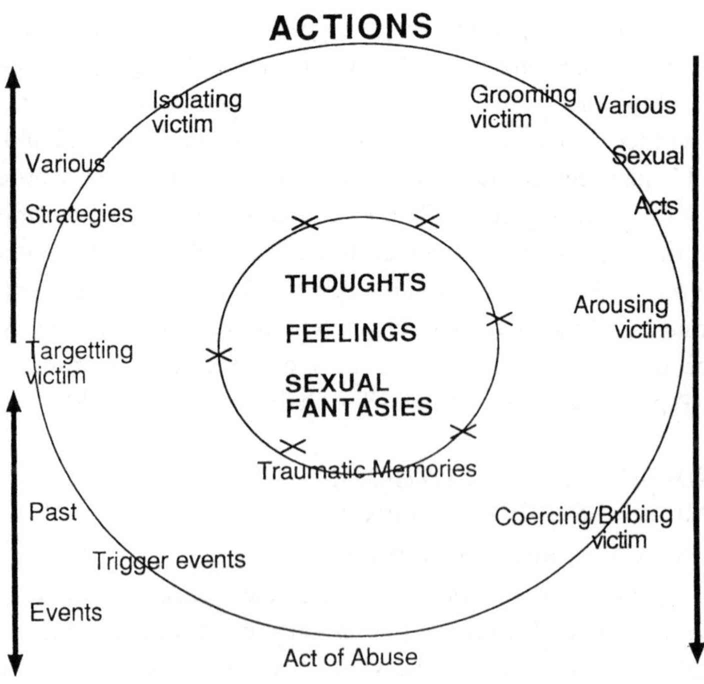

Figure 8.1 Integrated abuse cycle – actions and thoughts

The integrated abuse cycle is a powerful diagnostic tool which helps make sense of events which are clouded in uncertainty through denial, resistance or, perhaps, lack of understanding. It is a simple diagram which chronologically links those thoughts and feelings which accompany the actions and events that precede, accompany and follow an abusive act. It is most important to stress that the essential task of the therapists is to listen carefully to what the child is saying and, with them, to try and make sense of what they have done. Each child will bring their own thoughts and individual interpretations of events and, although an experienced practitioner may identify common themes and patterns, it would be counter-productive and poor practice if the therapist approached each assessment in the expectation of uncovering or confirming an anticipated blueprint. The integrated abuse cycle, despite it's circular shape, is a tool which, when used correctly, opens discussion and emphasises choice, rather than one which represents an inevitable and repetitious progression of events.

An outer circle depicts actions and events and an inner circle tracks the thoughts and feelings which coincide with them. The cycle is intended to be a graphic representation of the assessment and therapeutic efforts to link the external (actions) and internal (thoughts feeling and emotions) worlds. The cycle is sufficiently flexible to be used by very young children or those who are not literate and is particularly helpful with those who can read and write. Prior to the meeting, potential difficulties in communication are identified and a decision made about whether to represent actions or feelings by symbols or drawing figures if this is necessary. If it proves possible to create a relatively complete diagram, the workers and the child will jointly produce a powerful tangible image of the part which the child has played in causing the sexual abuse to occur and his/her motives for acting in this way. This is an invaluable contribution to the information required to assess risk and to co-operatively identify those events which trigger sexual abuse. In this optimistic scenario plans for treatment can begin to take shape from this point. Where the diagram remains less complete, with significant gaps in information or a failure to link thought to action, the professionals are, nevertheless, better equipped to assess risk and to identify areas for future work with the child.

The construction of the diagram is an activity in which the child is encouraged to actively participate and to take the lead role. In other words, children are asked to get up from their seat and draw or write items on to the abuse cycle on the flip chart. In this way, in addition to providing information for the benefit of the professionals involved in assessment, the child is also presented with a challenging representation of their sexual behaviour, which they have helped to produce. The exercise has a profound effect because it requires children to explain, in their own terms, abusive thoughts and sexual arousal which they have tried to suppress or to account for in a distorted or untruthful way. The definition of the problem is, as far as possible, one which they own and not one imposed on them.

There are a number of decisions to be made before and during the assessment interview which enhance the effective use of the diagram.

Adjusting to the developmental needs of the individual child

Some of the adjustments necessary to meet the intellectual or developmental needs of the child have already been commented on. In our clinical experience children as young as nine years of age or those with mild learning disability have been able, with help, to provide the written information necessary to construct a reliable diagram. However, with younger or less able children imaginative use of toys, symbols and figures can be equally effective and is a standard part of any child psychiatric assessment. For instance, the scene of a sexually abusive incident can be represented with toys or dolls on a table or on the floor of the interview room and the child helped to show what happened by moving the figures around and explaining the sequence of events to the therapists. The approach requires sufficient time prior to the interview for discussion between the members of the assessment team so that the timing of activities and the allocation of tasks can be decided.

Introducing the integrated cycle diagram

The cycle diagram may be introduced at almost any point in the interview, although, because it can evoke such powerful reactions, it is wise to leave sufficient time to allow a child to recover and to be reassured before the end of the session. If a child comes to assessment having spoken openly about the sexual things he has done, the assessment team, depending on the response of the child to the initial description of worries held about him, may decide (normally, in the first break for discussion) to move directly to an exploration of his actions. One or other of the therapists asks the child to try and explain why he/she has abused and, in almost every case, the child cannot give an explanation. This then provides an opportunity to state that this is a problem that they share with many other children we have seen and that there is a way to help them to understand what has happened. The assessment interview lasts only two hours and so the introduction of the diagram is made in a matter-of-fact way, with any movement of materials and chairs achieved as quickly as possible.

If the child being assessed has been more resistant, the introduction of the integrated cycle will be delayed in order to create a more positive rapport. The therapists will take care to note whether the child is more easily engaged with one or other of them and, if this is the case, he or she will introduce the idea of using the cycle diagram to unlock the puzzle of the child's worrying behaviour. The child is encouraged to move their chair close to the flip chart or board. The active therapist will then start the exercise by explaining, in simple terms, that the diagram is a way of looking at what the child did and what their thoughts and feelings were.

Starting the integrated cycle diagram

The two circles will then be drawn and the therapist will mark on the outer circle, usually where five o'clock would be on a clock face, the known or suspected sexual acts. The child will be asked to say what sexual acts they committed and what their thoughts were at the time. If they fail to do this, or leave out important information, the therapist will take responsibility, using words which the child understands. It is essential that this includes a brief but accurate account of the sexually abusive acts. It would not be sufficient to put 'John sexually abuses Mary'; instead, the therapist might write 'John puts his penis into Mary's vagina and ejaculates inside her', if these are terms that the child has said he understands, otherwise more age-appropriate words would be used. Where the abusive behaviour has taken place over an extended period, or where a number of different sexual acts have occurred, only the details of the last event would be written at this stage, unless the child volunteers a more complete version. This allows an opportunity for the assessment team to see the extent to which the child can move on to talk honestly about their behaviour at a later stage.

Moving on

A child's reactions to initial questions about their behaviour and feelings at the point of the sexually abusive act will provide the assessment team with an early impression of how easy or difficult the process of eliciting information is likely to be. It is inevitable that a substantial degree of resistance will be encountered and this may be manifest in a blanket denial of events, forgetfulness or silence. In order to free them from this blocked position the therapists will shift attention to an earlier or pre-aroused stage of the diagram and enter information concerning less anxiety-provoking incidents. The importance of thorough preparation is crucial here and the therapists will need to have as clear a picture as possible of where the abuse occurred and a willingness to enter into the perceptions of a child with an urge to sexually abuse.

Let us suppose that the sexual abuse is known to have taken place at about nine o'clock in the evening in the victim's bedroom. The choice may be to move back to an exploration of what was happening at school and on the journey home before going on to put on the diagram when he arrived home, who was there and what happened earlier in the evening. As far as possible, this exploration is carried out in a relaxed fashion with the child being given the opportunity to tell the story at his pace and to get into the habit of using his own words to describe both the internal and external process. In addition to establishing a baseline of information for the assessment team about an individual's ability to recall and accurately relay details, the child is encouraged to give his impression of other important people, especially other children and, of course, the victim of the abuse. This exploration of the arousal period often reveals underlying feelings of resentfulness and jealousy towards other children and anger, or a sense of anger or humiliation, which may link up with the subsequent sexually abusive acts.

The therapists will then move back to try and obtain more detail about the onset of arousal and what happened next.

Deconstructing obstructions and using strategic thinking

Difficulties will always be encountered when the therapists move into that part of the cycle which deals with sexually aroused thoughts and actions. The strategy of creating empathy and of approaching these issues indirectly is helpful but not foolproof. However, within a relatively short period of time it is possible for workers to develop the ability to analyse the reasons for a child to place obstructions in their way and to use that knowledge to work with, rather than against, causes of resistance.

A number of simple strategies often help to engage a child in more honest exploration, for instance:

1. *Circular questions.* It is more effective to use open-ended or circular questions than those which close down responses or invite a 'yes' or 'no' answer. If a child is known to have carried out penile penetration of another, it would be more productive to pose a question which assumed that erection had occurred and to establish when this happened rather than to ask if it had taken place.

2. *Objectifying issues and involving the child in the puzzle.* If the child being assessed still does not provide information, or, as is often the case, gives a patchy account with no description of thoughts feeling or intentions, a second tactic is for the therapist to step back from the diagram, sit next to the child and ask for their comments on it. The child may acknowledge that there is little information about the relevant part of the cycle or the therapists may need to point this out, stating that this gives the assessment team a puzzle to solve as it appears that it has been possible to recall details of events before and after the abuse but no details of what happened when it took place. One therapist will then comment to the child or to the other therapist that it is almost as though the abuse was carried out by a body or penis without any mind in control of it. A little time is allowed for this concept to sink in and it may be repeated or reframed to help the child to understand before they are asked whether a judge (if they are due to appear at court), a social worker or a psychiatrist would think that a child with a body that carried out sexual abuse without any brain attached to it was more or less dangerous than one who was able to tell people about the thoughts that they had before and during the abuse. In most cases the child identifies the abuser with the 'empty'

head as the more dangerous and the therapists confirm this, pointing out that neither the child nor any one else could predict when he might sexually abuse again because he had no idea why he had done it in the first place. This approach, which does not directly accuse the child of lying but encourages them to join the therapists in an examination of their problem, displayed objectively on the diagram, usually brings a positive response.

3. *Arranging the room.* The physical arrangement of the room is an important factor and, as suggested earlier, the avoidance of direct physical as well as verbal challenge prevents the child from slipping into a resentful or self-pitying victim frame of mind. The focus on an inanimate object, the cycle diagram, is helpful and the therapists may choose to pose questions or make comments without direct eye contact with the child, perhaps looking at the diagram or at each other. For instance, one worker may offer a hypothesis for a missing element of diagram, asking the other's opinion and then checking out the accuracy of the supposition with the child. In this way even the most difficult issues, such as the likelihood of the assessed child having been aroused by thoughts of hurting or even killing the victim, can be named in a contained fashion and a reaction observed.

4. *Appropriate challenge.* Although the intention is to create a sufficiently relaxed atmosphere to encourage the flow of reliable information, a direct challenge may be necessary when enough evidence is available to show that a continued denial is untenable. However, the risk of a child providing a response to appease, or at the suggestion of the therapists, should be anticipated.

Bringing the cycle to a conclusion

When as much information as possible has been obtained in the time available, the therapist who has been active in drawing the diagram sits down and, keeping the focus on the picture, makes a statement which encompasses what has been achieved and what is missing. Once this overview is complete, the child is asked to give their reaction and will often say something about how creating the picture has been difficult but has given them a sense of relief. The therapists then try to use the extracted information to make a link with the conclusion of the interview by asking the child to say whether what they see on the diagram suggests to them that they have a problem and, if so, what it is. If the child struggles to find appropriate words, the therapists might ask where in the body the problem might be located or further speed up events by stating what they believe the problem to be. This provides an opportunity to explore the issues of what therapeutic assistance is necessary and allied questions such as where the child should live while this is provided.

Alice, a 12-year-old girl who, initially, denied any sexually abusive thoughts or behaviour but, after completing a cycle diagram, was able to tell the therapists and her social worker that she had experienced thoughts of penetrating the vagina of younger girls, continued to have these thoughts and thought that it would not be safe for her to live in a home where younger children were present until she had got this problem 'sorted out'.

The integrated cycle diagram exercise can then draw to a conclusion and the therapists can explain that they will take a short break to discuss developments and then return with the other professionals who have accompanied the child to the assessment. During this break the child may be left with the task of trying to fill in any remaining gaps in the diagram.

CLINICAL EXAMPLES

Child A

The first example is of a 10-year-old girl who been sexually abused by an adult male paedophile, with previous convictions for the sexual assault of children, who had changed his name and moved to live next to child A's parents, whom he befriended as part of the process of targeting and then sexually abusing the child. This continued for approximately two years before the abuse was disclosed and the perpetrator prosecuted. The following year it emerged that child A had been sexually abusing her younger sister, both digitally and with objects, since her own experience of abuse.

When child A was referred to the Project she had admitted penetrative sexual abuse of her sister, explaining that she had done to her sister what had been done to her, although at this point she had disclosed only non-penetrative abuse by the man who assaulted her.

In this case the construction of the cycle was relatively straightforward with child A revealing the extent to which she continued to blame her sister for what had happened, acknowledging the calculation she put into the abuse and the degree of detachment from her sister's distress which she maintained. This, together with other information, helped in the design of child protection measures and therapeutic treatment for both siblings. One theme, present here and which often appears in assessment, is that of feeling pushed out or made to feel one's place as a child in the family threatened and of seeking to deal with these feelings in acts of abuse.

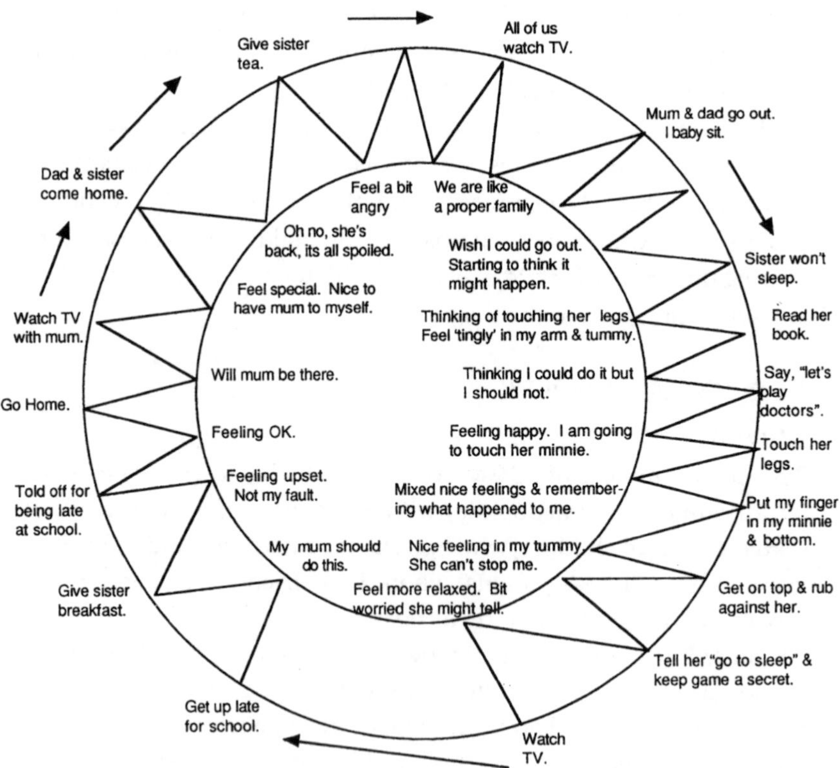

Figure 8.2 Child 'A', female aged 10 years. Victim, sister aged 2 years

Child B

The cycle relating to child B was drawn up while he was held on remand in a secure unit while awaiting trial for the murder of a woman, a stranger to him who he had stabbed in an apparently motiveless attack. He was a grossly overweight with a lengthy history of what was described to us by a number of different professionals as 'odd' behaviour. Child B had become increasingly isolated and bullied by fellow pupils and some six weeks prior to the murder had been excluded from school for threatening a teacher with a knife and setting fire to waste paper bins.

The process of completing the diagram helped child B to explain that he continued to have vivid fantasies, quite paranoid and hallucinatory in quality, of boys who had bullied him at school having the power to make their way into the secure unit and attack him. Given the link displayed in the cycle diagram between these

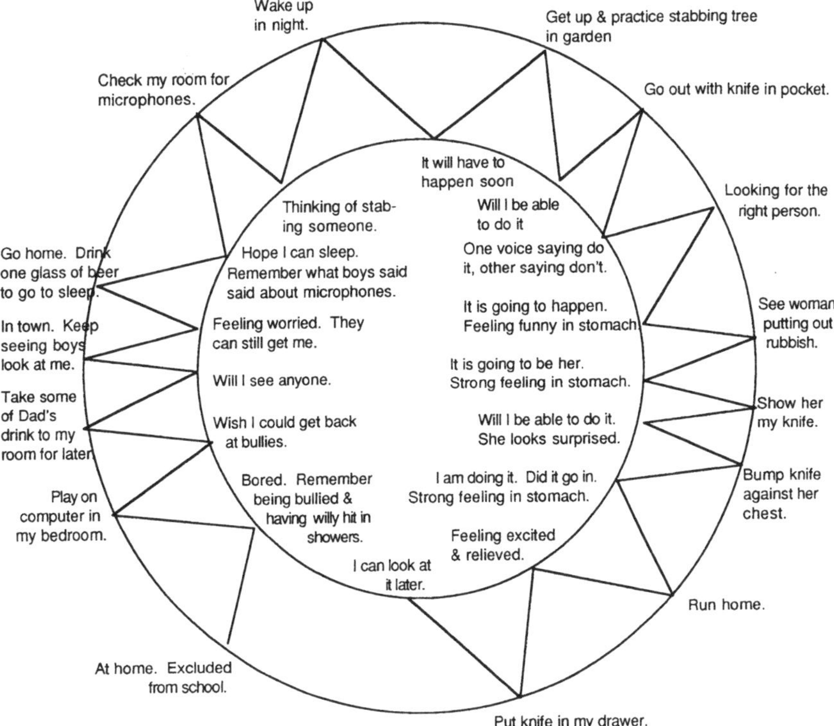

Figure 8.3 Child 'B', male aged 16 years. Victim, adult woman

feelings and his murderous attack, this information helped staff managing him to gain insight into his actions and to anticipate the risk he posed to fellow residents.

Child C

Child C, aged 15 years, was also accommodated in a secure unit before being interviewed at the Project. He had carried out a very serious and sadistic assault on a eight-year-old boy, a stranger to him, approximately a year earlier. In the intervening time he had refused to talk about what he had done, despite considerable efforts to engage with him in individual and in group settings.

In the assessment interview he was initially taciturn and uncommunicative but it proved possible to create an empathic link by discovering that, despite his age, he continued to have an imaginary friend to whom he told his secrets. The therapists helped

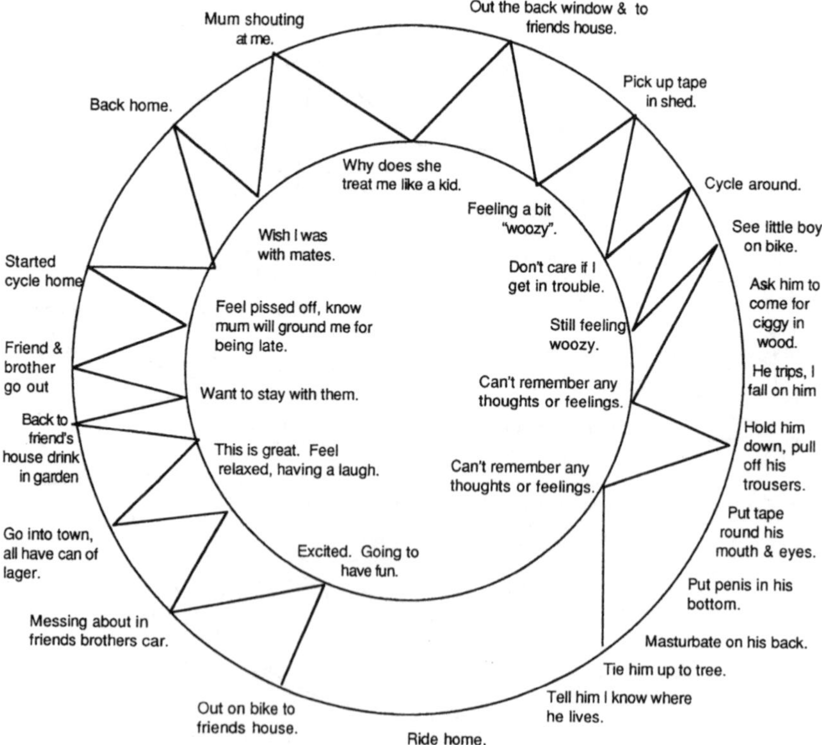

Figure 8.4 Child 'C', male aged 15 years. Victim, boy aged 9 years

him to talk about his feelings through this friend before moving on to talk about the more powerful and adult side of child C which had carried out the assault.

As the cycle diagram shows, he was able to describe most of his thoughts and feelings apart from those relating to details of the assault. The missing elements of the diagram, together with the noticeable absence of acknowledgement of or concern for the feeling of his victim, helped in the assessment of risk which child C posed to others and in advice about the treatment package necessary to work with him and his family.

Child D

Child D, an eight-year-old boy, had been referred to the Project because of concern stemming from inappropriate sexual behaviour towards younger children of either gender but, in particular, his repeated digital penetration of the vagina and anus of his four-year-old half-sister and the nine-month-old daughter of a neighbour. Child D had suffered long-term and extreme sexual abuse from the first months of his life. This was initially inflicted by his natural father, although his mother was also suspected of involvement.

For several months child D had not given any explanation for his behaviour beyond saying that it was an accident and that he had simply fallen on top of his half-sister and that his hand had brushed against his half-sister's vagina outside her knickers. This was not in keeping with either the medical evidence that the child victims had experienced repeated penetration nor the account given by child D's half-sister.

Child D was initially nervous but was reassured to hear that many other children who had done similar things had been seen and helped at the Project.

He described how he had ambivalent feelings about his half-sister, both envying, resenting and liking her. He responded in a spontaneous way to drawing up the abuse cycle and, when asked to consider it and to give his feelings, explained that he felt relieved and worried and wanted his social worker, who was observing by means of the video link, to know that it was important that he should not be accommodated in a family where other younger children were

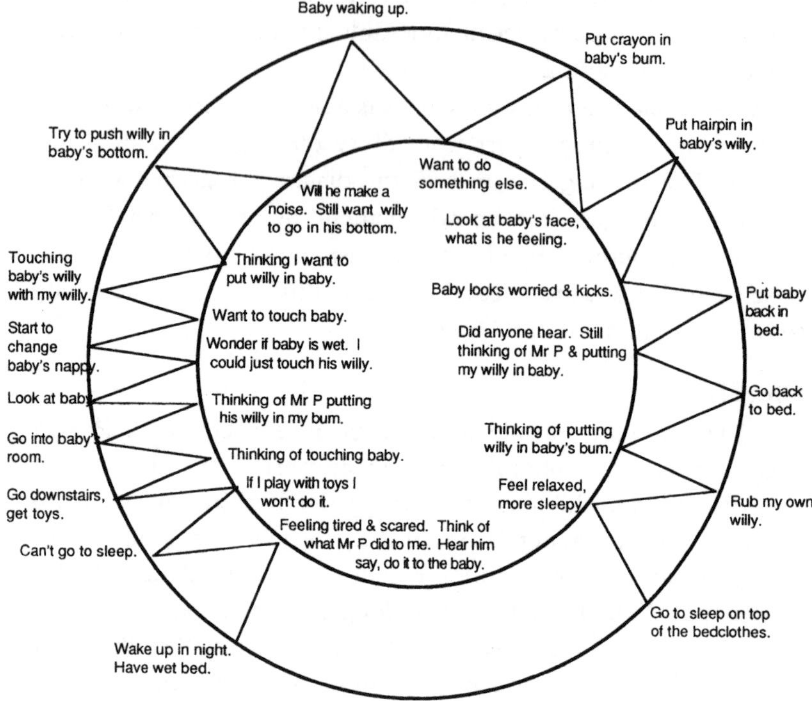

Figure 8.5 Child 'D', male age 8 years. Victim, sister aged 1 year

present because he continued to think about doing sexual things to them and thought he would need help to get the problem 'sorted out' before he could be considered safe.

CONCLUSION

This chapter has described the use of the integrated abuse cycle in the assessment of children at the Young Abusers Project. The technique is not universal in application but has been useful in other settings, such as probation officers' analyses of offending behaviour. We suggest that the idea of linking thoughts and actions in this concrete way could also be employed in the investigation of child abuse allegations and, perhaps, in other police interviews.

The concepts underlying the cycle have helped in individual and group treatment provided by the Project where they assist in the identification of triggers for abusing behaviours and, through understanding the repetitive aggressive or sexual fantasies which children experience, enable alternative and more acceptable patterns of behaviour to develop.

CONFIDENTIALITY

The names and details of the children referred to in this chapter have been altered in order to maintain the confidentiality of this vulnerable client group.

REFERENCES

Vizard, E., Wynick, S., Hawkes C., Woods, J. and Jenkins, J. (1996) 'Juvenile sexual offenders. Assessment issues.' *British Journal of Psychiatry*, 168, 259–262.

FURTHER READING

Hawkes, C., Jenkins, J. and Vizard, E. (1997) 'Roots of sexual violence in children and adolescents.' In V. Varma (ed) *Violence in Children and Adolescents.* London: Jessica Kingsley Publishers.

CHAPTER 9

Children in Danger of Violence from their Carers

Lessons from the Literature and Practice

Ann Hagell and Renuka Jeyarajah Dent

Despite media panics about attacks by strangers, it has always been the case that the main risk of violence to children comes from their carers. While it is sadly true that many children are the subject of violent abuse in the home, relatively few are in situations of intense danger where it is possible that they will be killed. While most cases are difficult, these children at the extreme end of the 'danger' distribution pose particular problems for multi-disciplinary child protection teams. In an ideal world we would like to be able to help welfare services to become more adept at detecting these particularly dangerous situations in order to intervene in ways of best possible advantage to the child or children. Yet, in reality, it is very difficult to predict danger and any exercise intended to help has to be set within the broader context of the local authority's risk management policy. In this chapter we discuss the background to a large, national project being undertaken in collaboration with six Area Child Protection Committees, Scope, Integrated Support Programme and the Baring Foundation, raising issues of prediction, interagency co-operation, risk management and resource limitations.

At the outset it is important to stress that danger to children can come in a variety of forms, both through acts of commission (such as physical violence) and acts of omission (such as neglect). However, given the topic of this book, we have focused in this chapter on danger through violence, where danger is the risk of a serious, negative outcome. In fact, the literature on violence is more established than that on neglect and, as a result, the information-gathering schedule that we will describe below also concentrates on predicting violent danger. It should be noted, however, that we also think that danger through neglect and emotional abuse is just as important and, in fact, that the schedule will prove useful for use with these children too as many child death inquiries have found that neglect and emotional abuse were present and evident long before the death of the child through violence from a carer (Department of Health 1991).

It is quite difficult to provide a clear definition of what is meant by violence in this context. In terms of risk of serious violence, at the broad level the definition is simply physically violent acts directed at the child, resulting in life-threatening injuries such as multiple broken bones, head injuries, burns or suffocation. However, much of what we discuss in this chapter is very reliant on context and other factors, and, in addition, the main thrust of child protection policy is currently against a very medical model concentrating solely on obvious injury, because this can lead to some patterns of child abuse being missed.

We start by presenting a brief description of the context for the study, which was based, in part, on a review of the literature on predicting danger to children and also arose from an understanding of issues arising from child death inquiries. The next section describes the results of a pilot project to help improve assessments of danger and we conclude, in the final section, with a discussion of the issues highlighted by the project in terms of future practice and research.

THE CONTEXT FOR THE PILOT STUDY

In the United States five children die as a result of maltreatment every day (Durfee and Tilton-Durfee 1995). In Britain at least one to two children are killed by parents or relatives each week (Central Statistical Office 1994), with approximately 120 child death notifications per year received by the Department of Health (Falkov 1996). Levels of fatal child abuse show little fluctuation on a year-to-year basis (Creighton 1995) but will represent an underestimation as some abuse cases will mistakenly be classified as accidents. Statistics also show that children are more likely to be killed in their own home and by members of their own family (including step-parents) than anywhere else or by anyone else (Browne and Lynch 1995; Reder, Duncan and Gray 1993). Most of these children will be very young, with infants and toddlers being more 'at risk' of homicide than any other age group (Creighton 1995).

A common perception in the study of child abuse and child homicide is that there is a continuum of violence ranging from mild physical punishment to severe abuse and homicide. The death of a child is thought to occur when there is a particular combination of factors. The role of chance is thus an important consideration, especially since, in the fluid and ongoing dynamic of family life, it is often difficult to be definitive about when, where, with whom, etc, an event will happen. However, Gelles (1991) claimed that child homicide was not simply an extreme form of child abuse but a distinct form of behaviour requiring a separate explanation, and others have also indicated that the relationship between child homicide and child abuse is complex (Browne and Lynch 1995). The current state of information is such that we cannot be conclusive about the distinctions between homicide and abuse. Both are bound to be complicated and, at the very least, overlapping to some degree.

The definition of abuse is influenced by professional, agency and societal values. Whether a case is accepted for work or investigation may depend, for example, on the seriousness of the alleged abuse or how easy it is to prove. However, this is not necessarily indicative of future re-occurrence or harm. A father who accidentally causes a head injury by unusually pushing a teenager into a chair in provoked anger may be less likely to harm the child in future than a stressed and depressed single parent who consistently fails to care. In many ways violent abuse to a child is easier to agree upon as the physical scars are easier to recognise, but the thresholds at which care is defined as violent can still cause controversy in working to protect children.

Abuse, while not always resulting in death, can present very serious danger to children in other ways and many children (32 in

10,000 in England – Department of Health 1995) require protection from maltreatment. Most abused and neglected children suffer harm from exposure to continual distorted family interactions, not just from isolated or sequential acts of physical violence. In fact, many children show a reaction to witnessing violence similar to that of having been abused themselves (Hurley and Jaffe 1990). Much more work is necessary to untangle causality and long-term effects and, at the severe end of the spectrum, one type of abuse is usually accompanied by others, so separating out effects is difficult in any case. However, it is known that there are facets of abuse which make it more dangerous for children. These are, essentially, the severity of abuse, the context in which it occurs, how long it goes on for and whether it includes several types of abuse at once. Physical abuse may be more likely to kill but emotional or sexual abuse could potentially have more serious, longer-term consequences than physical abuse in terms of affecting the child's developing schema for appropriate behaviour in relationships. Much will depend on the quality of the existing relationships apart from the abusive element (Gibbons *et al.* 1995).

When a child dies in England and Wales as the result of non-accidental injury or extreme abuse, it is a legal requirement that an inquiry takes place. Between the Maria Colwell Inquiry in 1972 and the end of 1989 there were 39 such inquiries, mainly dealing with the death of children through abuse. These are now known as 'Part 8 Inquiries', after the section of an inter-departmental publication entitled *Working Together*, which sets out the requirement for them to be undertaken (Department of Health 1991). In 1991 The Bridge Child Care Development Service completed a Part 8 Inquiry into the death of a child, called Sukina, at the hands of her father (The Bridge Child Care Consultancy Service 1991). The report concluded – as they often do – that no single professional or agency could be blamed for failing to prevent her death. However, there was evidence that the danger might have been averted had one agency taken responsibility for collating alerting information. The failure of this to happen meant that the information available did not impact on professional perceptions of risk or danger.

As a result of the Sukina enquiry, The Bridge began to raise the funding for a research project to look more closely at the failures to predict danger and to investigate the possibility of improving practice. The aim was to achieve this by developing a new information-gathering interview schedule for use in interagency child protection procedures with particularly risky cases. A crucial first step in the process was the identification of key issues in the field and assessment of what was already known about 'dangerousness'. To this end, The Bridge commissioned a literature review from Ann Hagell.

THE LITERATURE ON PREDICTING DANGER TO CHILDREN

There are several sources of literature on predicting danger. For example, there is the work set within the child abuse and child protection literature, although this tends to have focused more on procedures and risk management than on large-scale empirical research projects and has tended to look at the range of abuse scenarios, including less dangerous as well as more dangerous. There is also a wide range of relevant (and complimentary) research in the fields of probation, forensic psychology and mental health, where the focus has been more directly on very serious violent behaviour. In fact, defined broadly, there is a tremendous amount of potentially relevant material. However, there are some major difficulties in drawing lessons for child care from these related fields.

Sampling problems: most of the studies in other fields have been conducted with very different samples to those presenting before child protection teams. Many studies of danger in forensic settings, for example, have been conducted on selected, incarcerated, male populations. While there will be some overlap with dangerous carers, we have to be very careful about generalising from these different types of studies. In addition, studies done within the child protection framework are often proved to rely on small selected groups from which it is difficult to generalise.

Type of danger studied: many studies trying to predict whether people will become dangerous do not differentiate between different kinds of violence. However, in the work of The Bridge and other agencies involved in child protection it is only danger to children that is of interest. Whether someone will go on to murder strangers, for example, is less important in these cases than whether they will injure their child. Yet the state of the literature is not such that we can be confident that some factors predict one type of violence rather than another.

The very low base rate for dangerous behaviour, and for child death in particular: this makes prediction of dangerous behaviour very difficult indeed and optimism fluctuates concerning the degree of accuracy actually achievable. The identification of 'false positives', where violence or danger is predicted but does not come to pass, is more likely than missing cases where it will happen.

Bearing these issues in mind, we brought together relevant information from the different fields and identified three important sources of information which could contribute to a dangerous situation – information about the child, information about the carer and information about the situation. This is in keeping with the general consensus among practitioners that 'child maltreatment is the end result of inter-play between predisposed caretakers who are caught in conflictual relationship patterns, vulnerable children and external stressors, with no single factor 'causing' the abusive behaviour' (Reder and Lucey 1995, p.6).

A range of empirical studies of varying quality have identified a number of different factors which may be important in identifying potential perpetrators of violence or other types of dangerous behaviour (the focus has usually been on violence). These factors generally relate either to the individual's past or to their present behaviour. They have included a history of:

- previous violence and criminal offending (Blomhoff, Siem and Friis 1990; Milner 1995)
- past mental health and personality disorder (Bowden 1996; Monahan and Steadman 1994; Swanson *et al.* 1990;), particularly with hospitalisation (Swanson 1994)
- difficult childhood's and relationships (Boswell 1996; Cichetti and Carlson 1989; Monck and New 1996).

In terms of current behaviour, they have included:

- substance abuse (Fagan 1990; Monahan 1981)
- current symptoms of mental disorder (Monahan and Steadman 1994; Webster 1995)

- certain cognitive and dispositional factors, such as high levels of anger and the need to control (Blackburn 1994; Genders and Morrison 1996; Milner 1995)
- distorted perceptions of what children should be able to do (Milner 1995).

Certain children in certain settings may also be more at risk than others and there is a slightly controversial literature concerning factors about the child which should be used as alerting information. In part, this derives from a growing interest within criminology in victimisation and the importance of characteristics of victims which has developed since the 1980s, although within child care there has been a sensitivity about seeming to 'blame' the child for the event. Children are most at risk in the early years of their life (Central Statistical Office 1994). Whether or not they are on the child protection register may not be critically important (Falkov 1996). Physical variables, such as being premature and/or of low birth weight, being disabled or temperamentally difficult, may play a role (Benedict and White 1985; Skuse and Bentovim 1994) because they may place extra stress and demands on carers already at risk. In terms of child-centred risk factors, the role of the child's own account in alerting adults may also be valuable (Harris-Hendriks, Black and Kaplan 1993).

Finally, certain factors about the family's background and the context may make the difference between generally stressed parenting, on the one hand, and serious injury to the child on the other. Studies have concluded that high levels of family problems (Caliso and Milner 1994; Skuse and Bentovim 1994), low levels of social support (DePanfilis 1996; Moncher 1995; Skuse and Bentovim 1994) and lots of general stress – such as problems with employment and finances (including chronic poverty) – all increase the chances that things might go wrong if other risk factors are present as well (Creighton 1995; Trickett *et al.* 1991). The cumulative effect of these types of problems is likely to be an important consideration. Also, organisational factors relating to the local authority may contribute to poor decision making (Dale *et al.* 1986; Department of Health 1988; Kelly and Milner 1996). It is very important that these types of factors are acknowledged and considered alongside information about the carers and their child.

IN PRACTICE: THE HISTORY OF RISK ASSESSMENT IN PROTECTING CHILDREN

Despite two decades of intense focus on child protection procedures and practices, the development of over-arching risk policies in child protection has been slow and risk assessment practice tends to vary enormously between, and sometimes within, local authorities. Guidelines and key questions that should be used do exist (e.g. those contained in the Children Act 1989 and the accompanying documentation on how to apply the Act in practice) but there are no schedules or screening instruments in wide usage in Britain. Indeed, there has been some resistance to developing anything more systematic than what already exists, because of, for example, concerns that families will become labelled as 'dangerous' and this will have further negative effects. This relates to a serious issue about the problem of false positives with respect to risk assessment schedules – because of the low base rate of the problem, any risk assessment exercise of this kind is likely to result in families being wrongly identified. This is also a problem in many other fields, such as in the labelling of children as having behaviour or reading problems at an early age in school. While this might result in increased resources for the child or family, it may also lead to them being stigmatised. The main solution is to ensure that the resulting interventions are benign and positively framed. This is most difficult in situations of serious child abuse.

The situation is rather different in the USA, where the use of risk assessment instruments grew in the 1980s and some of the professional reservations have been overcome. However, these are varied and diverse and tend to be developed locally for use by particular departments, rather than for general application (Tatara 1989). In addition to having risk assessment components, some have diagnostic, case planning, treatment monitoring and case closure features. Pecora (1991) has provided a useful overview and a means of classifying the available schemes but it is clear that significant problems still exist, even after years of development, including, for example, psychometric limitations such as an inability to deal with interactions between factors, threshold effects and non-linear relationships. However, despite these difficulties, there are also advantages and a number of positive overall effects are being reported as a result of the move towards systematic collation of information about risk factors and structured decision making in America. For example, worker attention is more focused on critical areas for assessment, documentation becomes more systematic, decision-making procedures are clearer and the influence of stereotyping and bias on decision making is reduced (Pecora 1991).

While we were unlikely to be able to overcome the many problems associated with risk assessment, the review of the literature and of existing measures suggested that there was room for a new instrument in the UK which could help systematise the existing information about the known risk factors for dangerous care and lead to increased confidence in consequent decision making. The literature emphasised the existence of some clear pointers concerning risks for violence, at least, if not as clearly for a wider range of dangerous behaviour (such as neglect). In addition, discussions with professionals and an informal analysis of child death inquiries confirmed the validity of these factors in the minds of child protection experts and in the details of earlier death investigations.

WHAT A GOOD RISK ASSESSMENT SCHEDULE SHOULD DO

A good risk assessment schedule should alert professionals to high levels of risk in parent behaviour and help to assess need in order to attempt to reduce that risk. It should have a clearly stated purpose and it should be targeted for use at a certain stage in the child protection process – the same tool is unlikely to work both at the earliest stages of referral and also with very large, old case files where the family is well known. This is partly a matter of resource limitations and other practicalities – there is a limit to what can be done in detail at the first referral of a case and it may prove more useful to target an information-gathering schedule at a later stage in the process (around the time of an initial review or case conference, for example). In order to assess risk, the schedule should be able to identify factors relating to the chance that the person will engage in particular conduct, 'measure' these factors as accurately as possible and assist in decision making about interventions to reduce the likelihood of abuse or neglect.

Ideally, a risk assessment system should specify the criteria for determining the relationship between a given level of risk and the decision to be made by the child protection system. This is very difficult and no existing system manages to do this. Even the most sophisticated of American systems can only rank cases along a risk continuum without indicating how close the case is to either end of the continuum or how much distance there is between the rankings. As already indicated, there are a variety of reasons for this, including the present lack of knowledge both about the routes between abuse and its effects (especially at the serious end of the spectrum where there is likely to be a combination of different abuses) and the success of interventions on people with different risk profiles in relation to child protection.

It is also crucial that a good risk assessment schedule should fit into existing child protection systems and become part of a much larger process of risk management. No one schedule will ever provide a panacea for dangerous care and the limitations should be clearly recognised. A good schedule will help to improve and systematise an existing system.

THE BRIDGE PILOT PROJECT

As a result of the factors highlighted by the literature review, and our thoughts on what made a good risk assessment schedule, we developed an interview schedule for use by multi-disciplinary child protection teams to bring together all the relevant information about the child, the carer's background and the context in which they were situated. Copies of the schedule, which is called the BridgeALERT, are available from The Bridge Child Care Development Service in London. The work we had done identifying themes in the literature, and talking to a range of practitioners and experts, led to the development of the BridgeALERT as a method of obtaining information that is known to correlate with dangerous people and situations. It was not designed as an instrument that would result in likelihood scores pertaining to risk. In addition, the main features of the BridgeALERT were:

- that it should act to focus attention on the most critical risk factors

- that it should advocate an approach which allows decision-making criteria to be shared amongst professionals, agencies and the individuals concerned – it was never intended that it should replace clinical judgement but it was intended to improve and inform those judgements
- that it should be simple and user-friendly – to this purpose, the items focus on behaviours rather than diagnoses and interpretations
- that it should represent a dynamic rather than a static approach, able to accommodate new data as they arose.

The pilot schedule consisted of three sections: five questions about the context (e.g. 'Does the family have very little social support?' and 'Is there any evidence that current problems that have been identified by professionals are not being dealt with?'); nineteen questions about the carer (e.g. 'Has this carer got a history of drug or alcohol abuse?' and 'Does this carer have a history of assault towards other adults in the family?'); and seven items about the child (e.g. 'Has there been a history of failure to thrive?' and 'Has there been a history of separations from the child's carers?'). Example questions are shown in Table 9.1.

The items were either drawn from the literature or, from clinical consensus amongst the practitioner and expert advisory groups, that they were (a) critical in their experience and (b) important for inclusion for face validity. Each item was accompanied by a set of notes describing how to rate the behaviour. In order to rate, each item was awarded an A, B, C or D score. An 'A' score indicated that there was evidence that the factor was present in the current case; a 'B' score indicated that the available information suggested that the factor was present but that the information was a little unclear; a 'C' indicated that there was information that the factor was not present; and a 'D' indicated that the rater could not tell either way from the available information. Towards the end of the schedule the pattern of scores (As, Bs, Cs and Ds) was converted into a picture, which allowed (a) an overall assessment of whether there were lots of factors indicating danger present in the case (and where these fell – within the carer, child or context sections) and (b) indicated whether there was a need for more information gathering before the picture was clear (lots of Bs and Ds).

Table 9.1: Examples of questions included in BridgeALERT

Example from context section

Does the family have very little social support?
People are considered to have low levels of social support if there is no one they can turn to for practical help with things such as baby-sitting, buying milk if the family is ill, taking children to school or appointments, collecting prescriptions, etc. Rate this a definite 'yes' (A) if there is no reliable person they can turn to. It does not matter if they are relying on several people who are all members of the family – this counts as social support.

- ❍ A Yes, they have no reliable social support
- ❍ B It looks from the information as if this might be the case but I'm not sure
- ❍ C No, they do have social support
- ❍ D I can't tell from the information available

SOURCE(s)

Example from carer section

Was the carer a victim of repeated sexual abuse as a child?
Here we are concerned with repeated exposure to inappropriate and disturbing parenting practices (or practices by other adults) which have had a significant effect on the carer, rather than on single but traumatising incidences. If there is evidence of single, traumatising incidences that were not part of a repeated pattern, rate this as a 'B'.

Carer__________	Carer__________
❍	❍ A Yes, definitely experienced this
❍	❍ B Not sure, I wouldn't like to be definite
❍	❍ C No, it is clear they did not experience this
❍	❍ D I can't tell from the information available

Example from child section

Has the child ever said that they thought they were in danger, or asked anyone for help either directly or indirectly?
Have they ever expressed any fear about their family (for example, being scared of going back home after nursery, etc.) talked about unexplained injuries or illness or made allegations about family members to anyone outside the family?

Child 1________________	Child 2________________		
❍	❍	A	Yes, this has happened
❍	❍	B	It looks from the information as if this might be the case but I'm not sure OR no one has ever asked the child
❍	❍	C	No, the child has been spoken to, but has never suggested danger
❍	❍	D	I can't tell from the information available

Once the schedule had been developed, a pilot study was designed with each of the participating local authorities and agencies who were funding the research. The pilot study had three main aims:

- to test the actual content of the schedule – for example, whether it was clear and understandable
- to find out what the strengths and pitfalls were when it was used in practice – how long it took to complete, how easily people could find the necessary information, etc
- to begin to assess how use of the schedule fitted into existing practice and at what point in the usual processes was it most useful, etc.

The six-month pilot commenced in the Spring of 1997. In fact, five of the six local authorities took part (the sixth declining due to internal restructuring), plus one organisation providing specialist foster care, education and support for children. Together, these teams undertook a trial of 89 cases where they filled in the BridgeALERT and responded to questions about whether this helped or hindered their practice. At the start of the six-month period researchers from the Bridge team introduced the project to departments and initiated use of the BridgeALERT. It was stressed that the document was not public and had no legal weight – it was only to be used in addition to the usual procedures, rather than instead of them.

In each of the pilot sites data collection took two forms: staff attempted to complete approximately 20 schedules on the basis of inter-agency discussions and interviews took place with social workers and their managers. Selection of pilot cases included some cases who were new referrals (initial risk assessment), some who were being prepared for a case conference or who were between case conference and a review conference, and some who were 'old' cases known to the departments for many years but not actually being prepared for a case conference at the time. The old cases were defined as families who had been on the 'books' for at least three years, had had at least three referrals made to social services and/or where accommodation had been offered for the children on at least three occasions.

Throughout the summer BridgeALERT's were completed and collated.

RESULTS OF THE PILOT

In total, 89 schedules were completed and 35 interviews conducted. Overall, the pilot suggested that the early version of the Bridge-ALERT was easy to understand and complete. The sample turned out to have consisted of approximately equal numbers of cases of boys and girls, all of whom were living with their mothers and most of whom (86%) also had a father figure present. Most of the social workers filling in the schedule rated it as a positive exercise (86% of those answering) but there was a high proportion of missing answers to this question (27% failed to answer it). When asked if the exercise had changed their perceptions of risk, the majority (74%) responded that it had not, although many responses indicated that the exercise had helped them to 'focus'. Written answers and interview questions showed a variety of responses to the exercise, and a selection of these are presented in Table 9.2.

Table 9.2: A selection of responses from social work teams to the BridgeALERT exercise as a whole

Examples of positive responses

'I found the details of risk factors located in research to be very interesting and a positive experience.'

'[The schedule] highlighted areas that need further discussions with parents about their backgrounds.'

'It was useful to look at assessments in relation to the overview – that is, context, carer, child.'

'It underlines the particular areas I need to look at – that is, carers' early history.'

'It highlighted the situation and focused my thinking.'

'It has helped me to focus on what exactly are the risks.'

Examples of negative responses

'Didn't feel a true picture could be given, did not take account of risk to child through parent having a learning disability.'

'The situation didn't always fit into any category.'

'By concentrating on the concerns felt for one parent, I felt the form ignored the strengths presented by the other parent'.'

'Mother appears to be in denial over a number of issues, and there is limited scope within the schedule to deal with this.'

One of the main aims of the pilot had been to improve the BridgeALERT and to develop a second version for further piloting. There were six main issues that arose from the pilot which indicated that changes were needed to the schedule. These are interesting in their own right as a reflection on the overall experiences of these social workers in undertaking the risk assessment exercise. Table 9.3 presents these six main findings.

As a result of these findings, a series of changes were undertaken with the BridgeALERT. It was obvious that more attention needed to be paid to the design, both to accommodate difficult and complicated family arrangements and also to make the schedule striking and easy to complete. The pilot results suggested that it was important that the schedule stood out from the run-of-the-mill paperwork that constituted much of the social worker's everyday

Table 9.3: Six main findings from the pilot indicating problems with this version of risk assessment
1) The need to be able to reflect several children and several carers on the one form. For the 89 cases who were the focus, in fact, a total of 201 combinations of child and carer were recorded. Some were filled in for up to four children and three different carers in the same situation.
2) The problem with missing information. Despite the fact that these pilot sites were all very interested in the project, and had contributed funding, there was still a failure at ground level to actually answer all of the questions. This extended even to very basic questions such as the gender of the child.
3) The variation in time taken to complete. This varied from ten minutes to four hours, suggesting very variable efforts on the part of the social workers.
4) Problems with finding time to do the schedule in the light of difficult and stressful workloads.
5) Little in the way of confirmed multi-agency co-operation. Although difficulties in co-operating were not widely reported, many people had not attempted to consult colleagues in other departments or professions.

experience, so that it was more compelling and interesting. Further attention to design might also address the problem of missing information, making it more difficult for people to skip sections or less likely for them to do so if the design was more interesting. Significantly, the one result we did not get was any negative response to the item set. Overall, most respondents felt comfortable with the actual content of the schedule and felt that, according to their experience, most items of importance were included.

Only further research work will identify how much of an issue it is that the exercise did not actually change people's perceptions of risk. This is not an uncommon finding with risk assessment schedules and, in addition, the teams completing this batch of BridgeALERT's were very experienced and were already overtly concerned with improving their performance with very dangerous families. It is very unlikely that these types of people will either admit that their initial judgement was wrong or have actually been wrong in the first place. It is more likely that, in the long run, the BridgeALERT's contribution will be to a fine-tuning or calibration of perceptions of risk rather than to a dramatic volte-face. Used properly, it will prompt professionals to actively work together and discuss information. This will be of great advantage in protecting children from abuse/neglect.

GENERAL ISSUES ARISING FROM THE PILOT AND LESSONS FOR PRACTICE AND FUTURE RESEARCH

The Bridge's 'Dangerous Care' project has raised a number of issues about risk assessment and has suggested lessons for practice. In addition, as a result of the pilot, we have also identified a need for future research, particularly in terms of evaluation. The lessons fall into three main groups and have applications for formulas of policy on protecting children as well as applications for practice and management.

One of the main issues raised is the question of whether or not the BridgeALERT can be definite about whether a child is in danger. The short answer to this is 'no'. This conclusion is one supported by the literature and all previous attempts to develop risk assessment schedules. Human behaviour is simply too unpredictable, and danger is too open to the influences of chance, for us ever to be definite about the risks posed to a child. It would be inappropriate for a schedule of this nature to even attempt this. However, the BridgeALERT will indicate those cases for which there certainly should be strong concern and cases which warrant a systematic revisit. The items contained within the schedule should be answerable and, if information is lacking about the answers, it is important that this is known. Lack of knowledge about what information is or is not available is a major part of risk. A related issue is whether it would ever be possible to rank cases in terms of their dangerousness on the basis of information in the BridgeALERT or similar schedules. At the present stage of development this cannot be done using information from the schedule because the schedule is not standardised and has not been validated through any long-term evaluation. As it stands, there is an element of double-counting in the items, so that previous violence and mental disorder are addressed in several questions, giving them undue weight if the items are added up. For this reason, assigning numerical scores has been avoided, but it is critical that we look in the longer term at how different patterns of results relate to different outcomes for children.

Another issue – particularly given that the use of the Bridge-ALERT does not result in a score – is what is to be done once the schedule has been completed. Decision making is a critical aspect of protecting children from risk and, properly used, the BridgeALERT will have enabled a multi-professional team to have collected information about the case which is known to be important in alerting workers to the presence of dangerous care. The value of the BridgeALERT is its ability to collect the information in once place and its encouragement of dialogue concerning cases. However, the BridgeALERT itself does not make decisions, it lays the groundwork for them. Anecdotal evidence points to examples of assessment followed by more assessment where the information contained does not lead to appropriate decision making, the reasons being manifold and including resource and training limitations. Munro (1996) notes that the most striking lesson to be learnt from child death inquiries is how resistant people are to altering their beliefs in relation to a case. The next version of the BridgeALERT, redesigned after the pilot, contains a decision-making module (Table 9.4) at the end, which is intended to raise issues and help to build on the information collected in order to develop a decision – a first step, in other words. In addition, there are other ways of making decision making easier, including the use of skilled case consultancy from professionals outside the team. Systematic recording of outcomes of decisions will also help as there is a clear lack of follow-up for many decisions made by child protection teams. Finally, developing overt and overarching risk management policies, which acknowledge the role of random chance but also help to structure support for good decision making, are critical.

The Children Act 1989 provides a legislative framework within which professionals operate. It cannot, however, resolve many of the tensions that exist between the state and the family and between

Table 9.4: What next?

Answering the following questions may help you to decide what steps you should take after you have completed BridgeALERT.

Personal context –

- Do I have the necessary information?
- May I be missing something in the current formulation of the case?
- Do I have strong feelings for or against the carer or the child?
- Does my formulation match my intuition?
- Am I qualified to make this decision?

Child –

- What are the risks to the child?
- Have I confirmed the risks with others working with the child?
- Are the risks worth taking now?
- What will be the gain to the child of doing nothing?
- What will be the loss to the child of doing nothing?
- Have I considered how the losses and gains might alter in the time it takes for the interventions to work?
- Will other children be affected?

Carer – (if appropriate)

- Does the carer want to change?
- What does the carer perceive as the gains in achieving change?
- What does the carer perceive as the loss in achieving change?
- Is there indication that the carer can change?

The action –

- What action should be taken?
- Would a smaller or bigger step be more appropriate?
- Who will take the action?
- Are there any other resources to be used?
- When will I review actions and re-evaluate risk?
- How will I recognise success?
- How will I recognise failure?
- What can I do to make this action more likely to succeed?
- Are relevant professionals aware of and in agreement with the actions?
- Is the carer aware of and in agreement with the actions?

Finally –

- What have I learned?
- What are the implications for my personal/professional development programme?
- How will my organisation learn from this decision?

children and their parents. Transparent decision making which indicates the basis on which decisions are made is important in reducing such tensions. Factors that are known to alert concern are important in aiding transparent decision making.

There are also some practical considerations. It seemed from the pilot that the BridgeALERT was broadly acceptable and useable, which is a significant conclusion. However, we want to emphasise again the necessity of its use in practice as part of a process, not as an alternative – as part of that message, the importance of local training on its use and limitations is seen as critical for the application of the BridgeALERT.

It is not possible to say which factors will certainly predict dangerous care. However, BridgeALERT has identified some factors which occur repeatedly in different contexts and with different samples. There is a developing consensus that integrative schemes bringing together individual, didactic and situational factors, using both actuarial and clinical assessment information, are likely to be most fruitful. Risk is frequently contextual and, therefore, simplified additive approaches that focus only on the perpetrator are likely to miss key indicators of danger. What is required is a multi-factorial, multi-dimensional approach which can alert professionals to dangerous care. This is what BridgeALERT is designed to do.

ACKNOWLEDGEMENTS

We are grateful to the funders of the Dangerous Care Project (six English Area Child Protection Committees, SCOPE, The Integrated Support Programme and the Baring Foundation) for their support and also to the many social workers and their supervisors who took part in the pilot project. This chapter has drawn on earlier publications by the authors, particularly Hagell (1998) *Dangerous Care: Reviewing the Risk to Children from their Carers.* Policy Studies Institute: London; and Jeyarajah Dent (ed) (1998) *Dangerous Care: Working to Protect Children.* The Bridge Child Development Service: London.

REFERENCES

Benedict, M. and White, R. (1985) 'Selected perinatal factors and child abuse.' *American Journal of Public Health*, 75, 780–781.

Blackburn, R. (1994) *The Psychology of Criminal Conduct: Theory, Research and Practice.* Chichester: John Wiley.

Blomhoff, S., Siem, S. and Friis, S. (1990) 'Can prediction of violence among psychiatric inpatients be improved?' *Hospital and Community Psychiatry*, 41, 771–775.

Boswell, G. (1996) *Young and Dangerous*. Aldershot, Hants: Avebury.

Bowden, P. (1996) 'Violence and mental disorder.' In N. Walker (ed) *Dangerous People*. London: Blackstone Press.

Browne, K.D. and Lynch, M.A. (1995) 'The nature and extent of child homicide and fatal abuse.' *Child Abuse Review*, 4, 309–316.

Caliso, J.A. and Milner, J.S. (1994) 'Childhood history of abuse and child abuse screening.' *Child Abuse and Neglect*, 16, 647–659.

Central Statistical Office (1994) *Social Trends for Children*. London: HMSO.

Cichetti, D. and Carlson, V. (1989) *Child Maltreatment: Theory and Research on the Causes and Consequences of Child Abuse and Neglect*. Cambridge: Cambridge University Press.

Creighton, S.J. (1995) 'Fatal child abuse: how preventable is it?' *Child Abuse Review*, 4, 318–328.

Dale, P., Davies, M., Morrison, T. and Waters, J. (1986) *Dangerous Families: Assessment and Treatment of Child Abuse*. London: Tavistock.

DePanfilis, D. (1996) 'Social isolation of neglectful families: A review of social support assessment and intervention models.' *Child Maltreatment*, 1, 37–52.

Department of Health (1988) *Protecting Children: A Guide for Social Workers Undertaking Comprehensive Assessment*. London: HMSO (the Orange Book).

Department of Health, Home Office and Department of Education and Science (1991) *Working Together for the Protection of Children*. London: HMSO.

Durfee, M. and Tilton-Durfee, D. (1995). 'Multi-agency child death review teams: experience in the United States.' In K. Browne and M. Herbert (eds) *Preventing Family Violence*. Chichester: John Wiley & Sons.

Fagan, J. (1990) 'Intoxication and aggression.' In M. Tonry and J. Wilson (eds) *Drugs and Crime Disorder*. London: Department of Health.

Falkov, A. (1996) *Study of Working Together Part 8 Reports: Fatal Child Abuse and Parental Psychiatric Disorder*. London: Department of Health.

Gelles, R.J. (1991) 'Physical violence, child abuse, and child homicide: a continuum of violence or distinct behaviours?' *Human Nature*, 2(1), 59–72.

Genders, E. and Morrison, S. (1996) 'When violence is the norm.' In N. Walker (ed) *Dangerous People*. London: Blackstone Press.

Gibbons, J., Gallagher, B., Bell, C. and Gordon, D. (1995) 'Development after physical abuse in early childhood: a follow-up study of children on protection registers.' In Department of Health (ed) *Child Protection: Messages from Research*. London: HMSO.

Harris-Hendriks, J., Black, D. and Kaplan, T. (1993) *When Father Kills Mother: Guiding Children through Trauma and Grief*. London: Routledge.

Hurley, D.J. and Jaffe, P. (1990) 'Children's observations of violence: II. Clinical implications for children's mental health professionals.' *Canadian Journal of Psychiatry*, 35, 471–476.

Kelly, N. and Milner, J. (1996) 'Child protection decision-making.' *Child Abuse Review*, 5, 91–102.

Milner, J.S. (1995) 'Physical child abuse assessment: perpetrator evaluation.' In J. Campbell (ed) *Assessing Dangerousness: Violence by Sexual Offenders, Batterers and Child Abusers*. Thousand Oaks: Sage.

Monahan, J. (1981) *Predicting Violent Behaviour: An Assessment of Clinical Techniques*. Beverley Hills, Calif: Sage.

Monahan, J. and Steadman, H. (1994) (eds) *Violence and Mental Disorder: Developments in Risk Assessment.* Chicago: University of Chicago Press.

Moncher, F. (1995) 'Social isolation and child-abuse risk, Families in Society.' *The Journal of Contemporary Human Services*, 421–433.

Monck, E. and New, M. (1996) *Report of a Study of Sexually Abused Children and Adolescents, and of Young Perpetrators of Sexual Abuse Who Were Treated in Voluntary Agency Community Facilities.* London: HMSO.

Munro, E. (1996) 'Avoidable and unavoidable mistakes in child protection work.' *British Journal of Social Work*, 26, 793–808.

Pecora, P.J. (1991) 'Investigation allegations of child maltreatment: the strengths and limitations of current risk assessment systems.' *Child and Youth Services*, 15(2), 73–92.

Reder, P. and Lucey, C. (eds) (1995) *Assessment of Parenting: Psychiatric and Psychological Contributions.* London: Routledge.

Reder, P., Duncan, S. and Gray, M. (1993) *Beyond Blame: Child Abuse Tragedies Revisited.* London: Routledge.

Skuse, D. and Bentovim, A. (1994) 'Physical and emotional maltreatment.' In M. Rutter, E. Taylor and L. Hersov (eds) *Child and Adolescent Psychiatry: Modern Approaches.* Oxford: Blackwell Scientific Publications.

Swanson, J.W. (1994) 'Mental disorder, substance abuse and community violence: an epidemiological approach.' In J. Monahan and H. Steadman (eds) *Violence and Mental Disorder: Developments in Risk Assessment.* Chicago: University of Chicago Press.

Swanson, J.W., Holzer, C.E., Ganuk, V.K. and Jono, R.T. (1990) 'Violence and psychiatric disorder in the community: evidence from the epidemiologic catchment area surveys.' *Hospital and Community Psychiatry*, 41, 761–770.

Tatara, T. (1989) 'CPS risk assessment project survey of states on CPS risk assessment practice: summary of preliminary findings.' In V. Murphy-Berman (ed) 'A conceptual framework for thinking about risk assessment and case management in child protection services.' *Child Abuse & Neglect*, 18, 2.

The Bridge Child Care Consultancy Service (1991) *Sukina: An Evaluation Report of the Circumstances Leading to her Death.* London: The Bridge Child Care Development Service.

Trickett, P.K., Aber, J.L., Carlson, V. and Cicchetti, D. (1991) 'Relationship of socioeconomic status to the etiology and developmental sequelae of physical child abuse.' *Developmental Psychology*, 15, 331–337.

Webster, C. (1995) *The Prediction of Dangerousness and the Assessment of Risk in Mentally and Personality Disordered Individuals.* Conference Paper, Faculty of Law, University of Southampton.

FURTHER READING

Department of Health (1995) *Child Protection: Messages from Research.* London: HMSO.

Hagell, A. (1998) *Dangerous Care: Reviewing the Risk to Children from their Carers.* London: Policy Studies Institute.

Jeyarajah Dent, R. (ed) (1998) *Dangerous Care: Working to Protect Children.* London: The Bridge Child Care Development Service.

CHAPTER 10

Managing Violence in Residential Settings

Angela Stanton-Greenwood

INTRODUCTION

This chapter will explore definitions of violence and clarify the concept of residential settings, and it will describe the factors peculiar to residential care that can intensify the propensity for, and severity of, violence.

Strategies for the management of violence are discussed, including recommendations about the use of restraint. The importance of looking beyond the relationship between the assailant and victim into the context in which they exist is stressed. This includes recommendations about the content of care and control policies and procedures, recording and monitoring systems and support and complaints procedures.

The residential settings included in the title are larger and smaller group settings where there is a residential aspect – for example, children's centres, schools and respite care for all client groups, including children, adults, people with a disability (learning, physical, sensory) and mental health problems.

Definitions of violence vary. The Health and Safety Executive definition (1992) states that violence is 'any incident in which an employee is threatened or assaulted by a member of the public in circumstances arising out of the course of their employment' (p.2).

This is defined in more detail by the Department of Health and Social Security Advisory Committee on Violence to Staff (1986) as 'severe verbal abuse or threat where this is judged likely to turn into actual violence; serious or persistent harassment (including racial or sexual harassment); threat with a weapon; major and minor injuries: fatalities' (p.36).

Whichever definition we prefer, definitions of violence should have the following common features:

- they should deal with observable behaviour that is explicitly described and judged as unacceptable and which possesses an element of intention to hurt
- they should allow for differences in tolerance thresholds and peoples' experiences of fear
- they should recognise the particular role played by the victim's reaction to the behaviour.

For the purposes of this chapter, violence will be viewed as one aspect of a whole range of challenging behaviours. It includes the threat or application of force which could have physically and psychologically harmful consequences, and behaviours of such intensity that the physical safety of a person or others is perceived by them as likely to be placed in jeopardy.

So, do residential settings and violence go together? There are factors peculiar to residential settings that can intensify the propensity for, and severity of, violence. As Payne and Douglas (1981) say, 'any discussion of violence in residential care must take into account the context in which violence occurs and the complex interplay of individual situations and social influences' (p.31).

Studies described by Wiener and Crosby (1988) indicate that residential care workers face more violent incidents than field social workers and suggest that this is because: residential care workers spend more time with their clients and may have more intense relationships. 'There may be evident a tension in daily work in that the client they are concerned for and to whom they wish to give the best possible attention could in certain circumstances threaten the very life of the staff member' (More and Nicholls 1997, p.2).

I would add to this that residential care workers and their clients may not be physically able to leave potentially violent situations – they form a captive audience of victims amongst peers and staff – and there can be a group or 'plague' effect in which violence or unrest in one client can affect the stability of others. Physical confrontation in a group can also risk a loss of self-esteem for those involved and the mere presence of others can distort the intentions of both the client and the staff.

Work by Wiener and Crosby (1988) demonstrates that residential settings can contain the very factors that contribute to violence. They state (p.8) that these factors are:

1. What the client brings.
2. What the staff bring (individual and team).
3. What interaction between and within the two groups brings.
4. How the institution is run and how well it meets the needs of clients and staff.
5. Outside constraints on the institution.
6. The techniques staff have or have not developed for dealing with potentially violent situations.

I propose to examine each of these factors in more detail.

What the client brings

> Many people in care appear to have a great deal of hurt and bottled up anger inside them and their opposition to authority can cause anger, aggression and violence depending upon the maturity and self control of the adult they confront. Situations which trigger this off are almost inevitable where people live at close quarters such as in residential care. (East Sussex County Council 1983, p.6)

It is possible to identify three different types of aggression that can be displayed:

1. manipulative – a cold calculated determination to obtain something of benefit to them. It is uncommon (although many young people may be accused of it) but the effect on staff and clients is out of all proportion to its rarity. These are the clients that both staff and other clients remember vividly, and who are emulated by others for a long time after they have left.
2. angry – this form of aggression and violence is far more common and is based upon modelling behaviours from others, such that clients are unable to demonstrate any alternative behaviour through which to communicate their emotions and needs. Such clients do not target anyone else

specifically after emotional arousal but may displace and transfer their anger to significant others around them. This can be exacerbated by substance or alcohol abuse and encouraged by peer groups. These clients may truly not know of any other ways of communicating their needs and when staff state the behaviour they *do not* want, they need to state the behaviours they *do* want in order to suggest an alternative.

3. defensive – in response to a perceived threat. Such violence is committed because the client is convinced that they need to 'get one in first'.

What staff bring

Staff bring beliefs about sources of violence which affect the way they respond to it – for example, 'she knew exactly what she was doing' – and, sometimes, long and bitter experience of violence, which kills the staff's concern for other people and makes them deaf to the needs of their clients. Research by the Studio III training group (McDonnell 1992) shows that staff can fall into negative traps (the quotes in italics are Studio III's names for the traps):

- the '*helpless*' trap (I've tried everything)
- the '*victim*' trap (taking the assault personally)
- the '*it's their fault*' trap (blaming the clients without analysing their own behaviour first)
- the '*I want to punish them*' trap (hard to admit and often legitimised as a consequence)
- the '*punishment works*' trap (except that it only has a short-term effect and does not educate the client)
- the '*they will not change*' trap (can become self-fulfilling)
- the '*they do not like me*' trap (it may be true)
- the '*that's the way they have always been*' trap (so therefore they will never change).

Staff also bring an awareness of their own contribution to any incident and their perceptions of, and reaction to, fear. Any analysis of an interaction with a client needs to start with the member of staff.

Interaction between and within the two groups

Physical violence may not be present but a spiralling interactive process between the aggressor and victim may eventually result in an eruption of violence as one reacts heatedly and destructively

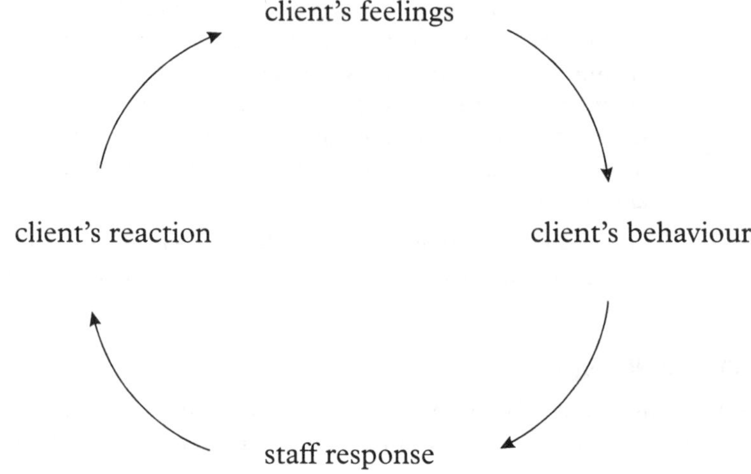

Figure 10.1: Cycle of conflict
Source: Budlong, Holden and Mooney (1993, p.175)

towards the other. This is typified as a cycle of escalating conflict (Figure 10.1).

The way in which an adult responds to the client's behaviour is crucial in either breaking the conflict cycle or sending it spinning into escalation.

How the institution is run

An assumption must be made that the managers of residential settings will be constantly striving to achieve the four components of providing quality care as described by Pearson (1992). These components are:

- a workforce that has self respect, feels in control, and acts with professional confidence and integrity
- an environment which offers the client a reasonable sense of comfort and safety
- a service which meets the clients' expectations or better
- a satisfactory completion of any activity which maintains the self-esteem of all parties involved.

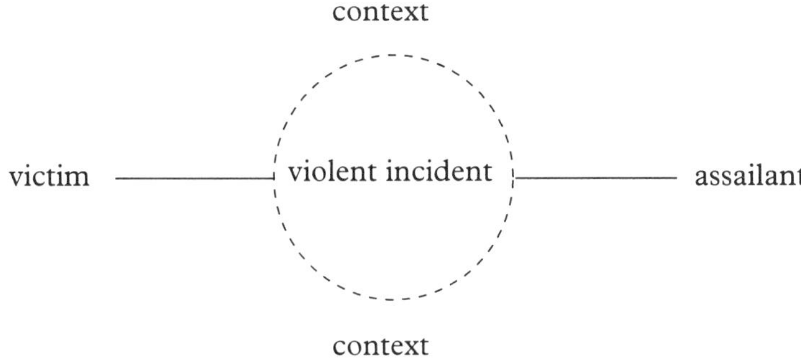

Figure 10.2: The context of violence
Source: McDonnell, Dearden and Richens (1991b, p.110)

In my experience, problems in this area develop when different people in different roles have different explanations about the sources and causes of violence. Thus people who are NOT involved in violent incidents may explain violence in terms of the people involved (i.e. they mishandled it). People who ARE involved invariably explain violence in terms of the context (i.e. not enough staff on duty).

Assaulted workers can then become stereotyped as provocative, authoritarian, inexperienced or incompetent. Hence incidents are not defined as violence and not reported or acted upon.

Managers who run institutions that subscribe to this model analyse violence in terms of the interaction between the victim and the assailant. They need to extend their debate/analysis beyond the sum of the individuals to include the context.

Outside constraints on the institution

Policies and procedures for intervention can be so vague as to be useless in practice, and funds can be so limited that the building is poorly ventilated, ill lit, unwelcoming, inaccessible, poorly furnished – all factors that contribute to an environment full of fear.

Techniques that staff have for managing violence

I have seen staff staggering away from the management of a violent incident shaking their heads and saying 'I can't believe I just did that'. So what have they done?

Have they been paralysed with fear or, in needing to be strong, stayed far longer in a dangerous situation than is wise; heard themselves shout 'well go on then and we can get it all over with!'; been unable to think what to do and lost all sense of what is 'common sense'; through poor training, or no training, responded unreasonably in the eyes of the law; lost control altogether and have not asked for someone else to intervene; responded to the behaviour only and have not considered or explored the meaning behind it. If all or some of these factors are present in a residential setting, the propensity for violence is higher than where they are not.

MANAGING VIOLENCE

> Carers should endeavour to understand why a behaviour occurs and attempt to prevent it rather than manage the behaviour when it happens. (McDonnell 1991b, p.151)

Trying to understand the cause of a behaviour can aid its management – in that if that cause can be altered or removed, the violence may also disappear. Research carried out by McDonnell (1992, p.5) in 39 children's residential settings shows eleven main causes of challenging behaviour:

1. Being unable to communicate a need other than through challenging behaviour.
2. Being confused. This can be caused by inconsistent staff requests. One member of staff may ask a client to do one thing then another comes along and chastises them for doing it when in their opinion they should be doing something else.
3. Medical problems.
4. Inactivity. Boredom and the time to worry about problems can trigger violence.
5. Demands and requests made by the staff or demands or requests refused by the staff.
6. Changes and inconsistencies in routines.
7. Environmental effects:
   a) lack of personal space
   b) excessive heat

   c) excessive noise
   d) seating, lighting, decor.
8. Relationship problems.
9. Early childhood traumas.
10. Being provoked or wound up.
11. Being bullied.

Triggers to violence can be external – for example, a stressful event – or internal, sometimes related to the previous causes. Examples of external triggers can be the presence of a certain person in a room, a phone call to say that they cannot go home for the weekend, the word 'no'. Internal triggers can be reminders of events, seeing a similarity of a hated figure in someone else. Carers should try and understand what triggers their clients have by:

- observing and relating to their clients
- knowing their social history; culture; history of violence
- knowing how they have responded to social work interventions before
- knowing any described triggers and successful interventions
- knowing the client's pathway to violence.

Some of these aspects can be described very vividly and repeatedly in a client's case history. The danger of taking some pre-admission materials at face value, however, is that the record may be made with intention of getting a disruptive client excluded from their present environment into a different one. I could have spent many a day tiptoeing around a supposedly dangerous and uncontrollable client who is new to us when what they need at that point is positive regard and a clear introduction to new structures.

Obviously, in an ideal world, all of the information required to help carers to manage violent behaviour will be at hand and be unbiased. New assessments can always be made, based on the fact that a change of environment can change patterns of behaviour, as, all too often, staff become trained into patterns of responses by the behaviour, or probable behaviour, of a client. I have seen clients take great delight in giving 'that look' and watching the changes in body language and behaviour of staff. They have no intention of developing their behaviour further (on this occasion) but enjoy the control that they have over staff's responses.

Case study

Consider client Adam. Over time, we began to recognise his pathway to violence, record it and agree responses. The first signs of his negative behaviours and high arousal were verbal and consisted, initially, of three facets:

1. Verbal threats (which should always be taken seriously, acknowledged and not ignored).
2. Ritualistic repetition (which wound him up and caused adrenalin to flow).
3. Depersonalising language (racist and sexist abuse, demeaning language), all designed to generate an aggressive response.

In tandem with these verbal patterns came non-verbal behaviours. He would walk restlessly around the project, muttering under his breath and, if spoken to, would give extended eye contact, moving in to invade personal space. Should this be ignored, or should staff intervention be unsuccessful or generate more anxiety, his behaviour would escalate to banging tables, doors and furniture and poking and pushing less able and/or smaller peers, towering over them. This was designed to force staff to intervene.

This picture of Adam's behaviour was built up over time and experience of some painful situations for Adam, peers and staff alike.

As with many clients, he seemed to feel more secure with some staff than others and patterns of poor behaviour were located on certain shifts. He responded positively or negatively to staff interventions dependent upon his perception of the adult's perceived status and influence in the project's pecking order. He, like others, became very adept at exploiting what he perceived as an adult's strengths and weaknesses – more particularly, their tolerance thresholds.

It was essential that we read his social and emotional barometer at all times, recognising that certain negative patterns of behaviour were likely to develop on certain shifts and/or if inactive. (We were careful to not view this as a self-fulfilling prophecy however).

Combinations of staff were chosen with care so that more and less vulnerable staff worked together. As Adam was so little in control or aware of his own behaviour it was essential that staff intervened early, decisively and effectively if preventative measures like shift combinations and activities did not succeed. It was crucial that they did not wait for Adam's contagious impact on other peers before they intervened.

Initially, the rest of his peer group had to be redirected and persuaded to move away from Adam rather than the other way round, which would have been more confrontative. The team had already discussed the acceptable distractors.

Once alone, Adam was observed from a distance and then offered a distractor – for example, to pass something to a member of staff, an invite to make a drink, etc. If Adam responded positively, or indifferently, contact was continued. If he responded aggressively, staff withdrew, still observing from a distance. The removal of his intended victims enabled Adam to begin to work his way out of trouble in isolation from the apparent source of it.

Over time, and many cold drinks, small tasks and Life Space Interviews, Adam was able to reluctantly recognise (if not own) his own pathway to violence. He was encouraged to recognise and name his own feelings and the related behaviour at each stage of the cycle to violence and to pull back from each stage. He did not appear to understand alternative behaviours that could help him to meet his needs in a less aggressive manner.

He still demonstrated a tendency to be disrespectful and invasive with staff that he did not respect, however, and this encouraged a plague effect with his peers. In agreement at a team meeting, staff who felt less effective with Adam, and who were judged in this manner by him, were encouraged to ask clearly that another member of staff enforce a consequence of behaviour with him. After initial sneerings of 'You've got to get someone else to do it for you', Adam began to realise that whoever he challenged he still received the same response, if not from that person themselves then under their direction. Several staff eventually felt enabled to carry out the behaviour management strategies themselves whilst the more 'effective' staff member loitered in the background.

A GUIDE TO GOOD PRACTICE

It is hard and, indeed, wrong to be prescriptive about ways of managing violent behaviour. There are too many combinations of factors to consider in any potentially violent situation for even a large number of approaches or strategies to work consistently. From experience, however, there are certain principles of good practice that could help to de-escalate a potentially violent situation. I list them below:

1. Know your client, his or her background, triggers and individual pathways to violence.
2. Know yourself, your own triggers. Be aware of your own internal bodily reactions. Fear can be confused with anger. If your own anger is rising, state the agreed cue that encourages another member of staff to take over.
3. Avoid confrontation – have a calm manner; be aware of body movements and position; do not corner your client.
4. Avoid physical contact and keep your distance.
5. Avoid the phrase 'because I say so' – you turn yourself into an instant victim. Talk of house rules instead.
6. Do not include other issues and pile on the agony.
7. Do not make an ultimatum you cannot keep. Stick to the adage 'say yes and do it. Say no and mean it'.
8. Repeat your request like a broken record, but remember that there is a fine line between that and nagging.
9. Assess the situation. Ask yourself these questions:
   - what am I feeling right now?
   - what does this person need or want?
   - what is going on in the group right now?
   - where is this person on the 'in control/aware' axis? (See Figure 10.3.)

If, when a client is displaying aggressive/violent behaviour, they appear to be not aware of themselves and not in control of themselves, they can be very dangerous. The client may have been out for the evening and appear intoxicated. Call for assistance.

If they are in control of themselves and aware of their behaviour, they are either being very intentional or are amenable to reason. Therefore, this can be a very negative state to be in or a very positive

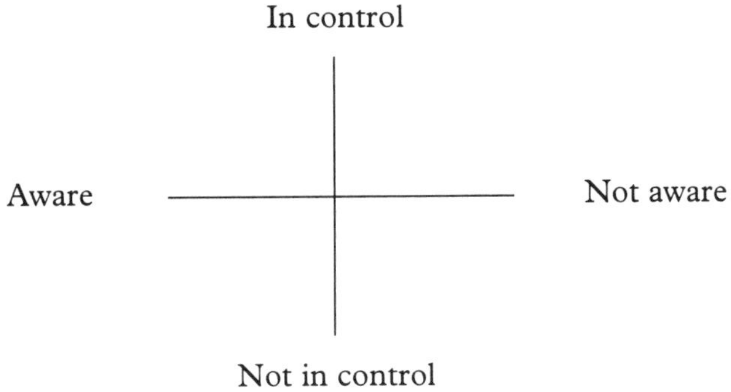

Figure 10.3: The control/aware axis
Source: Studio III training event (November 1997, Bristol)

one. If you are the target, remove yourself and observe at a distance with a colleague. The latter may intervene more effectively simply because they are not you.

If a client is aware of their negative behaviour but not in control of it, provide structure until their self-control is restored. This client will be very distressed and to ignore their behaviour may drive them into an unaware/not-in-control state. Their behaviour is designed to attract you to manage them. Encourage them to give you a sign when they are losing control.

If they are in control but not aware that their behaviour is unacceptable, they may need education or counselling and to be offered the opportunity to practise alternative, acceptable behaviours. This may be a client who is demonstrating unacceptable sexual behaviour in public which, by law, should be conducted in private. It is probably better to assume that a client knows no different until they are enlightened than to assume that they are being deliberately provocative.

After considering some of these issues, decide how you will respond. Record cycles of behaviour and successful/unsuccessful interventions so that others may learn from this and so that clients need not be constantly practised on.

In Adam's case the client group was amenable enough to rewards to remove themselves if offered an acceptable distractor. Where this is not the case, and violence is occurring, other steps may need to be taken.

THE USE OF RESTRAINT

Only reasonable force can be used in the management of physical behaviours in general. Staff would have to prove that the force they used was reasonable if their action was questioned or a complaint made. Government guidance on the Permissible Forms of Control in Residential Homes (DoH 1993) states that 'staff should intervene positively'.

A distinction has been made between open and secure accommodation but a myth abounds that staff have no rights to physically restrain children in open accommodation. As Brayne and Martin (1997) say, 'the Control of Children in Public Care: Interpretation of the Children Act 1989 guidelines make it clear that the use of physical restraint to prevent children from putting themselves or others at serious risk or to prevent serious damage to property can be justified. Staff in these situations should act as a parent would' (p.223).

However, physical restraint is *not* a behaviour management strategy and, if conducted as such, is *not* a therapeutic intervention. Physical restraint is a *last resort* and could be regarded as a failure of preventative measures. There are certain principles and practices that I believe must be included in restraint procedures:

- the method of restraint should be effective and socially acceptable where possible
- an effective restraint procedure should be able to contain the behaviour without tissue damage to the client or carer
- pain should *never* be used as a means of control
- joints should be avoided at all costs and *never* locked
- the procedures used must be such as to make the possibility of their use as a physical punishment impossible
- the method of restraint should be effective and socially acceptable where possible
- care staff should learn to use their body weight effectively and carefully
- restraint should not be viewed as a end in itself but as an attempt to control the client until they re-establish self-control. Ways of avoiding this situation in the future must be discussed and agreed with the client and other carers.

The employment of restraint procedures must be located within the policies, procedures and guidelines of the establishment and should be included in the risk assessment for each individual client, the environment, activities, etc.

Vague statements in care and control policies, like 'use minimum force', are of little use to someone confronted with a violent person (McDonnell, Dearden and Richens 1991c). However, although it is true that a care and control policy cannot possibly anticipate every violent situation, it can state examples of good and bad practice and what is acceptable and what is not. Having studied care and control guidelines, the best policies and procedures seem to emphasise that prevention is better than intervention – that is, the avoidance of violent situations is always a preferable solution; state specific criteria for intervening in violent situations; state the intervention procedure; specify a training system; specify recording procedures/ monitoring; specify support and complaints procedures.

We have already considered issues pertinent to prevention and intervention, so let us look in greater depth at training systems, recording procedures and support and complaints procedures.

SPECIFIC TRAINING SYSTEMS

Once a training system has been specified, it should be experienced and re-visited by all staff members. Such training should:

- involve staff in practising releases and getting away (not self-defence)
- concentrate to a large extent on methods of defusing negative behaviour
- be explicit about the fact that restraint is a last resort and that they must only use techniques in which they have been trained
- help staff to be aware of how they may personally cause a threat and in what way
- help staff to understand their power if in a position to allocate/deny resources
- when to call for help and how
- when and how to intervene between a staff and client, and between clients.

Such training should:

- reduce client and staff injury rates
- increase the confidence levels of the carers, who may defuse incidents more effectively
- clarify grey areas, including the reasons for restraint

- clarify for staff which specific restraint methods and principles are acceptable and avoid other forms
- clarify for clients which specific restraint methods and principles are acceptable.

SPECIFIC RECORDING AND MONITORING SYSTEMS

Risk assessments should be completed which analyse and assess the severity and frequency of risk, likelihood of violence and potential hazards in any given activity, with a given client in a given environment.

Managers should ask their staff questions about:

Tasks – do you have some tasks that are more likely to get an aggressive reaction? For example, budgeting, encouraging independence skills

Places – do some places feel inherently more hazardous than others? If so, why? For example, no exit other than through main door, isolated and ill lit

Times – are there times when something is more likely to happen? For example, the 'Sunday night syndrome' before school on Monday

People – are some people more likely than others to pose a threat? (More and Nicholls 1997, p.6)

The purpose of risk assessment is to know the factors likely to affect the risk of violence and make plans before, or when work begins, to reduce or compensate for as many of these as possible.

Risk reduction is the phase for thinking of both the techniques and logistics for reducing risk. This may help to directly reduce the anxieties of a carer who has an accessible exit, who never works alone, etc, and, thereby, reduce the factors which could contribute to an escalation towards violence.

A risk evaluation (Small 1985) states the action the carer is to take if violence is occurring, or has occurred, and can take the form of care and control guidelines. Recording procedures should include:

- health and safety reports
- incident reports written within 24 hours of the incident and which include (where possible) the client's views of the incident and the action plan agreed to avoid the incident happening again

- behaviour management strategies/reactive plans which include an agreement with the client about areas of their behaviour management that need to be focused on; agreed strategies to help the client to manage their own behaviours; agreed methods of restraint (e.g. none required, chair, floor).

Incident reports should be monitored regularly in order to ensure that staff are only using the specified behaviour management and restraint procedures and only in appropriate circumstances; patterns of staff behaviours are analysed and discussed in supervision; patterns of client behaviours are analysed and discussed with the client and in team meetings (where appropriate).

SPECIFIC SUPPORT AND COMPLAINTS PROCEDURES

Should restraint be required, it is not enough that it is done within all guidelines. All participants in such an event need support and to be able to talk through what has happened, how and why, and to develop a plan in order for it not to happen again. This means:

- crisis-incident stress debriefing for clients and staff or a Life Space Interview. Both sets of participants should be individually encouraged to analyse their own behaviour in any given situation and agree a plan as to how to manage it next time if it should occur
- counselling support for work-related stress, confidential to staff and counsellor
- a complaints procedure which is advertised and explained to the client before they take up residence.

CONCLUSION

There are no panaceas in the management of violence. Nor is there a stock of behaviour management strategies that staff can follow which will always work. There are principles and practices that will enable the incidences of violence, and severity of it, to be reduced.

Each analysis of a violent situation needs to include an analysis of the assailant, the victim and the context at that time. The context can often contribute as much to the escalation of a violent incident as the two protagonists. For this reason, risk assessments are crucial, as is working through 'worst possible scenarios'.

What this chapter has sought to describe and illustrate are principles of good practice in the management of violent behaviour which do not belong in the minds or hands of front-line staff alone.

They belong firmly upon the agenda of clients as individuals and a group, staff as individuals and a team, and managers who provide the context in which violence may or may not take place and who strive to maintain quality care in residential settings.

REFERENCES

Brayne, T. and Martin, G. (1997) *Law for Social Workers*. 5th ed. London: Blackstone.

Budlong, M., Holden, M., Mooney, A. (1993) *Therapeutic Crisis Intervention, Fourth Edition.* New York: Family Life Development Center.

Department of Health (1993) *Permissable Forms of Control in Childrens' Residential Homes*. London: HMSO.

East Sussex County Council (1983) *Handling Aggression and Conflict*. London: ESCC.

Health and Safety Advisory Committee (1986) *Violence to Staff in the Health Service*. London: HMSO.

Health and Safety Regulations Commission (1992) *The Management of Health and Safety at Work. Approved Code of Practice*. London: HMSO.

McDonnell, A.A., Dearden, R. and Richens, A. (1991b) 'Staff training in the management of violence and aggression. 2. Avoidance and escape principles.' *Mental Handicap*, 19, 109–112.

McDonnell, A.A., Dearden, R. and Richens, A. (1991c) 'Physical restraint procedures.' *Mental Handicap*, 19, 151–154.

McDonnell, A.A. (1992) *Managing Challenging Behaviour in Young Children.* Bath: Studio III training Systems.

More, W. and Nicholls, D. (1997) *Managing Aggression and Violence.* Birmingham: Pepar.

Payne, C. and Douglas, R. (1981) 'Planning to deal with the violent ones.' *Social Work Today*, 12, 38, 12.

Pearson, V. (1992) *The Causes of Aggression.* London: Pavic Publications.

Small, N. (1985) 'Minimising the risk.' *Community Care*, 14–16.

Wiener, R. and Crosby, I. (1988) *Handling Violence and Aggression. Training Pack*. Leeds: University of Leeds.

FURTHER READING

Barnardos (1980) *Dealing with Violence and Aggression.* Training pack. London: Barnardos.

Department of Health (1997) *The Control of Children in Public Care: Interpretation of the Children Act 1989.* Guidelines. London: HMSO.

Leadbetter, D. and Trewartha, R. (1996) *Handling Aggression and Violence at Work.* Lyme Regis: Russell House Publishing.

McDonnell, A.A., Dearden, R. and Richens, A. (1991a) 'Staff training in the management of violence and aggression: 1. Setting up a training system.' *Mental Handicap 19,* 73–76.

McDonnell, A. (1996) *The Physical Restraint Minefield: A Professional's Guide.* Bath: Studio III.

More, W. (1988) *Aggression and Violence: Steps to Safety at Work.* Birmingham: Pepar.

Tutt, N. (ed) (1976) *Violence.* London: HMSO.

CHAPTER 11

Violence in High Secure Hospital Settings

Measuring, Assessing and Responding

Colin Dale, Phil Woods, George Allan and Walter Brennan

INTRODUCTION

The National Health Service Act (DHSS 1977) places a duty on the Secretary of State 'to provide and maintain services… for persons subject to detention under the Mental Health Act (DHSS 1983) who in his opinion require treatment under conditions of special security on the account of their dangerous, violent or other criminal propensities' (section 4). In Great Britain these arrangements are executed by the provision of four high secure 'Special Hospitals', namely Ashworth Hospital in Merseyside, Rampton Hospital in Nottinghamshire, Broadmoor Hospital in Berkshire and Carstairs Hospital in Scotland.

Patients are cared for in such a way as to protect the public, patients and staff from harm. Such care only differs essentially from NHS psychiatric hospitals in that patients are treated within highly secure buildings, paying particular attention to dangerousness and its reduction. The Butler report (DHSS 1975) defined dangerousness as a 'propensity to cause serious physical injury or lasting psychological harm'.

Patients are admitted to these hospitals because they are judged to be 'a grave and immediate danger' if they were to remain in the wider community. Some are determined and accomplished absconders. The majority suffer from mental illness (see Figure 11.1) and have a history of assaultiveness (see Figure 11.2). Most of the patients eventually leave but a small number stay because they are never considered safe enough to be transferred to conditions of lesser security. Eighty per cent of patients have been convicted of an offence, some of which are of a very serious nature.

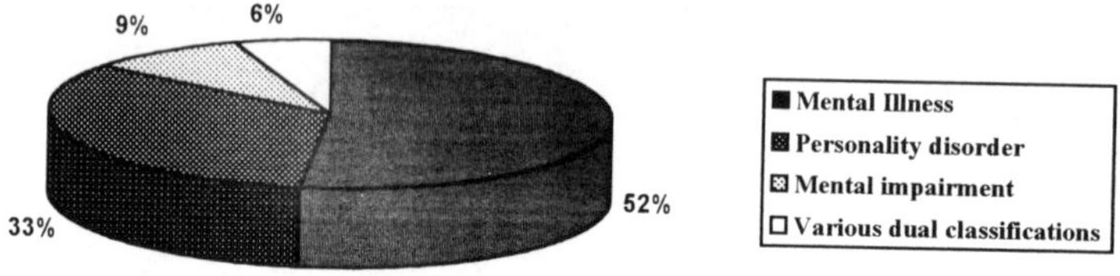

Figure 11.1: Admissions by diagnosis to Ashworth Hospital between 1975–1994 (n=1463)

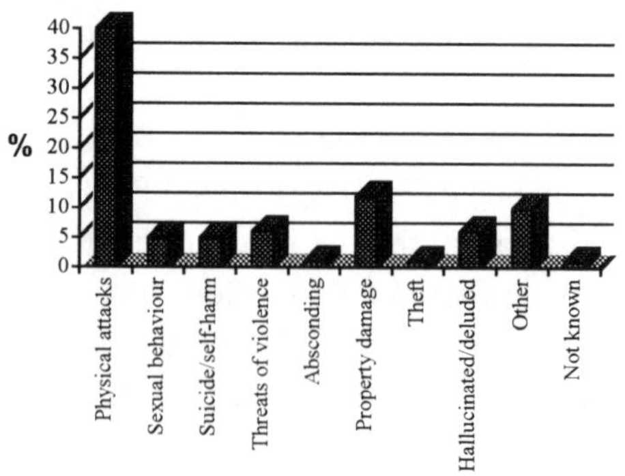

Figure 11.2: Reason for admission for all patients admitted between 1975–1994 (n=1463)

REVIEWING THE LITERATURE

Psychiatric hospitals account for the largest proportion of violent incidents in health care settings. Conn and Lion (1983), in a study of a large university hospital in the USA, reported that assaults were distributed throughout the hospital with 41 per cent in the psychiatric unit, 18 per cent in emergency rooms, 13 per cent in the medical unit, 8 per cent in a surgical unit and 7 per cent in the paediatric unit.

Much of the literature is contradictory and difficult to compare due to differences in the following factors: the variable operational definitions of what is being studied; the types of study undertaken (retrospective versus prospective); and the differences in the sample populations.

When defining and measuring violence, descriptions vary from the very vague – for example, 'untoward events that adversely affect the well-being of patients' (Way *et al.* 1992, p.361) through to definitions which include passive aggression, verbal abuse, threatened aggression and actual aggression. Many studies categorise the violence directly in relation to seriousness of injury, which is a questionable premise as it takes no account of the intent of the assailant or the sufferings of the victim.

One of the other key issues relates to under-reporting of incidents. Lion, Snyder and Merrill (1981) reported that up to five times as many assaults occurred as were actually reported. Explanations offered for this include: frequency of minor assaults is so high that staff become inured to them and therefore do not report all incidents; staff consider it too troublesome to fill out reports, especially when they see no change forthcoming as a result of reporting; and staff fear accusations of negligence and inadequate performance when assaults occur. Carton and Larkin (1991) found that even with a prospective study there was under-reporting, with only 42 per cent of incidents being reported.

Predisposing factors to violence

The factors reported can be grouped together under the headings 'patient characteristics' and 'environmental factors'. Patient characteristics would include the following:

- Age – assailants tend to be relatively young.
- Gender – a high level of violence amongst female patients has been reported. Larkin, Murtagh and Jones (1988) found that female patients, who account for 25 per cent of the population in English special hospitals, accounted for 75 per cent of the violent incidents.
- Ethnic background – there is a paucity of published research in this area. What is published provides contradictory evidence.
- Previous history of violence – a number studies have identified that a previous history of violence is associated with increased involvement in violent incidents. Many of the studies have indicated that a small proportion of patients were responsible for the majority of the incidents. This held true in most types of psychiatric hospitals.
- Diagnosis – schizophrenia is identified as being the most commonly represented diagnosis in violent patients (Tam, Englesmann and Fugere 1996; Noble and Rodger 1989; Coldwell and Naismith 1989; Fottrell 1980). Some researchers narrowed this diagnosis down further to paranoid schizophrenia (Kennedy 1993; Hunter and Carmel 1989). Studies have also shown that many of the diagnoses have been exacerbated by substance abuse (Walker and Seifert 1994; Davis 1991; Palmstierna and Wistedt 1989; Krakowski, Convit and Jaeger 1989).
- Length of stay – a number of researchers have identified an association between the patients' length of stay in a psychiatric hospital and involvement in violence, that is, the violent patients tended to have a longer length of stay.

Environmental factors

There is considerable agreement that the wards housing the less stable patients – for example, admission, intensive care and locked wards within general psychiatric hospitals – have the most incidents (Powell, Caan and Crowe 1994; Coldwell and Naismith 1989; Hodgkinson, Hillis and Russell 1984; Fottrell 1980). Some studies have also identified that those wards which house patients with alcohol and drug abuse have a higher level of violence than general psychiatric wards (Powell *et al.* 1994; Palmstierna and Wistedt 1989; Krakowski *et al.* 1989).

Studies in secure and forensic settings have indicated that there is an even greater rate of violent incidents than in general psychiatry

(Kelsall, Dolan and Bailey 1995; Larkin *et al.* 1988; Rix and Seymour 1988; Dietz and Rada 1982).

Of those studies that have looked at sub-locations, most of them agree that the majority of incidents occurred on the ward, with very few incidents in off-ward areas (Kelsall *et al.* 1995; Coldwell and Naismith 1989; Hodgkinson *et al.* 1984; Fottrell 1980). The dining-room area was identified as having the highest level of incidents. Other studies pinpointed communal areas of the ward, with very few incidents occurring in sleeping areas.

Patient density has been examined and a more recent study (Brooks *et al.* 1994) argues that there is a strong positive relationship between incidents at high patient density. There is considerable data relating to the time of day when most incidents occurred. However, much of this data is conflicting. Data suggests that patient activity is more important than time of day and that the differences may be accounted for by different levels of patient activity during the different time periods. Studies reporting on days of the week have also been conflictual. Again, this supports the notion that patient activity is more important than day of the week.

Nature of incidents

A survey commissioned by the Health Advisory Committee (1987) confirmed the increasing impact of violence on the work of health service staff. It reported that about 6 to 7 per cent of all staff were assaulted in a three-month period. There is almost universal agreement that nursing staff bear the brunt of assaults (Carton and Larkin 1991; James *et al.* 1990; Noble and Rodger 1989; Larkin *et al.* 1988; Fottrell 1980), with evidence that attacks on male nursing staff are 50 per cent higher than on female nurses. Coldwell and Naismith (1989) and Larkin *et al.* (1988) found that the second most common group of victims are other patients, whilst Dooley (1986) found that they were more likely to be assaulted than nursing staff.

Several studies found that most of the incidents that occur are minor in nature (Kelsall *et al.* 1995; Noble and Rodger 1989; Rix and Seymour 1988; Fottrell 1980). Larkin *et al.* (1988) found that within the special hospitals incidents tend to be more serious in nature. This finding was confirmed in a replicated study by Carton and Larkin (1991) but they found that the number of incidents had decreased since the previous study and argued that this was due to greater confidence engendered in staff by control and restraint training. The beneficial effect of training and restraint was supported by evidence from the United States (Poster and Ryan 1989; Lion 1977). Probably, one of the most extensive literature reviews is by Davis (1991), who proposed that violence is a result of interaction between the various types of factors and simply not an expression of individual pathology.

STUDY INTO VIOLENT INCIDENTS IN A HIGH SECURITY HOSPITAL

Recommendation 88 of the 1992 Ashworth Inquiry stated: 'We recommend that a system of reporting all incidents (untoward events) occurring in the hospital must be established, and we suggest a form the system might take' (Department of Health 1992, p.261). In light of this, a small working group was established to consider incident reporting and set up a classification system for incidents, which would extend the scope of incident reporting to include the documenting of relatively minor incidents.

Incidents were categorised into four groups, which are in descending order of seriousness:

Category A	Any unexpected death
Category B	Life-threatening activity – e.g. attempted suicide, severe assault with a weapon or attempted strangulation
	Escape
	Hostage taking
	Serious fire
Category C	Serious assault
	Significant destruction of property
	Drug/Alcohol abuse
	Security breaches – e.g. escape plot
Category D	Others within the definition of incidents above, including:
	Minor assaults
	Verbal altercation between patients
	Verbal abuse against staff

The list was not intended to be exhaustive and staff were expected to exercise judgement regarding this. It was further agreed that a computerised system be designed to capture all categories of incidents with the following aims:

1. To provide an accurate record of all relevant information appertaining to incidents.
2. To produce a system of incident reporting which is accessible, versatile and would assist in reviewing the patient's care.
3. The system should be viewed positively by those involved, including patients, and should underpin good practice and help improve standards of care and treatment.

This computerised Incident Reporting System was satisfactorily piloted in July 1994 and implemented on all wards. During the implementation period incidents occurring on wards which did not have the computerised system were recorded on the system centrally.

The following is an analysis of all incidents occurring during a three-year period, 1 December 1994 to 30 November 1997, which met the following definition: 'any behaviour which could physically damage the individual, another individual or property' (Kelsall *et al.* 1995, p.151).

Results

There were a total of 687 patients who were resident in the hospital at some time during the study. Of these, 64 per cent (n=436) were involved in an incident; 84 per cent (n=367) males and 16 per cent (n=69) females. A total of 5009 incidents occurred; 55 per cent (n=2779) involving males and 44 per cent (n=2214) involving females, and 16 unknown patients. This in itself is interesting as females only accounted for 10 per cent of the total patients during the period of the study. The total number of incidents for each individual ranged from 1 to 194 incidents. Interestingly, only a small number of patients (n=32) were responsible for 50 per cent of these incidents and, for the incidents involving females, 8 patients were responsible for 49 per cent. Furthermore, 69 per cent of the individuals involved in greater than 75 incidents were female.

SEVERITY OF INCIDENT

The severity of incident was examined using three criteria: serious, moderate and minor. A serious incident was defined as category A or B, as previously identified; a moderate as category C; and a minor as category D. Figure 11.3 shows the results. In summary, 3 per cent (n=136) were serious; 31 per cent (n=1566) moderate; and 66 per cent (n=3291) minor.

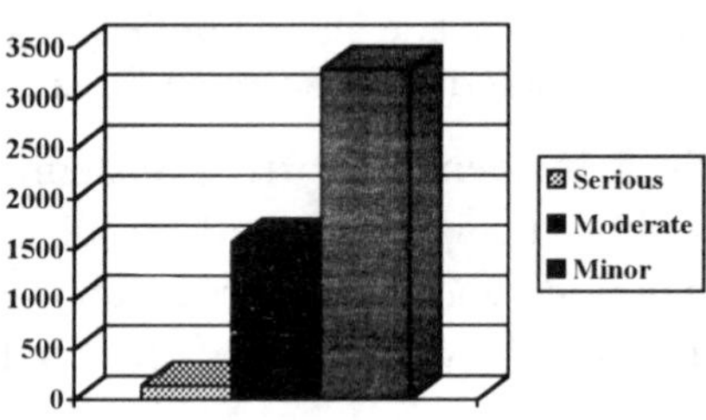

Figure 11.3: Severity of incident

Differences between gender revealed strong evidence that males were involved in more serious and moderate incidents, with females tending to be involved more in the minor ones. Ethnicity examination revealed that black patients tended to be involved in more serious incidents.

Examining age differences, indications were that individuals between the age of 18 to 39 carried out 81 per cent of the most serious incidents and 78 per cent of moderate ones. However, when stratified by gender, the percentage of serious incidents in this age range rises to 89 per cent for incidents involving females. This phenomenon is also seen in incidents of minor and moderate severity. In males, however, the same age range is responsible for 77 per cent of serious incidents but, although still responsible for the majority of other incidents, it is less striking with a greater spread.

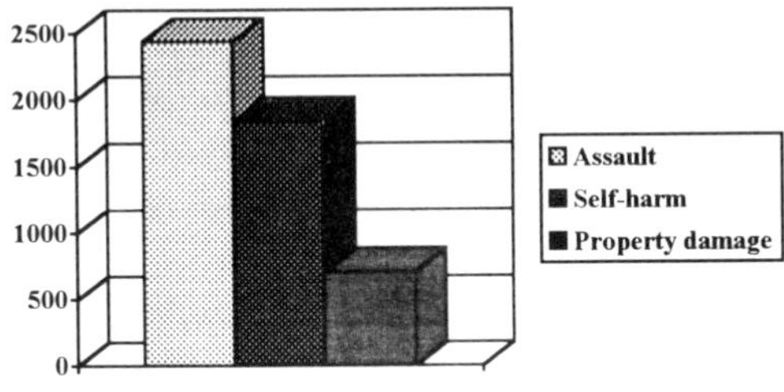

Figure 11.4: Type of incident

TYPE OF INCIDENT

Data were conflated into three main types of incident: assault, self-harm and property damage (see Figure 11.4). In summary, 49 per cent (n=2437) of incidents were assault, 37 per cent (n=1841) self-harm and 14 per cent (n=709) property damage.

Again, in examining gender differences, interesting, but not unexpected, results were obtained. Males tended to be involved in more incidents of assault than females (78% versus 22%), whereas incidents of self-harm occurred more frequently for females than males (76% versus 24%). This is even more striking considering that females consist of 10 per cent of the total patient population. Sixty-two per cent of property damage was by males and 38 per cent by females.

VICTIMS

There were 2437 incidents of assault of which 51 per cent (n=1245) involved assaults on other patients, 47 per cent (n=1137) on staff and 2 per cent (n=55) on others – for example, visitors. No differences were found between the victim and severity of the assault.

LOCATION OF INCIDENTS

The majority of incidents – 98 per cent (n=4891) – were found to occur on the ward. An analysis of the frequency of incidents by type of ward showed that 57 per cent of all ward-based incidents occur on high-dependency type wards, with only 2 per cent on low-dependency type wards. Further conflation of data revealed that almost half of all ward-based incidents occurred in two areas of the ward. The largest proportion of incidents – 28 per cent (n=1383) – occurred in the patients' bedroom area, whilst the day areas of the ward accounted for 20 per cent (n=961) of incidents.

However, further conflation by gender illustrated a rather different picture. The majority (25.5%) of incidents involving males occurred in the day area of the ward, followed by the bedrooms, then other communal areas of the ward (toilet and bathroom areas). A significant number of incidents occurred in the night station and staff areas of the ward, whilst the majority (40.1%) of incidents involving females occurred in bedrooms, then the day area of the ward. A significant number of incidents (10.6%) occurred in the toilets, but very few in the staff areas.

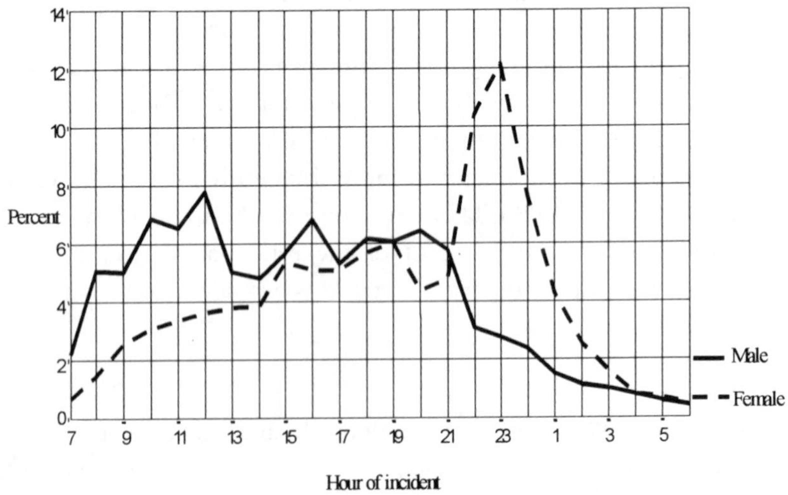

Figure 11.5: Percentage of incidents by hour for males and females

The majority of assaults took place in the communal areas of the ward – for example, day area, night station – whilst incidents of self-harm took place predominantly in the bedrooms and toilets.

TIME OF INCIDENTS

An analysis of the frequency of incidents for each hour stratified by gender is illustrated by Figure 11.5. It can be seen here that although both genders have a steady increase throughout the morning, males have a steeper incline and are responsible for the majority of this.

Incidents involving female patients continued to rise until eight in the evening before falling slightly. The most interesting point is the dramatic peak for females between ten and eleven o'clock in the evening (mostly due to self-harm when females initially retired to bed). The frequency then declined significantly over the next two hours and continued to fall throughout the remainder of the night.

RISK ASSESSMENT

Within high security psychiatric care, risk assessment is the guiding force for care continuums (Woods 1996). Fundamentally, concern is with how dangerous an individual has been in the past, presently is, and is likely to be in the future. The aim, ultimately, is how best to manage the risk or risks that have been identified.

Two main methodological approaches have evolved around risk assessment. First, there is the actuarial or statistical approach, based on static and pre-determined variables such as age at first violent offence and failure on previous discharge. Current research focus is on grounding actuarial predictions along with the second approach: clinical risk assessment.

Clinical risk assessment is grounded in the individual's clinical and behavioural presentation. Furthermore, if assessments are systematic and person-focused, they can ultimately inform treatment and discharge planning. Good base assessments can thus contribute to a dynamic assessment of risk.

The Behavioural Status Index (Reed *et al.* 1996) offers clinicians such a systematic approach to risk assessment and is theoretically grounded in previous risk assessment research. It integrates both actuarial and clinical approaches, where variables measured are treatment- and person-specific but, through regular assessment, an actuarial, but dynamic, picture can be produced for the individualised risk assessment.

The Behavioural Status Index

The Behavioural Status Index (BSI), a behaviourally based assessment instrument (Reed *et al.* 1996), focuses on the therapeutic assessment of social 'risk', insight and communicational skills through its combination of three related sub-scales (Woods, Reed and Robinson 1998). The BSI consists of 70 items that are measured on an ordinal scale ranging from 1 through 5 (that is, from worst to optimal status). Underpinning the scalar items are normative behavioural performances, seen in the optimal state for each, where a higher score indicates more socially adaptive or 'acceptable' behavioural performance.

The risk sub-scale contains 20 items measuring constructs associated in the literature with violence or dangerousness: the influence of supportive family links; elements of violence to others; violence which is directed towards the self; verbally directed aggression; violence directed towards property or objects; breaches of security; more generalised disruptive episodes; behaviours which are copied from observation of member(s) of the peer group; inappropriate sexual behaviours; sado-masochistic behaviours, macho gear and adornment; threatening fixations involving other individuals; substance abuse; and, finally, psychiatric illness (see Box 11.1).

The insight sub-scale contains 20 items and examines an individual's cognitive constructs of reality. The influence here is one of an eclectic perspective which developed from psychodynamic, cognitive-behavioural and phenomenological theories. Included are: tension-orientated items; anger-related items; the ability to identify and describe methods for reducing feelings of tension or anger; items that relate to features of personal relationships and shared situations; the ability to identify attributes liked or disliked in others; self-appraisal; prioritisation of problems; goal planning; realism of expectations; compliance with therapy; identification of pre-admission events; and sense of personal responsibility (see Box 11.2).

Box 11.1: Risk sub-scale

NO:	ITEM:
1	Family support
2	Serious violence to others without apparent trigger event
3	Serious violence to others following trigger event
4	Minor violence to others without apparent trigger event
5	Minor violence to others following trigger event
6	Serious self harm
7	Superficial self harm
8	Verbal aggression without apparent trigger event
9	Verbal aggression following trigger event
10	Attacks on objects without apparent trigger event
11	Attacks on objects following trigger event
12	Breaches of security
13	Disruptive episodes
14	Imitative disruption
15	Inappropriate sexual behaviours
16	Sado-masochistic behaviours
17	Macho gear and adornment
18	Obsessive-compulsive behaviours
19	Substance abuse
20	Psychiatric disturbance

The communication/social skills sub-scale contains 30 items which fundamentally examine adaptive social behaviour and the processes by which interpersonal relationships are established. Items measured are required for effective verbal and non-verbal communication and include items which examine *inter alia*: habitual facial expressions; aspects of proxemics; paralinguistic features; aspects of conversational interaction; potential conflict; and self-presentation (see Box 11.3).

The BSI is currently undergoing extensive empirical examination with four principle aims to the study: (1) to determine the clinical validity of the BSI; (2) to study implications of pooled

Box 11.2: Insight sub-scale

NO:	ITEM:
1	Awareness of tension
2	Description of tension
3	Tension-reducing strategies
4	Recognition of negative or angry feelings
5	Tension-producing thoughts
6	Tension-producing events
7	Personal strategy for reducing tension
8	Identifying relaxing thoughts
9	Identifying relaxing activities
10	Attributes disliked in others
11	Attributes liked in others
12	Events producing insecurity
13	Events producing security
14	Antecedent events leading to treatment
15	Ascription of responsibility
16	Self-appraisal
17	Prioritisation of problems
18	Goal-planning
19	Compliance with therapy
20	Expectations

data for validity and reliability; (3) to describe emergent trends within and between the three sub-scales; and (4) to examine the potential utilisation of outcome data in planning individualised care through the care programming approach.

Data has been collected at the two principle sites: Rampton and Ashworth Hospitals (n=503); contributory data are being drawn from a variety of clinical contexts, including similar forensic facilities in the Netherlands and other European countries (Reed *et al.* 1997; Robinson 1997). Face and content validity have been established through the extensive empirical work, with all the items based on sound clinical usage and therapeutic value. Examination of data has

Box 11.3: Communication and social skills sub-scale

NO:	ITEM:
1	Facial expression
2	Eye contact
3	Orientation to others
4	Body posture
5	Expressive gestures
6	Social distance
7	Tone of voice
8	Voice modulation
9	Verbal delivery
10	Conversational initiative
11	Amount of speech
12	Fluency
13	Turn-taking
14	Listening skills
15	Response to questions
16	Conversational topics
17	Egocentric conversation
18	Frankness
19	Expressing opinions
20	Disagreement
21	Arguments
22	Making requests
23	Assertiveness
24	Self-presentation
25	Social activities
26	Emotional control
27	Relationship with others
28	Ease of communication
29	Sociability and support
30	Deferring to others

proved high test/re-test reliability and acceptable inter-rater reliability. Internal consistency and item homogeneity is high. A distinctive factor structure is evolving. Inter-item and scalar correlations are indicative of strong relationships emerging between the items.

Since an important aspect of any assessment is to identify predictive behaviours that are displayed systematically, the factorial structure discussed above can only be of considerable interest to clinicians. Thus this is, therefore, the subject of ongoing statistical analysis by the researchers. Clinically, the logic is that there may exist certain patterns or behavioural 'diatheses' which predispose to (that is, increase the risk of) occurrence of offending behaviour (Woods *et al.* 1998).

Such a 'diathesis' has been described as maybe consisting 'of behavioural elements or skill repertoire; thus allowing for assessment of baselines, appropriate interventions designed to ameliorate specific deficits or promote insightful adjustment and social learning; and evaluation of remeasurement data' (Woods *et al.* 1999). Through this the probability exists that the BSI will move toward meeting the needs of professionals seeking an appropriately operationalised version of constructs commonly used in multidisciplinary planning of individualised treatment in forensic care (Robinson, Reed and Lange 1996).

It is envisaged that as the work progresses, knowledge and inferences around the prediction of dangerousness and its relationship to factors of insight, communication and social skills will unfold. Therefore, clinical care and its outcomes can be more focused within the forensic contexts that are involved in the study. For example, where complementary items are shown to be related within and between scales, it becomes possible to focus care and treatment around these items and thus to move the risk assessment process along interventive and therapeutically useful lines (Woods and Reed 1998).

RESPONDING TO THE VIOLENT INCIDENT

If seclusion prompted serious debate amongst mental health professionals in the late 1980s and early 1990s, the question of physical restraint as a therapeutic intervention for managing aggression is increasingly becoming the vexed question as we move towards the millennium.

Coping with violent patients has troubled psychiatry for hundreds of years. During the past two decades clinical guidelines designed to address the problem of violence have been, at best, ambiguous and, at worst, non-existent. The common situation was where maybe six members of staff piled upon a hapless patient on the floor. Any hopes of systemising such a physical intervention was dependent on the person in charge and his/her favoured route of attack. The physical well-being, or dignity, of the patient were simply not for consideration.

In 1981 a system of interventions based around the martial art of ju-jitsu was introduced by the Home Office via the Prison Service (Tarbuck 1992). The aim of these techniques – known as control and restraint – was to manage violence in a consistent and effective method, described as a systematic controlled method of intervention (Tarbuck 1992).

Obviously impressed with the effectiveness of these techniques, hospitals throughout the country, previously at a loss for coping satisfactorily with violent behaviour, embraced control and restraint and, rapidly, staff were being trained in these techniques. Aggression and violence could be almost completely relegated to the status of a minor problem now that control and restraint was here.

Sadly, despite acknowledgement from the Mental Health Act Code of Practice (DHSS 1983), all is not well with physical restraint, including control and restraint. Anecdotal evidence suggests that control and restraint is open to disparity between the perceptions of those applying such techniques and those receiving them – that is, the patients. The disparity ranges from misinterpretation as to when restraint should be used through to misuse (Department of Health 1992). One of the major principles underpinning control and restraint was the use of pain-inducing techniques to reduce the act of violence from the aggressor and induce co-operation from the patient. However, as a method of intervention, control and restraint seemed to be viewed by many clinicians as the best choice from a poor menu.

Physical restraint encountered a number of problems. These included:

- Misinterpretation: the teaching of practical skills of physical restraint were, and, to date, remain, non-standardised – meaning that different establishments seemed to have their own interpretation and method considered most effective for dealing with a particular type of client group.
- Misuse: reports of injuries to patients increased. Cases of bruising (Department of Health 1992), severely damaged ligaments and even fractures occurred to patients who had been restrained. Sadly, there seems to be a culture that promoted restraint as a response from staff, not only to aggression or violence but to non-co-operation, such as refusing to get out of bed.
- Reduction in Communication Skills: worryingly, there still seems to be anecdotal reports of staff returning from such courses with the firm belief that aggression management is about developing the necessary dexterity to physically apply the restraint techniques – a worry highlighted by Morrison (1990).

Restraint, whether in the form of Mental Health legislation, seclusion, control and restraint, or medication, can conflict with a nurse's respect for an individual's autonomy (Stilling 1992). Coercive controls directly manipulate body processes physically or chemically and bypass the patients own thinking mechanism (Sciafani 1986). A sense of helplessness and loss of control can itself lead to increased levels of violence (Stilling 1992). Worryingly, if the teaching of control and restraint techniques is not underpinned by a research, educational and value base of respect for the patient's needs for autonomy and well-being, acknowledgement of anxiety and desire to restore dignity, the sense of justifiable disquiet currently associated with such physical restraint will be compounded by critics and service-user advocates alike.

The efficacy and therapeutic value of control and restraint should be measured and monitored not by how proficiently staff are able to recall and apply the techniques taught on such a training course but by how reassured, pain-free and dignified the service user reports back when interviewed post-incident. It is clear that much needs to be done before physical methods of restraint, such as control and restraint, can be considered to be a safe, therapeutic, measurable intervention that is compatible with the role of carer.

A philosophy of care must influence how and when control and restraint teaching and its application to the patient occurs. It has been suggested that a culture that is aimed at control and safety is likely to yield a violent environment (Morrison 1990). A possibility for the evolution of such cultures is the fact that staff often seem to have a less than rudimentary knowledge of the factors that can cause aggression and violence – not only within a mental health context but aggression *per se*.

With an emphasis on physical interventions, the net result is that staff may have some expertise in coping with violence but absolutely none in areas such as triggers of violence (Breakwell 1995) and de-escalation techniques (Brennan 1997; Patterson, Leadbetter and McCormish 1997), stress management, anger management (Novaco 1978) and the concept of victimology (Fisher 1992).

This can enable care staff to successfully prevent anger from becoming aggression or aggression developing into violence. It seems quite illogical that staff are provided with training in just one aspect of aggression management when it is clearly evident there are vital aspects being neglected. The teaching of physical restraint techniques should be grounded on a knowledge and value base and be incorporated within an overall framework aimed at offering skills in aggression management. Learning theories to support this argument include cognitive (Kenworthy and Nicklin 1995), humanistic (Ogier 1989) and psycho-motor skill acquisition.

Ethical dilemmas surrounding the management of aggression are becoming increasingly important for carers of patients or clients today (Tarbuck 1992; Aitken and Tarbuck 1995). Hopton (1995) considers the issues from a different perspective, suggesting that as some psychotherapeutic or psychiatric interventions are both oppressive and damaging, the patient may express what he calls justifiable anger. Fannon (1986, 1990) analogised the function of patient aggression with that of any colonised indigenous populace whereby the people were made to feel inferior for refusing to embrace the cultural norms of the colonisers. Thus rebelling and displaying violent resistance to the colonisers restored their self-respect and esteem. It may be that a proportion of the institutionalised aggression encountered is a bid by patients to reject the so-called therapeutic agents' (colonisers') cultural norms.

The need to both develop and restore non-touch interventions cannot be over-emphasised. By having a repertoire of interventions, practitioners need not rely upon only one. By having an extended number of responses, carers can indulge in systematic risk taking – talking or negotiating with clients in situations they may previously have resolved by using techniques like control and restraint. To have hands placed on a person can be described as – depending on the administrators' and patients' perceptions – therapeutic or a violation. We believe that a disparity does exist and further believe that the ultimate measure and mode of evaluation needs to be those expressed by the latter group.

While methods of coping with violence and aggression within mental health settings have improved, there is still a need to address certain areas of concern. Control and restraint interventions have started to respond to the need of the patient and this has been compounded by the need for physical interventions to be taught within a framework of antecedent analysis, trigger awareness, theories and philosophical models, and victimology, not to mention post-traumatic stress disorder. This can hopefully challenge the myth that those considered most suitable for coping with aggressive patients need to be of a machismo disposition.

DISCUSSION AND GUIDANCE FOR PRACTICE

The issues for ensuring good practice in high secure environments are not that dissimilar for that in general mental health and learning disability services. Perhaps what is more evident is the extent and severity of incidents.

The core elements that we believe are essential factors would include:

- a clearly formulated and understood policy in managing and responding to violent incidents
- a system of incident reporting (ideally, for analysis purposes, computer based) system with built in reviews by the Patient Care Team and Management Board (this a requirement of Health and Safety legislation)

- responding to identified service shortfalls by adjusting resources accordingly (for example, the deployment of additional staff at key times – in our study, late evening for female and at weekends for male patients)
- the consideration of alterations in treatment regimes for 'difficult to manage' patients responsible for high levels of incidents – examples would include both medication and cognitive/behavioural programmes
- trend analysis of ward areas can help with early warning signs of destabilised environments, poor patient mix and the need to consider managerial and clinical interventions
- we have detailed a specific clinical risk assessment system (BSI) which we believe provides clinicians with both information to facilitate care planning and has predictive qualities for transfer and discharge consideration. Whether or not services adopt the BSI approach, what is imperative is that a clearly articulated system of risk assessment is operationalised within the service – preferably, as part of a broader risk management strategy for the service
- it is now more accepted in high secure and most regional secure services that training of staff in physical response techniques is a valuable tool in engendering confidence in the workforce in dealing with physical aggression and ensuring as much safety from injury for the patient. What is less widespread is the availability of this training in general services and outside the health sector. Also, within high secure services the guarantee of both training and updating rarely gets close to full coverage. We feel that these essential skills are mandatory from both an initial (usually five days) and update (usually two days) basis
- the more serious incidents will require a separate investigation to determine the full circumstances involving antecedents, the incident itself and its management and consequences. Consideration will need to be given to the independence of this investigation (depending on involvement and severity), the training of key investigators, reporting mechanisms and follow-up.

Violence in high secure hospitals is, unsurprisingly given the background of patients, both a common occurrence and with a high proportion in the more serious range. This requires a high level of preparation and vigilance for the staff of these services with the emphasis on prevention and analysis.

It will be impossible to eradicate violence from these environments but it can be minimised and, when intervention is necessary, the safety and protection of all involved can be enhanced by a structured system of response.

NOTE

For further details in relation to the Incident Reporting system or data contact George Allan at Ashworth Hospital (e-mail: gallan@cableinet.co.uk). For details on the BSI contact Phil Woods (e-mail: philwoods@cableinet.co.uk).

REFERENCES

Aitken, F. and Tarbuck, P. (1995) 'Practical ethical and legal aspects of caring for the assaultive client.' In B. Kidd and C. Stark (eds) *Management of Violence and Aggression in Health Care*. London: Gaskell.

Breakwell, G. (1995) 'Theories of violence.' In B. Kidd and C. Stark (eds) *Management of Violence and Aggression in Health Care*. London: Gaskell.

Brennan, W. (1997) 'Pressure points.' *Nursing Times*, 93(43), 29–32.

Brooks, K.L., Mulaik, J.S., Gilead, M.P. and Daniels, B.S. (1994) 'Patient overcrowding in psychiatric hospital units: effects on seclusion and restraint.' *Administration and Policy in Mental Health*, 22, 133–144.

Carton, G. and Larkin, E. (1991) 'Reducing violence in a special hospital.' *Nursing Standard*, 5, 29–31.

Coldwell, J.B. and Naismith, L.J. (1989) 'Violent incidents on special care wards in a special hospital.' *Medicine Science and the Law*, 29, 116–123.

Conn, L.M. and Lion, J.R. (1983) 'Assaults in a university hospital.' In J.R. Lion and W.H. Reid (eds) *Assaults within Psychiatric Facilities*. Florida: Grune and Stratton.

Davis, S. (1991) 'Violence by psychiatric inpatients: a review.' *Hospital and Community Psychiatry*, 42, 585–590.

Department of Health (1992) *Report of the Committee of Inquiry into Complaints about Ashworth Hospital, Cm 2028-I*. London: HMSO.

Department of Health and Social Security (1975) *Report of the Committee on Mentally Abnormal Offenders (The Butler Report). CMND6244*. London: DHSS.

Department of Health and Social Security (1977) *The National Health Service Act*. London: DHSS.

Department of Health and Social Security (1983) *The Mental Health Act*. London: DHSS.

Department of Health and Welsh Office (1993) *Code of Practice*. London: HMSO.

Dietz, P.E. and Rada, R.T. (1982) 'Battery incidents and batterers in a maximum security hospital.' *Archives of General Psychiatry*, 39, 31–34.

Dooley, E. (1986) 'Aggressive incidents in a secure hospital.' *Medicine Science and the Law*, 26, 125–130.

Fannon, F. (1986) *Black Skin White Masks*. London: Pluto.

Fannon, F. (1990) *The Wretched Earth*. London: Penguin.

Fisher, A. (1992) 'Violence and victims in the psychiatric setting.' In H.S. Wilson and C.R. Kneisl (eds) *Psychiatric Nursing*. California: Addison Wesley.

Fottrell, E. (1980) 'A study of violent behaviour amongst patients in psychiatric hospitals.' *British Journal of Psychiatry*, 136, 216–221.

Health Services Advisory Committee (1987) *Violence to Staff in the Health Service*. London: HMSO.

Hodgkinson, P., Hillis, T. and Russell, D. (1984) 'Aggression management: assaults on staff in a psychiatric hospital.' *Nursing Times*, 80, 16, 44–46.

Hopton, J. (1995) 'Control and restraint in contemporary psychiatric nursing: some ethical considerations.' *Journal of Advanced Nursing*, 22, 110–115.

Hunter, M. and Carmel, H. (1989) 'Staff injuries from inpatient violence.' *Hospital and Community Psychiatry*, 40, 41–46.

James, D.V., Fineberg, N.A., Shah, A.K. and Priest, R.G. (1990) 'An increase in violence on an acute psychiatric ward: a study of associated factors.' *British Journal of Psychiatry*, 156, 846–852.

Kelsall, M., Dolan, M. and Bailey, S. (1995) 'Violent incidents in an adolescent forensic unit.' *Medicine Science and the Law*, 35, 150–158.

Kennedy, M.G. (1993) 'Relationship between psychiatric diagnosis and patient aggression.' *Issues in Mental Health Nursing*, 14, 263–273.

Kenworthy, N. and Nicklin, P. (1995) *Teaching and Assessing in Nursing Practice*. London: Scutari Press.

Krakowski, M.I., Convit, A. and Jaeger, J. (1989) 'Inpatient violence: trait and state.' *Journal of Psychiatric Research*, 23, 57–64.

Larkin, E., Murtagh, S. and Jones, S. (1988) 'A preliminary study of violent incidents in a special hospital (Rampton).' *British Journal of Psychiatry*, 153, 226–231.

Lion, J.R. (1977) 'Training for battle: thoughts on managing aggressive patients.' *Hospital and Community Psychiatry*, 38, 8, 882–925.

Lion, J.R., Snyder, W. and Merrill, G.L. (1981) 'Underreporting of assaults on staff in a state hospital.' *Hospital and Community Psychiatry*, 32, 497–498.

Morrison, E. (1990) 'The tradition of toughness: a study of non-professional nursing care in psychiatric settings.' *Journal of Nursing Scholarship*, 22(1), 32–38.

Noble, P. and Rodger, S. (1989) 'Violence by psychiatric in-patients.' *British Journal of Psychiatry*, 155, 384–390.

Novaco, R.W. (1978) 'Anger and coping with stress: cognitive behavioral interventions.' In J.P. Foreyt and D.P. Rathjens (eds) *Cognitive Behavioral Therapy*. New York: Penguin.

Ogier, M.E. (1989) *Working and Learning*. London: Scutari Press.

Palmstierna, T. and Wistedt, B. (1989) 'Risk factors for aggressive behaviour are of limited value in predicting the violent behaviour of acute involuntarily admitted patients.' *Acta Psychiatrica Scandinavica*, 81, 152–155.

Patterson, B., Leadbetter, D. and McCornish, A (1997) 'De-escalation in the management of aggression and violence.' *Nursing Times*, 93, 36, 58–61.

Poster, E.C. and Ryan, J.A. (1989) 'Nurses' attitudes toward physical assaults by patients.' *Archives of Psychiatric Nursing*, 3, 315–322.

Powell, G., Caan, W. and Crowe, M. (1994) 'What events precede violent incidents in psychiatric hospitals?' *British Journal of Psychiatry*, 165, 107–112.

Reed, V., Robinson, D., Woods, P. and Henderson, S. (1996) *The Behavioural Status Index: Named Nurse Assessment Manual for the Assessment of Dangerousness and Risk*. Unpublished.

Reed, V., Robinson, D., Woods, P. and Van Erven, T. (1997) *Clinical Relevant Assessment in Everyday Forensic Reality and Better Recidivism Prediction on the Future: The Behavioural Status Index (BSI) Offers the Means to do Just That.* Minisymposium, Congrescenter, GgzEindhoven, Netherlands.

Rix, G. and Seymour, D. (1988) 'Violent incidents on a regional secure unit.' *Journal of Advanced Nursing*, 13, 746–751.

Robinson, D. (1997) *The Behavioural Status Index (BSI) Euro Collaborations.* Research News, issue 13. Retford: Rampton Hospital Authority.

Robinson, D., Reed, V. and Lange, A. (1996) 'Developing risk assessment scales in psychiatric care.' *Psychiatric Care*, 3, 4, 146–152.

Sciafani, M. (1986) 'Violence and behaviour control.' *Journal Psychosocial Nursing*, 24, 11, 8–13.

Stilling, L. (1992) 'The pros and cons of physical restraints and behavioral controls.' *Journal of Psychosocial Nursing*, 30, 3, 18–20.

Tam, E., Engelsmann, F. and Fugere, R. (1996) 'Patterns of violent incidents by patients in a general hospital psychiatric facility.' *Psychiatric Services*, 47, 86–88.

Tarbuck, P. (1992) 'Use and abuse of control and restraint.' *Nursing Standard*, 6, 52, 30–32.

Walker, Z. and Seifert, R. (1994) 'Violent incidents in a psychiatric intensive care unit.' *British Journal of Psychiatry*, 164, 826–828.

Way, B.B., Braff, J.L., Hafemeister, T.L. and Banks, S.M. (1992) 'The relationship between patient-staff ratio and reported patient incidents.' *Hospital and Community Psychiatry*, 43, 361–365.

Woods, P. (1996) 'How nurses make assessments of patient dangerousness.' *Mental Health Nursing*, 16, 4, 20–22.

Woods, P. and Reed, V. (1998) 'Measuring risk and related behaviours with the Behavioural Status Index (BSI): some preliminary psychometric studies.' *International Journal of Psychiatric Nursing Research* (In press).

Woods, P., Reed, V. and Robinson, D. (1999) 'The behavioural status index: therapeutic assessment of risk, insight, communication and social skills.' *Journal of Psychiatric and Mental Health Nursing* (In Press).

CHAPTER 12

Public Protection, Potentially Violent Offenders and the Role of Senior Managers

Gill MacKenzie

INTRODUCTION

How can senior managers promote and develop within their organisations the safe and constructive supervision of potentially violent offenders? Much has been written about the role of the practitioner (and, to a lesser extent, about the role of the first-line manager) but scarcely can I find in the literature any reference to the roles and responsibilities of senior managers or any guidance on how to fulfil those responsibilities. It is in an attempt to encourage a more active consideration of the role of the senior manager in developing services with a public protection focus, rather than offering a definitive seal to the subject, that I write this chapter. I write as someone on the journey under no illusion that the destination is in sight. It is based on my experiences and observations as a senior manager in the probation service, although the reflections could apply, no doubt, to any organisation, independent or statutory, which offers services to, or has responsibility for, potentially violent offenders.

Defining terms such as 'public protection' and 'potentially violent offenders' is notoriously fraught with difficulty. Within criminal justice, 'public protection' is often used as a short-hand term for any activity aimed at reducing offending *per se*. The definition of 'public protection' to be employed here is one which describes the activities of agencies designed to reduce the likelihood of the commission of offences which would cause serious physical or psychological harm to the victim(s). A potentially violent offender is someone assessed, according to agency or inter-agency requirements, as having an above-average propensity to commit an offence which would cause serious physical or psychological harm to the victim(s).

My central argument is that the pre-dominating emphasis of public protection which has been recently placed on the probation service requires senior managers to build an organisational framework deliberately and systematically designed to cope with the nature of the new responsibilities. The ability of staff to carry out this difficult, taxing and, sometimes, threatening work is largely determined by the quality of this framework. An holistic approach is required if an organisation is successfully to carry the burden of working with violent offenders and remain healthy as an organisation, especially in the prevailing societal climate of blame. The unprecedented decision of the Home Office to release a probation circular to the press in July 1997, which surveyed serious incidents (not convictions) occurring during a thirteen-month period (PC 1998), illustrates the point: 'Stop this scandal of prisoners being freed to commit murder' (*The Express* 1997a); 'Officers facing blame as sex crimes also soar' (*The Express* 1997b); 'Killing and raping while on probation' (*The Daily Mail* 2 July 1997).

PUBLIC PROTECTION

Certainly, 'public protection' and allied phrases such as 'risk management' are ubiquitous phrases nowadays falling readily from the lips and pens of politicians, government officials, journalists and those working in the criminal justice system. Yet in the 1980s these phrases were rarely employed in the context of criminal justice. The first 'Statement of National Objectives and Priorities' for the probation services (Home Office 1984) makes no reference to any Home Office concept of dangerousness or risk assessment, or of public protection in respect of these two possibilities. Indeed, the service was urged to allocate resources to through-care only sufficient 'to enable the Service's statutory obligations to be discharged'. The statement's over-arching concern was the reduction of the prison population by ensuring that community penalties were imposed whenever possible, whilst retaining the confidence of the public. Statham and Whitehead's *Managing the Probation Service: Issues for the 1990s* (Statham and Whitehead 1992), wide-ranging as the issues were, contains no discussion of the service's public protection role; the preoccupation of the time was managerialism.

Yet in the seven years since the enactment of the 1991 Criminal Justice Act, the legislative, governmental and public requirements and expectations of the probation service in respect of public protection have been transformed. Section 31(3) of the Act permitted longer custodial sentences to be imposed if the court thought it 'necessary to protect the public from serious harm from the offender' – since which time a series of further conditions laid upon the service have increasingly sharpened the focus on public protection. In response to a significant report published in 1995 by the Probation Inspectorate (HMIP 1995), Home Office Plans published in 1997 and 1998 have gone a step further and both describe a service priority to be 'to reduce the risk to the public from dangerous offenders' (Home Office 1997; PC 1998).

Even though the probation service has supervised potentially dangerous offenders for decades, and, probably, from the beginning, this explicit focus represents a shift in the organisational paradigm. The probation service now protects the public by the accurate assessment and management of potential offenders and by working to rehabilitate the offender. It does not, as previously, work to rehabilitate the offender and thereby protect the public. Whether that is a desirable shift in emphasis is a matter of debate; my concern here is with the implications of this shift for senior managers.

When the Probation Inspectorate published *Dealing with Dangerous People: The Probation Service and Public Protection* (HMIP 1995), one of the key findings was that 'the identification of potentially dangerous offenders is a corporate responsibility but too often managers at all levels are insufficiently involved' (p.15). The report also observed that 'objective setting and review, information and resource management had become dominant in their [managers'] working lives' (p.54), leading the report to speculate that those 'changed definitions about what constituted a *good manager*' (p.54) detrimentally affected the way in which they managed staff in relation to high-risk cases. If the dominance of 'objective setting and review, information and resource management' (p.54) is unhelpful in an era of public protection, what is helpful as a dominant management style?

Foremost, senior managers need to recognise that the pre-eminence of public protection as an organisational duty has an impact on the whole organisation. Thinking of public protection as a bolt-on to existing structures and practices invites a mechanistic response to a subject that is too complex and too challenging for such an approach. Instead, it requires a whole agency model that involves and commits the entire organisation to the primacy of public protection. It is an approach that extends well beyond ensuring that policies and procedures are in place and that the right reports are written at the correct time (important as those things are). Senior managers should aim to imbue their organisations with an understanding of the concept of public protection and its relationship with rehabilitation in ways that develop confidence in staff and which exhibit a true corporate responsibility for intrinsically difficult and, sometimes, dangerous work. This is impossible to achieve quickly. It requires a comprehensive strategy that takes full account of all aspects of the organisation from the ethical rationale for actions taken to the training and support of clerical staff.

RESPONDING TO UNCERTAINTY

The ethical debate could be seen as being the locomotive by which the necessary cultural change is initiated. Given the power that agencies such as the probation service have over the lives of offenders, it is the duty of senior managers to keep ethical discussions buoyant at all levels in the organisation. The consequences of an assessment that places an offender on a register, designating that person as likely to commit a violent offence, or the consequences of initiating recall procedures for, say, a life sentence prisoner, are too profound to be left to an agency that lacks the confidence and sensitivity to question the legitimacy and wisdom of its actions (and the reliability of its evidence). Nurturing an organisational culture that can cope with the ambiguities and uncertainties of a public protection role is an essential role for senior managers. It is, doubtless, a perpetual quest, but a vital one if the supervision of potentially violent offenders is to be conducted in the open, thoughtful and challenging way that is the pre-requisite of good case supervision. It should be the antithesis of what is often referred to as 'macho management', whereby staff are required to follow procedures, deliver the outputs and, in the words of so many staff, 'make sure the agency's back is covered'. As in all dangerous philosophies, there is more than an element of truth in that phrase. No chief executive wants to explain to the media why procedures were not followed when a disaster occurs. However, staff who operate within a blame culture, who may feel very frightened and alone in a procedure-driven environment which ignores the, sometimes, daunting emotional and intellectual content of their work, are so much more likely to deliver just those very disasters. As Tony Morrison (1996) observes of a middle manager in a social care agency who was required to 'think' in her own time and never to feel, the consequences for the organisation are harmful in terms of critical reasoning, planning, working relationships, reflective analysis, staff stress and motivation.

Any agency which recognises, and is seen by its staff to recognise, the anxiety generated by potentially violent offenders is already on the right track. This is achieved not only by ensuring that the obvious components of good service delivery are in place (training, supervision, attention to Health and Safety issues) but, equally importantly, by paying attention to elusive factors such as the availability and approachability of managers, their responsiveness and, above all, their ability to make workload decisions that are equitable and acknowledge the huge impact that cases 'on the boil' have on workload.

Something of an ideal world is being described here, but unless we, as senior managers, have a vision of the climate we wish to create, an anxiety-prone or defensive culture will predominate, anti-pathetic to the sure handling of difficult cases.

Good work with damaged and violent offenders is labour intensive and resource hungry. Co-working, inter-agency meetings, even the careful scrutiny of a thick case file are time consuming. The active involvement of the agency in public protection makes a major impact on workload. Resources are at a premium and it is tempting to cut down on labour-intensive activities. Some probation services have curtailed specialist work with sex offenders as a result of funding crises. Juggling resources is the senior manager's perpetual nightmare and, of course, there are no easy solutions. If, however, public protection work is the first priority, should that not be preserved at the expense of other activities? If public protection is the first priority, should not our information systems, workload measurement tools and the arguments assembled for resources reflect that priority?

EQUIPPING STAFF FOR A PUBLIC PROTECTION ROLE

A whole-agency concept for public protection means that every member of staff must be trained and supervised to enhance their understanding and skills in their particular contribution to the agency's responsibilities. In the probation service context, receptionists and community service supervisors, for example, alert to the signals of an offender in trouble and, sufficiently confident to respond appropriately, are just as much part of the agency's safety net as specialist practitioners. All staff need appropriate support in dealing with the impact of encounters with destructive and shocking aspects of human behaviour. In relation to clerical staff, the 1998 Probation Inspectorate Report *Exercising Constant Vigilance: The Role of the Probation Service in Protecting the Public from Sex Offenders* (HMIP 1998) rightly and commendably draws attention to the effect of 'some very explicit and disturbing material... The impact of such material should not be underestimated' (p.146). Unsurprisingly, the report also found that the support and induction needs of clerical staff working in non-specialist terms were not adequately met.

A programme of training for all staff, including senior managers, is vital. Within this programme the scope for joint training with other agencies should be identified. Joint training with social services and the police is often a well-established feature of provision, but routine consideration should also be given to training agreements with partnership agencies who often share the burden of risk of violence. If the key to good public protection lies with the training and support of staff, particular attention should be paid to the skills of first-line managers in their supervision of those staff.

Countless inquiries have identified poor communication as a key factor in failure and tragedy. The first line of communication is invariably with one's manager. Listening, questioning, consulting, advising are real and subtle skills that were deprecated in the objectives-driven 1980s. Now they are central to the task of public protection.

Multi-agency work in relation to violent offenders has undergone something of a revolution in recent years. Senior managers have been astute and energetic in formulating strategic agreements and protocols to give shape, consistency and direction to joint working. It would be tempting to fall back on our laurels at this point but multi-agency work should be as dynamic and developmental as single-agency work. Protocols are part of the beginning, not the pinnacle of completion. Perhaps the next phase is to draw up multi-agency strategic plans, subject to review and evaluation, as are corporate ones. A powerful message is conveyed if Chief Officers meet regularly (but necessarily frequently) to review the strategic approach to public protection.

No discussion of violent offenders would be complete without consideration of Health and Safety, the importance and legal obligations of which have a substantial literature of their own. The concern here is with some of the particular provisions necessary for the health of an organisation dealing with potentially violent offenders. Few managers will have missed the significance of the case of Walker v Northumberland County Council (1995) in which Mr Walker, who had been employed as an area social services officer, successfully sued his employers for breach of duty of care in failing to take steps to avoid exposing him to a health-endangering workload (Spicer 1996). Every employer has a common duty of care to safeguard the health and safety of employees and, as this case demonstrates, mental well-being comes within the ambit of 'health', and budgetary constraints are not, in themselves, a satisfactory defence.

The sensitivity and responsiveness of an organisation to the signs of overwork, burn-out, or even temporary battle fatigue, are one of the yardsticks by which staff measure their trust in their employers. Is a confidential counselling service available? Is an independent consultant employed to work with staff on those horrifying, troubling cases that can haunt sleepless nights? Indeed, is the culture one in which such feelings can be expressed openly and treated with respect?

Incidents of violence and aggression towards staff deserve the very special, consistent and high-priority attention of senior managers. It is insufficient to have systems in place that only treat such incidents as events to be dealt with by middle managers and logged by senior managers. All incidents should receive some interactive response, and, of course, serious incidents demand the swift and personal involvement of senior managers. As with other forms of offender violence, lessons of benefit to the whole organisation can be learned and incorporated into future practice if debriefing is perceived as being helpful and purposeful.

Managerial anxiety about public protection can often express itself in weighty volumes of guidance. Too many manuals, procedures and forms only serve to create confusion and important messages can be lost in a welter of words. It pays dividends to concentrate on crisp, straightforward messages which are easily remembered rather than on reams of guidance that no one understands properly and, therefore, rarely reads. Perhaps whatever essential guides must be written should be composed as if to gain the approval of the Plain English Society!

CONCLUSION

It is inevitable that, from time to time, tragedies will occur; no organisation can completely nullify the frailties of human nature. These are awful times for everyone involved and it is only too easy for anxiety to distort what should be a calm and rational process. Acknowledgement that tragedies can occur should already be contained within agency policies and a general procedure to be followed known and agreed – it will help staff to understand the reasons for any inquiry and assist the smooth undertaking of any such investigation. This is a time when the performance of senior managers can make or break an organisation's confidence. Unless someone has been wilfully negligent, the incident is either an unavoidable tragedy or it is a failure of your system. Staff should be supported and protected, especially from the media. Good staff may feel a quite unwarranted sense of responsibility. That burden will either be shared and alleviated by sensitive management or it will descend into a feeling of being scapegoated if management react defensively or angrily. Try to ensure that the organisation learns positively, rather than defensively, from an inquiry. The legal context so helpfully described by Carson (1996) is an invaluable aid to managers and staff alike in trying to establish for one's own agency the over-arching principles.

Any tragedy is likely to attract media interest, the handling of which is clearly a senior management responsibility. Of course, you will not have started from here! Positive accounts of your agency's work and success stories will have regularly found their way into the local press, radio and TV. Although appropriate confidentiality and legal requirements must be preserved, these should not be used as a cloak behind which to hide. Admit that there is a problem and describe the steps being taken to deal with it. If you have access to public relations advice, use it. Consider issuing a rapid press statement containing the essential points you wish to convey; amongst other benefits, it will enable you to clarify the key points you want to emphasise. If a major emergency or crisis has taken place, issue a press release as soon as possible, recognising that something significant has happened, and stating that a press conference will be held in the near future. Issuing such a swift press statement can help to reduce misinformation and journalistic speculation. If the case is shared with other agencies, liaise urgently with them and consider holding a joint press conference. It can also be helpful at times of intense media interest to use the PR of your professional or employing association to act as a clearing house.

Even if something has gone horribly wrong, the public (and your own staff) can still discern integrity.

REFERENCES

Carson, D. (1996) 'Risking legal repercussions.' In H. Kemshall and J. Pritchard (eds) *Good Practice in Risk Assessment and Risk Management*. London: Jessica Kingsley Publishers.

Daily Mail (1997) 'Killing and raping while on probation.' 2 July.

Express (1997a) 'Stop this scandal of prisoners being freed to commit murder.' 2 July.

Express (1997b) 'Officers facing blame as sex crimes soar.' 2 July.

Her Majesty's Inspectorate of Probation (1995) *Dealing with Dangerous People: The Probation Service and Public Protection*. London: HMSO.

Her Majesty's Inspectorate of Probation (1998) *Exercising Constant Vigilance: The Role of the Probation Service in Protecting the Public from Sex Offenders*. London: HMSO.

Home Office (1984) *Probation Service in England and Wales – Statement of National Objectives and Priorities*. London: Home Office.

Home Office (1997) *The Three Year Plan for the Probation Service 1997–2000*. London: Home Office.

Morrison, T. (1996) 'Emotionally competent child protection organisations: fallacy, fiction or necessity?' In J. Bates, J. Pugh and M. Thoroughson (eds) *Protecting Children: Challenges and Change*. Aldershot: Arena.

Probation Circular (1998) *Plan for the Probation Service 1998–1999*. London: Probation Unit, Home Office.

Spicer, R. (August 1996) 'Stress-related anxiety and psychiatric damage.' In Croner *Health & Safety Briefing No. 108*. London: Croner Publications Ltd.

Statham, R. and Whitehead, P. (eds) (1992) *Managing the Probation Service: Issues for the 1990s*. London: Longman.

CHAPTER 13

Training on Violence and Aggression

Ron Wiener

INTRODUCTION

This chapter outlines the content and structure of a one-day training course in dealing with violence and aggression. It is based on courses run with staff in public sector organisations, such as social services departments, the health service and probation departments.

It is divided into four parts – course introduction, before incidents, during incidents and after incidents – corresponding to the four sessions of a training day.

COURSE INTRODUCTION

Setting the scene

There are many different aspects in getting a course going. These include:

a) Helping the participants to move from being a collection of individuals into a working group. A good way of starting is to have people in a circle explaining how and why they have come on the course (for a fuller description of course beginnings, see Wiener 1997).

b) Doing the house rules – that is, timings, when and where refreshments will be, etc.

c) Confirming the agenda/learning outcomes.

d) Agreeing ground rules, such as those relating to anti-discriminatory practice, confidentiality and no physical violence.

Agenda for the first session

In the first session the trainer needs to cover the following issues.

DIFFERENT THEORIES AS TO THE CAUSES OF VIOLENCE AND AGGRESSION

More (1990), for example, gives three theoretical explanations: that it is something we all inherit; that we learn to be aggressive either by being rewarded for exercising it or via observation; or that it arises from frustration. Other suggested causes are: drugs and alcohol lowering inhibitions; a consequence of sexual and/or physical abuse; a result of how people view the world; the XYY syndrome, where aggressive individuals are hypothesised to have an extra chromosome; or violence existing as part of the sub-culture within which an individual lives. For most practitioners, while this is useful background information, they are more interested in what is likely to set an individual off in a particular situation.

Some of the more immediate factors to consider are the colour of walls, the availability of weapons, such as glass ashtrays in waiting areas and triggers like over-long waiting times.

The trainer can run this part of the session as a short lecture backed by overhead projections and handouts. An alternative way would be to do it as a pub quiz with competing sub-groups. In terms of group building, it is useful for the trainer in the first session to have participants working in a variety of sub-groups.

AGREEING A DEFINITION OF WHAT IS MEANT BY VIOLENCE AND AGGRESSION

The Local Government Management Board (1991) report points out that:

> violence and aggression mean different things to different people. The conditions for defining an incident as aggressive or threatening, or as involving violence, differ among individuals and across occupational groups and may differ between policy makers and recipients of such behaviour. (p.3)

Another definition is 'violence is purposeful or reactive behaviour intended to produce damaging or hurtful effects, physically or emotionally, on other persons' (Strathclyde Regional Council 1986, p.1). However, should it also include sexual and racial abuse or harassment? And what about self-harm when aggression is turned on oneself? This might be as emotionally traumatic for a staff member as being on the receiving end of verbal abuse. It is also important to realise that the definition covers client/client, staff/staff, staff/client interactions as well as the more usual client to staff assault.

One way of thinking about the definition is as a continuum. At one end there is the out and out physical assault by a client on a staff member with resulting physical injury. There is no doubt in anyone's mind that this is an act of violence. At the other end there might be a phone call from an angry client to a receptionist in which some swearing takes place. Three out of four receptionists might brush this off but the fourth might find any swearing offensive. At this end of the continuum the definition is more subjective and it is difficult to get consensus of what to record. Incidents down this end of the scale are much less likely to be recorded consistently.

As a trainer, there are different ways of getting the group to look at the issue of definition:

a) Small groups brainstorming with the trainer pulling together the different versions.

b) Small group discussions based on existing definitions used by practitioners in their workplace.

c) The trainer distributing different definitions for small group discussion.

d) The trainer enacting different scenarios as a basis for group discussion. This could be done by:

    i) The trainer choosing a large person from the group as a volunteer and saying to the group: 'if the volunteer was a client and s/he the trainer was a professional worker, everyone would agree that an act of violence had occurred if the volunteer was to punch and kick the trainer.'

    ii) The trainer then, after warning the volunteer that there will be no physical contact, coming up close to him or her and saying in a loud voice: 'I'm going to get you one day', then getting the volunteer to sit back down.

    iii) The trainer getting a pen, sitting down and saying: 'what if I'm a client who sits all through an interview fiddling with a knife like this but makes no actual threat?'

iv) The trainer saying: 'what if a client says to me, *sotto voce,* "I know where you live" but makes no more threat than that?'

v) The trainer then asking: 'as a worker, what if I were black (assuming trainer is white) and someone made a racist remark?'

vi) The trainer then raising the question: 'if, as a rugby player, I elbow someone, I might be praised for my play. Why is the same action wrong if done by a client to a worker?' – the aim here is to raise the issue that the context defines the interpretation of an action.

The trainer can enact or describe the scenes and then get people to come up with a definition which covers them all.

PUTTING THE VIOLENCE INTO CONTEXT

It is more dangerous to be a patient in hospital – one in five accident victims treated by the NHS is left needlessly injured or disabled due to poor care (Milhill 1992) – than it is to be a worker. Similarly, there is more chance of being hurt if one is a resident in a hostel than if one is a worker. Staff members are only there for shifts. If there is a potentially violent client, the other residents have to be with them for 24 hours a day in what will be a threatening atmosphere.

One way of putting this into perspective is to ask the group for information as to how often they have been on the receiving end of violence. The questions to ask are: How often have you been physically attacked badly enough to need time off from work? How often have you been physically attacked and needed medical treatment? How often have you been physically attacked but needed no treatment? How often have you been threatened? How often have you been verbally abused?

What one finds is:

a) A pyramid with the worse the incident the smaller the number of cases.

b) Few people have been physically attacked badly enough to require medical treatment. This is not to diminish how traumatic this might be for these people and this needs to be acknowledged.

c) How much at risk people are. This can be done by going round the group and adding up how long people have been working in the service. Let us suppose that a group of 15 have worked, on average, for 10 years each. If we now multiply this by 50, it gives an approximate number of weeks worked – that is, 7500. If one then asks the group how many potentially serious incidents they are involved in each week, say 2 on average, this gives the group a collective history of 15,000 possible incidents. This can then be contrasted with the number of times people have been seriously hurt, say 5, which this leads to 1 in every 3000 incidents. This line of argument leads to:

   i) A recognition of the defusion skills that exist in the group. This provides the basis for moving the training to a group sharing model rather than the trainer as expert.

   ii) Comparing this to other activities: car driving (4229 people were killed on the roads in Great Britain in 1992); smoking (the Health Education Authority claims that passive smoking kills some 11,000 adult Britons each year (O'Kane 1993); one category of pollutants – particulates – routinely kill 10,000 Britons every year (Lean 1995); domestic violence (one in ten women have been victims of violence from their partners in the last twelve months (Campbell 1993)).

   iii) A need to compare the figures from the training group with known figures for that client group – for ambulance staff, for example, Nethercott (1997) found in a survey that 10 per cent of respondents had been the victims of physical assault requiring medical assistance.

d) In general, the more time that people spend with clients, the more likely they are to be involved in incidents. This is one of the reasons why residential staff have a higher incidence rate than field social workers.

RECORDING OF INCIDENTS

There are a number of factors to be highlighted:

a) The failure of a clear definition, as we have seen, often makes it difficult for staff to know what to record.

b) There is a general under-reporting of incidents. A report on one social services department (SSD) (Leeds 1985) found that, of 200 incidents in residential and day care centres over a month, only 25 were reported up to the next level of management. There are many reasons for this:

   i) Staff feel: 'why bother if nothing ever changes?'

   ii) The amount of paperwork involved.

   iii) It might reflect badly on the staff member/workplace involved.

   iv) It might be seen as part of the job – in establishments working with older people, hair-pulling by clients on staff during dressing is taken, in many places, to be the norm.

   v) The staff member does not want to get the client into trouble.

c) There is a need for accurate recording because:

   i) Many incidents are repeat incidents. The Leeds SSD (1985) report found that 167 of the 200 incidents recorded were repeat episodes. Repeat incidents are predictable and, therefore, strategies can be devised to minimise their re-occurrence.

   ii) Similarly, incidents do not happen everywhere with equal regularity in terms of time, place or conditions. The Leeds (1985) study found that incidents occurred most often in communal areas when there was little structure. In residential establishments, going to bed and getting up are often high-risk times and those cases involving loss of liberty in mental health sections or children in child work always carry potential danger.

   iii) Again, just as there are high-risk clients, so some staff get involved in more incidents than others. This could be because of a lack of skill on the part of these staff; different gender expectations – 'you're the man, you deal with it'; staff role differences – 'you've been on a self-defence course, therefore you are the best person to deal with them'; the staff are key workers with high-risk clients. In contrast, senior staff, because of their power, usually have least difficulty in defusing confrontations.

Therefore, accurate records provide the information which enables an analysis to take place as to the causes of violence and, hence, to plan an appropriate response.

There are three ways in which the trainer can deal with recording of incidents:

a) Small group discussion of possible reasons for under-reporting.

b) Trainer giving a short talk to group with overhead projections.

c) Trainer setting up one or more role plays which highlight recording problems and using these as a discussion base for how they would/should be recorded in people's workplaces.

PHYSICAL RESTRAINT

It is not possible in a one-day course to safely teach physical restraint. The Rampton course, for example, lasts for two weeks. What is important is to talk about the usefulness or otherwise of restraint courses. The advantages of such courses are:

a) They equip staff to restrain violent clients.

b) They give staff confidence in difficult situations, which means it is more likely that they will have the confidence to intervene positively without needing to use force.

c) Because the world both in and out of the workplace is seen to be more dangerous for women, there might be a case for a women-only self-defence class.

The disadvantages are:

a) It raises the risk of people resorting to physical responses when a less risky one might be equally effective.

b) There is a risk of people being hurt – if the worker engages physically, it gives the client permission to retaliate in kind.

c) There is a risk of the worker being sued for assault unless he or she can show that they were only using the minimum force necessary and following organisational guidelines.

d) Many strategies for successful restraint require a team of two or three workers. Many places have only single staff

> cover. Sometimes, this is why teaching release holds is an effective compromise. Even here, though, sufficient time must be allocated for people to learn them properly and then to practise them on a regular basis.

It is often useful to give people the space to have a short discussion about the pros and cons and, therefore, whether this is something they want to pursue with their employers.

SUPPORT

Successful interventions require team work. Inconsistency in the way that different members of the team deal with individuals or incidents will result in ongoing problems. One aspect of this is how well staff feel supported. There are three disabling support rules that operate in teams.

The first of these is the macho rule. This applies in teams which pride themselves on being tough or having a difficult client group and, in practice, means that newcomers have to show that they are tough enough to fit in. Translated, this means that you can only get help when you can show that you no longer need it.

The second rule is the wimps rule. This means that you have to show that you are a potential victim before help will be offered. In reality, the person has to say to team mates: 'I don't think I can cope with X. Will someone come with me?' Good teams have rules which minimise the risk of this happening – for example, all first home visits involve two workers going together.

The third rule is the support that is formally offered but in such a way that it can never be acted on. A good example is the manager who says: 'I can be reached at home', but says it in such a way that staff know not to ring.

The trainer can introduce the first rule and then ask if anyone can think of any others.

SHARING

The last thing that is useful to do in this session is to put people into small groups and get them to share a confrontation they have been involved in. This enables them to bring their own experiences into the workplace; brings to the fore possible incidents that the trainer might want to use later in role plays; provides people with a possible

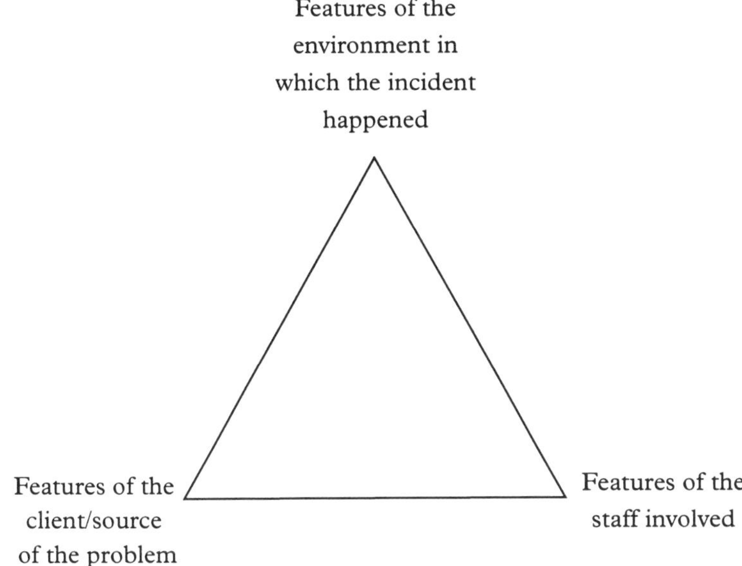

Figure 13.1: Problem Analysis Triangle

opportunity to off-load a 'bad' experience they have been hanging onto.

One way to structure the feedback from the sub-group discussions is to use the problem analysis triangle (Figure 13.1).

SESSION TWO: BEFORE INCIDENTS

There are a large number of areas to consider in looking at what needs to be in place to either reduce the chance of incidents happening or to minimise their effects. These include:

a) The need for the organisation to have a policy in place. The Strathclyde Regional Council Report (1986), for example, covers: relations with the police; financial, legal and personal support; and the right of individual employees 'to make a formal complaint to the police or to pursue a civil action'.

b) Training for staff in defusion skills and in recognising possible dangers and, where appropriate, in restraint and release holds.

c) Effective risk assessment procedures. An example of a simple risk questionnaire is given in Breakwell (1989).

d) Analysing the physical layout of the workplace for dangerous places. Attention needs to be paid to:

   i) Separation of the public from the staff offices – for example, by doors with coded locks.

   ii) The design of reception areas – colour of the walls, availability of magazines, toys for children, etc.

   iii) Lighting, especially around the edge of the building on winter nights.

   iv) Design of the interview rooms – no objects that can be used as weapons, other staff can see and/or hear what is going on, alarm systems, etc.

e) Insurance and compensation for physical damage to staff property.

f) Alarm systems. These need to be tested occasionally, just as fire alarms are. They are only as effective as the staff drills that go with them. It is important to recognise that there are two types of call for help:

   i) 'I'm in serious trouble – get here quickly' – this is the call that alarm systems are set up to meet.

   ii) 'This is a tricky situation, I want someone standing by just in case'. In this case the ringing-bell alarm system might well provoke the incident that the worker is trying to avoid. Here other systems need to be set up. One example is the coded telephone message from the interview room: 'could I have a cup of tea with three sugars' – where the 'three' is the code word.

g) Good communication with other agencies, particularly in terms of dangerous behaviour. There are enough inquiries into deaths caused by people with mental health problems which have highlighted poor communication as one of the factors. One thing which fuels the lack of openness is the need to minimise someone's dangerousness if the purchaser is trying to place him or her with a reluctant provider.

h) Good internal communication – for example, effective shift handovers, case reviews.

j) Having plans for known trouble makers. As we have seen, the majority of incidents are repeat episodes involving the same small percentage of clients. It makes sense to identify these individuals and have specific strategies in place for dealing with them. These might include:

  i) Always seeing them at the office.

  ii) Never seeing them alone.

  iii) Having an express system so that they are not kept waiting.

  iv) Marking their files in some way so that new workers picking them up are immediately aware of the need to take precautions.

k) Analysing potential difficult scenarios:

  i) Carrying money.

  ii) Single-cover working in residential units.

  iii) Meal times in day centres when there are lots of people crowded together and few staff available.

  iv) First visits to new clients.

Trainer strategies

a) Getting individuals to draw their workplaces on a flip chart and identify weak points in terms of safety. People are then put into pairs, taking turns to be the safety inspector looking at the other's plan. People are then asked to depict the changes they want to make. These need to be divided into those that can be done with minimum resource implications and those which require significant investment.

b) Getting people, in pairs, to describe, step-by-step, their typical working day. While one person talks, the other asks questions as to whether there are any potential dangers.

c) Re-creating a workspace in the training room, using the available furniture. The trainer then puts people into role as potentially difficult clients, receptionists, workers, managers, other clients, etc. The difficult clients are then followed through in terms of what happens typically at each stage of being processed through the system. Among the issues that often arise when doing this are:

i) How welcoming the reception area is.

ii) Who is responsible for the reception and waiting areas.

iii) How the receptionist communicates to other staff that a 'difficult' person is in the waiting area.

iv) Who keeps the waiting people informed of delays.

v) Who explains the informal rules of the waiting room – for example, why people are not necessarily seen in the order in which they arrived.

vi) Who knows who is in the interview rooms and how long they have been in there.

vii) The centrality of the receptionist in terms of communication and knowledge systems.

d) A similar scenario can be worked out to examine how to make home visits safe. Here two scenes are set up. The first is the office where workers are making a decision about who should go. Here the factors that need to be highlighted are:

i) How can the one worker ask the other to accompany them if they feel anxious?

ii) What are the rules for joint visiting?

iii) How will the worker know if this is a 'high risk' visit?

iv) If it is 'high risk', what precautions need to be taken?

v) Who in the office will know where the worker is?

vi) What procedure is in place if the worker does not report back in by a set time?

vii) Does the worker need to take a mobile phone?

The second scene is set in the home the worker(s) is going to visit. The issues here are:

i) Where should the worker have parked their car? – ideally, under a street light facing the way they want to leave.

ii) What should they be looking out for as they approach the house? – signs of anything different, broken windows, uncollected milk bottles, etc.

iii) At the door, before they enter, they should ascertain who else is in the house, what state they are in, what the vibes are, whether there are any dogs in the house (dogs can be a cause of aggression in their own right). This step is important because, as soon as someone steps over the threshold, they are on the client's territory and, once the door has shut behind them, it is that much more difficult to get out.

iv) Once inside, where should people sit? – ideally, this should be near the door.

v) The parts of the house people should avoid if there is any sense of danger – upstairs, bedrooms and kitchens. Kitchens are problematic because although they are the room with most weapons – that is, knives, hot things – they are also the place where, in many houses, most entertaining takes place.

e) Brainstorming and discussions in big and small groups.

f) Providing examples of good practice from other organisations.

SESSION THREE: DEFUSING

Post-lunch, the trainer might well need to do something which energises the group. This is not a good session for a lecture or similar input, as it will sink into the after-lunch stupor.

The first aim in defusing is to make people aware of the warning signs that violence might be about to happen. Braithwaite (1992, p.38) lists the following non-verbal signs as ones that workers need to be aware of:

physical closeness – defensible space

positioning – yours in relation to an aggressive person

physical contact – cultural differences

posture – as indicator of mood

facial expressions – what indicates aggression

eye movement – appropriate eye contact

gestures – what do you do which might irritate the client

head movements – used to indicate listening

mirroring – used to defuse situations.

Verbal warning signs, according to Braithwaite (1992, pp.57–61), are:

threats

depersonalised language – 'you are all the same'

repetitive language – it is also important to stress here how essential it is that warnings are taken seriously.

The trainer could use the following ways of introducing this material:

a) Questionnaires and small group discussion.

b) In pairs, getting people to sculpt (physically position) each other to show:

   i) Non-verbal warning signs – for example, head jutting forward.

   ii) How non-verbally not to defuse a situation – for example, aggressive hand gestures.

   iii) How non-verbally to defuse a situation – for example, by sitting down.

The second aim is to make people aware of the do's and don'ts of defusing potentially violent confrontations. As in most cases of training, the group will already know 80 per cent of the answers and we saw in the first session how you can reflect back to the group the reservoir of knowledge they will possess from having dealt successfully with hundreds of such events:

a) The do's:

   i) Defuse before you negotiate. The 'A's are useful here:

   Acknowledge the anger.

   Agree, where possible, that the situation is anger provoking.

   Apologise, if appropriate, for what has happened.

Care needs to be taken, otherwise they may come over as patronising.

- ii) Stay calm, which is easier said than done. Getting people to slow their breathing down helps.
- iii) Be non-judgmental.
- iv) Set limits.
- v) Use the broken record – this is where you keep repeating over and over what it is you want the other person to do.
- vi) Breakwell (1989, p.66) suggests that 'you keep talking using as normal a voice as possible'.
- vii) Breakwell (1989, p.66) also suggests the use of diversionary tactics, the making of a cup of tea, taking care not to equip the other person with a dangerous weapon.
- viii) Use active listening skills.

b) The don'ts include:

- i) Don't argue, put down, stereotype, criticise, patronise or blame the person.
- ii) Don't make threats that you can't back up.
- iii) Don't jump to conclusions.
- iv) Don't respond with anger – it simply raises the temperature.
- v) Don't corner the other person or yourself.
- vi) Don't have an audience unless it is necessary that they can and will summon help.

The trainer, again, has a number of ways of getting the group to explore this issue:

a) Brainstorming do's and don'ts they would like to give a new and inexperienced worker coming to join their team.

b) Putting the group into pairs. A to repeat 'yes, yes, yes' and B, at the same time, to say 'no, no, no'. The trainer then interrupts and asks A to do everything s/he can to make the situation worse (the don'ts), short of physical violence. The roles are then reversed. The exercise is repeated and this time B is asked to defuse the situation (the do's).

c) Using role plays. These can be:

  i) Based on real situations that the group members volunteer.

  ii) Examples introduced by the trainer.

  iii) Set in motion by trigger videos (Wiener and Crosby 1986). These are short scenes involving violence looked at through the eyes of the worker who comes to the scene. The trigger videos can also be used to start a discussion of do's and don'ts.

The role plays will only work if the group feels safe enough for individuals in it to take risks. The role plays can be:

a) Done in small groups with people trying out different roles and exploring strategies.

b) Done as forum theatre (Boal 1992), where the scene which ends in a confrontation is played through once. The second time, it is played through, to begin with, exactly as happened the first time, but now group members can stop the action when they see another way of handling it. The person who said 'stop' now comes out and tries their option and the group can see if it produces a different response from the aggressor. The person then sits down again. The original person carries on with the action, as in the first run through, until someone else says 'stop' and tries out their strategy at this stage.

SESSION FOUR: AFTER THE INCIDENT

This session contains two parts: what needs to happen after an incident and how the course needs to finish.

After the incident

The issues that need to be considered for:

THE WORKER

a) In the short term:

  i) Immediate support. Straight after an incident the victim needs to spend time with someone who they feel supported by, whether this is a colleague, someone from another team or a friend outside the workplace.

ii) Medical treatment. Often, the victim is not in the best position, unless the injury is serious, to determine whether they need to be examined. This is partly because the adrenalin pumping around their system is likely to mask injuries and also the victim might want to vacate centre stage as part of their emotional recovery.

iii) A decision whether they need to be at work or at home. Home is not always the best alternative, especially if the person lives alone. Staying at work might be the only option in times of staff shortages.

b) In the intermediate term:

i) Completing an incident form. The sooner this happens the better, as details are either forgotten or distorted to fit the remembered version of what happened.

ii) The provision of counselling in order to deal with the emotional impact of the event. People are, for example, likely to feel guilty, as if they were to blame for the aggression. Sometimes, the impact will only become apparent days after an event, so it is not sufficient for the team leader to ask someone the following day how they are and, if they hear there is nothing to worry about, to assume that that is the end of it.

iii) Advice – which might be to do with compensation, legal rights, worker protection with the trade union.

iv) Supervision with the line manager as to what happened so that the incident can be reviewed and any learning for the individual taken on board.

c) Long term:

Sometimes, after an incident, the emotional effect does not go away and we are left with the possibility of the worker having post traumatic stress disorder. According to Braithwaite (1992, p.13), there are five possible symptoms:

i) Performance guilt – an over-critical examination of what one did or did not do.

ii) Focused resentment or anger – usually anger which is difficult to express against the client and is directed elsewhere.

iii) Reconstruction anxiety – the memory of the violence being triggered off at unexpected times.

iv) Irritability.

v) Loss of motivation.

In this case there is a need to find appropriate skilled counselling.

In all of this there are a number of things that need to happen for the worker. They do not all have to be done by the line manager personally but the line manager has a responsibility to ensure that they are happening when and if required. Therefore, some incident forms will carry a checklist of what needs to happen for the worker, which can be ticked off once they have been met.

THE STAFF TEAM

They might need to:

a) Have time to reflect and share their feelings about the incident. If it has been traumatic for most of the team, there might be the need for some psychological debriefing. According to Hodgkinson and Stewart (1991, p.131), this has seven phases: the introductory; the fact; the thought; the reaction; the symptom; the preparation; the re-entry.

   Among the aims of the debriefing are:

   i) The ventilation of impressions, reactions and feelings.

   ii) The promotion of cognitive organisation.

   iii) Decrease in individual and group tension.

   iv) Increasing group support and solidarity.

   v) Identification of avenues of further assistance.

b) Consider the implications of the event for their practice in terms of:

   i) How they deal with this particular client.

ii) How they deal with this sort of client/behaviour.

iii) What lessons are there to be learnt for the team in terms of decision making, communication, knowledge and skills, layout of the building, inter-agency working and the working environment.

THE CLIENT(S)

There is a need to consider:

a) Their emotional/physical state post-incident, what they need and who should provide it.

b) What changes need to be made to care plans.

c) The appropriateness of their placement with the team.

THE TRAINING OPTIONS

There are a number of different ways the trainer can deliver this session. These include:

a) Brainstorm what should happen after an incident.

b) Ask people to think of a confrontation that someone in their workplace has recently been involved in, consider what happened after the event for the staff and what should have happened and draw up a list of what needs to change.

c) Ask for a real incident from group members or use the trigger videos and ask what should happen for the staff member once the incident is over.

d) Divide the group into three and take an incident. One group takes the worker, one the staff team and one the client, and each group decides what needs to happen next. These can be written up on flip chart sheets which are then passed around so that each group gets to contribute to each aspect.

e) Write a protocol for your workplace on what should be in place for post-event support.

The ending

The first task for the trainer is to ensure that the learning points from the day are summarised. This can be done by:

a) Handouts.

b) People making their own handouts from the information written on flip chart sheets and blu-tacked to the wall during the day.

c) Trainer highlighting key points.

The second task is to help participants take the learning back to their workplace and apply it. This can be done by:

a) Group members drawing up protocols/checklists. These can be compared with other members' contributions and samples of good practice given by the trainer.

b) Participants making public statements as to five things they will do differently back at work.

c) Participants working with others from the same workplace to be able to support each other to combat the resistance to change that they are likely to find, especially if they are quite junior members of staff.

d) Pre-course arrangement that course members will have a meeting with their line manager to discuss the learning and how it might be enacted.

e) Having a follow-up session three months later so that people can report on the progress or otherwise of implementing change.

The third task is for the trainer to check that the emotional business of the day has been resolved and that no one is going home carrying, for example, remnants from role plays they were involved in. For this:

a) The trainer needs to be observant.

b) People in pairs sharing about how they feel about anything that has gone off during the day.

The last task is to receive feedback as to the usefulness of the event. This can happen via:

a) Evaluation questionnaire.

b) Everyone sharing in a circle as to what they got out of the day.

REFERENCES

Boal, A. (1992) *Games for Actors and Non-Actors*. London: Routledge.

Braithwaite, R. (1992) *Violence: Understanding, Intervention and Prevention*. Oxford: Radcliffe Professional Press.

Breakwell, G. (1989) *Facing Physical Violence*. London: Routledge.

Campbell, D. (1993) 'One in 10 women have been victims of domestic violence in past year.' *The Guardian*, 17/2.

Hodgkinson, P. and Stewart, M. (1991) *Disaster: A Handbook*. London: Lewisham Social Services Department.

Lean, G. (1995) 'Where did the fresh air go?' *The Independent on Sunday*, 5–9.

Leeds Social Services (1985) *Report of the working group on conflict and aggression*. Leeds: Department of Social Services.

Local Government Management Board (1991) *Violence at Work: Issues, Policies and Procedures*. Luton: Local Government Management Board.

Milhill, C. (1992) 'Poor NHS care leaving 20pc of accident victims with disability.' *The Guardian*, 3/12.

More, W. (1990) *Aggression and Violence*. Birmingham: Paper Publications.

Nethercott, K. (1997) 'Defence mechanisms.' *Health Services Journal*, 4 September, 30–31.

O'Kane, M. (1993) 'Anti-smokers threaten action.' *The Guardian*, 28/1.

Strathclyde Regional Council (1986) *Violence to Staff: Policies and Procedures*. Strathclyde: Regional Council.

Wiener, R. (1997) *Creative Training*. London: Jessica Kingsley Publishers.

Wiener, R. and Crosby, I. (1986) *Coping with Violence and Aggression: Trigger Videos*. Leeds: University of Leeds, Audio-Visual Service.

FURTHER READING

Brennan, W. (1997) 'Pressure points.' *Nursing Times 93*, 43, 29–32.

Clode, D. (1987) 'Recipe for reducing risks.' *Social Services Insight*, 13 March, 6–7.

Crane, D. (1986) *Violence on Social Workers*. Norwich: University of East Anglia.

Crine, A. (1982) 'An occupational hazard.' *Community Care*, 11 November, 25–27.

Department of Health and Social Security (1988) *Violence to Staff*. London: HMSO.

Fanning, F. (1998) 'Skills for preventing aggression.' *Nursing Times 94*, 8, 60–61.

Gibbs, A. (1988) 'Violence and the organisation.' *The Professional Nurse*, January, 116–118.

Hatchett, W. (1988) 'Violence at work.' *Care Weekly*, 17 June, 10.

Health and Safety Executive (1993) *Prevention of Violence to Staff in Banks and Building Societies*. London: HSE Books.

Health Services Advisory Committee (1987) *Violence to Staff in the Health Services*. London: Health and Safety Commission.

Littlechild, B. (1996) 'The risk of violence and aggression to social work and social care staff.' In H. Kemshall and J. Pritchard (eds) *Good Practice in Risk Assessment and Risk Management I*. London: Jessica Kingsley Publishers.

McDonnell, A., Dearden, G. and Richens, A. (1991) 'Staff training in the management of violence and aggression.' *Mental Handicap 19*, December 151–154.

Osborne, J. (1988) 'Dealing with victims of domestic violence.' *Social Work Today,* 9 June, 12–13.

Owens, R. and Ashcroft, J. (1989) *Violence.* London: Croom Helm.

Paterson, B. Leadbetter, D. and McCornish, A. (1997) 'De-escalation in the management of aggression and violence.' *Nursing Times 93,* 36, 58–61.

Thompson, A. (1996) 'All in a day.' *Community Care,* 1–7 August, 14–15.

Tonkin, B. (1988) 'Quantifying risk factors.' *Community Care.* 13 November 22–25.

The Contributors

George Allan RGN, RMN, MA is currently responsible for the management of Clinical Support Services at Ashworth Hospital Authority and is the designated lead officer for incident reporting. He recently completed his MA in Applied Research and Quality Evaluation at the University of Sheffield where the subject of his dissertation was Reporting and Management of Violent Incidents in a High Security Psychiatric Hospital.

H.H. Judge David Bentley Q.C was born in Sheffield and read law at London University. In 1994 he was awarded a PhD by Sheffield University for a thesis on the nineteenth criminal justice system. He was called to the bar in 1969 and thereafter practised on the North-Eastern Circuit. He was appointed Q.C. in 1984 and became a Recorder of the Crown Court in 1985. He has been a circuit judge since 1988 sitting mainly in Sheffield and Hull trying crime and in London as a Deputy High Court judge. He is the author of two books on legal history *Selected Cases from the Twelve Judges' Notebooks* (1997) and *English Criminal Justice in the Nineteenth Century* (1998).

Dr Gwyneth Boswell is a Senior Lecturer at the University of East Anglia, currently on attachment to the new Degree/Diploma in Probation Studies Programme at the De Montfort University. She is former Probation Officer and Senior Probation Officer. Her research interests centre around violent young offenders and the parenting role of imprisoned fathers, on which subject she is preparing a report for the Department of Health. She is co-author, with Davies and Wright, of *Contemporary Probation Practice* (Avebury 1993) and author of *Young and Dangerous* (Avebury 1996).

Walter Brennan RMN, FETC is currently Lecturer in conflict and aggression management at Ashworth Hospital. He previously worked as a Charge Nurse and Ward Manager within Forensic Mental Health Settings. He has spoken nationally and internationally on violence and has written more than a dozen articles on the subject.

Karen Buckley is a Senior Probation Officer in Nottinghamshire. She also writes and teaches primarily on topics related to gender and sexuality. She is currently co-editing a book on sexuality and power to be published in 1999.

Colin Dale MA, RN, DipN (London), Cert Ed, RNT, DMS was recently appointed to the University of Central Lancashire as a Senior Research Fellow to project-manage a UK-wide study into nursing in secure environments on behalf of the United Kingdom Central Council for Nursing, Midwifery and Health Visiting. Previously, he was the Executive Nurse Director at Ashworth Hospital Authority with a very varied career to date as clinician, educator, policy advisor and manager at the most senior levels. He has worked with national bodies as the Nursing Development Officer of the Special Hospitals Service Authority and lectured to Master's degree programmes in Community Care.

Umme Farvah Imam is a Lecturer in Community and Youth Work Studies at the University of Durham. For over twenty years she has been an activist in women's groups and projects both in India (where she was born and educated) and in England. She worked as a community and youth worker for several years at Roshni, Asian Women's Association in Newcastle-upon-Tyne supporting and developing several projects for black and South-Asian women in the region. Her research focuses primarily on violence against South-Asian women and children.

Dr Ann Hagell BA, MSc, PhD, AFBPsS, C. Psychol is Co-Director of the Policy Research Bureau, a centre for applied social policy research on children, young people and families. She has extensive research experience in the areas of at-risk young people, offenders and anti-social behaviour. Recent publications include *Antisocial Behaviour by Young People* (with Michael Rutter and Henri Giller, Cambridge University Press) and *Dangerous Care: Reviewing the risks to children from their carers* (Policy Studies Unit).

Colin Hawkes qualified as a social worker in 1971 after completing a postgraduate Diploma in Applied Social Studies at the University of Leicester (School of Social Work). Since then he has worked in North-East London Probation Service – for the last six years on a part-time basis, the remainder of his employment being as a Consultant Social Worker at the Young Abusers Project, part of Camden Health Trust. Colin has a particular interest in training and development and in designing group treatment programmes for the wide age and ability range of children worked with at the Project.

Renuka Jeyarajah Dent is an Educational Psychologist and Deputy Chief Executive of The Bridge Child Care Development Service. Before taking up her current position, Ms Dent worked for BAAF and in Inner London as an Educational Psychologist specialising in working with children known to social services. This was done in a multi-disciplinary setting and included gathering evidence for courts. Ms Dent's work at The Bridge includes consultancy, training and research at the local and European level. She also serves on the management board of the National Foster Care Association.

Hazel Kemshall is currently a Senior Research Fellow with the Department of Social and Community Studies at DeMontfort University. She was previously a Probation Studies Lecturer with Birmingham University and has practice and management experience with the Probation Service. She has written extensively on risk assessment and risk management, and has recently completed research for the Economic and Social Research Council entitled *Risk in Probation Practice,* grant number L211252018.

Gill Mackenzie is Chief Probation Officer of Gloucestershire, Vice-Chair of the Association of Chief Officers of Probation and its lead officer on risk and dangerous offenders. She has a long-standing interest in issues of violence and public protection, stemming from working in prisons in the 1970s.

David Morran is a Lecturer in Social Work at the University of Stirling. He has extensive previous experience of working with offenders in a range of prison and fieldwork settings. His principal interests are in violence and masculinity and in crime and deviance with marginal communities.

Judith Rumgay, a former probation officer, was probation tutor for the post-graduate social work programme at London School of Economics for several years. Currently, as Lecturer in Social Policy in the Department of Social Policy and Administration, LSE, her teaching mainly focuses on the areas of psychology and crime, and rehabilitation of offenders. Her research interests and publications concern the probation service, drug and alcohol related crime, and women offenders. She is the author of *Crime, Punishment and the Drinking Offender*, has recently completed research into partnership programmes for substance misusing offenders and is presently engaged in a study of a voluntary organisation dedicated to provision for female offenders.

Angela Stanton-Greenwood is a residential care co-ordinator for Barnardos. She has worked for twenty years in residential care with clients with challenging behaviour and is presently working with clients with moderate to severe learning disabilities. She is a trainer in Therapeutic Crisis Intervention.

Ron Wiener, Independent Training Consultant and Associate Consultant in the School of Continuing Education at the University of Leeds. He works for organisations in the public, educational, voluntary and private sectors training trainers and improving team functioning and skills development in areas such as management of change and staff supervision. His work is characterised by the use of creative action methods involving the whole group.

Monica Wilson started her career as a researcher on a study of wife abuse. She went on to work as a researcher on various projects and then into higher and health education before joining CHANGE as Joint Co-ordinator with David Morran in 1989. In 1997 she completed the Diploma in Person Centred Counselling. She is currently working part-time for CHANGE and as a Counsellor in Primary Care.

Phil Woods RMN, Dip H C Research is a lecturer in Nursing at the University of Manchester with the role of research into personality disorder and mentally disordered offenders. He has many years experience in high secure psychiatric care and publishes widely in the academic press. He is presently in the final stages of his PhD focused on the development of a behaviourally based instrument to assist in the risk assessment process. He is collaborating in a European risk assessment project with the Norwegian forensic services.

Subject Index

Name Index